Graham McColl is a writer and journalist who contributes regularly to *The Times* and whose work has appeared regularly in a variety of newspapers and magazines. His many books include *England – The Alf Ramsey Years*, *Scotland in the World Cup Finals* and *'78: How a Nation Lost the World Cup*. He lives in Glasgow with Jackie, his wife, and Anna-Maria, Dominic and Joseph, his children.

How to Win the World Cup

Graham McColl

BANTAM PRESS

LONDON • TORONTO • SYDNEY • AUCKLAND • JOHANNESBURG

TRANSWORLD PUBLISHERS
61–63 Uxbridge Road, London W5 5SA
A Random House Group Company
www.rbooks.co.uk

First published in Great Britain
in 2010 by Bantam Press
an imprint of Transworld Publishers

A CIP catalogue record for this book
is available from the British Library.

ISBN 9780593066225

Addresses for Random House Group Ltd companies outside the UK
can be found at: www.randomhouse.co.uk
The Random House Group Ltd Reg. No. 954009

The Random House Group Limited supports the Forest Stewardship
Council (FSC), the leading international forest-certification organization. All our
titles that are printed on Greenpeace-approved FSC-certified paper carry the FSC
logo. Our paper procurement policy can be found at
www.rbooks.co.uk/environment

Typeset in 12/15.5 pt Sabon by Falcon Oast Graphic Art Ltd.
Printed and bound in Great Britain by CPI Mackays, Chatham, ME5 8TD

2 4 6 8 10 9 7 5 3 1

For Dominic Nicholas, born 30 April 2009,
while this book was under construction

Contents

Acknowledgements

Special thanks to Giles Elliott, my editor at Transworld, for backing this project and for providing inspirational encouragement in seeing it through to publication. Thanks also to copy-editor Julian Flanders, to Rachel for her work in collating the picture sections, and to Stan, my agent.

Thanks to all the players, managers, World Cup winners and others, whose insightful reflections have helped to illuminate my work on this book.

Introduction

WINNING THE WORLD CUP SHOULD BE A FAIRLY SIMPLE matter, shouldn't it? All you do is play the best, most entertaining football in each of your matches, overwhelm the opposition, captivate the world with an irresistible attacking style and win the Final in memorable fashion to establish your team as indisputably the best in the world.

The problem is, the World Cup has been won in this way on only a handful of occasions and the last time it happened was forty years ago, when Pelé inspired the brilliant Brazilians of 1970 to victory. That wonderful victory is still rolled out frequently as the way to win a World Cup but, as the nine champions of the world since then would tell you, that's not the only way to win. Indeed, on only a handful of occasions in the 80-year history of the World Cup have the eventual winners been indisputably the finest team in the tournament.

Finishing first is as much a test of nerve, adapting to the World Cup environment and combating circumstances as it is of pure footballing skill. No one will be more aware of that than Fabio Capello. Italy, his native country and the world champions in 2006, did not do much in that tournament to win over too many people outside their own country. Their approach to hurdling each stage of that tournament was not one designed to entertain people around the globe. Did that matter to the Italians? The two million people who turned out to welcome them back to Rome and who commandeered the country's fountains and squares to parade their delight after that triumph answered that question emphatically.

It goes against all our romantic preconceptions but if you are going to win the World Cup it is probably better if you are clearly not the best team in the competition. Those who have done most to light up a World Cup tournament by playing memorably attractive football tend to be more fondly remembered by the world at large than the winners themselves – such beautiful losers as the mesmerizing Brazilians of 1982, the Hungarians of 1954, the Dutch of 1974; even, to a degree, the Argentinians of 2006, though their general good impression was somewhat spoiled when they reverted to type and began a fantastic mass brawl at the conclusion of their quarter-final defeat to Germany. But you can still be sure that those teams would have instantly exchanged all the kind words and airy praise they have received in the years since for a good deal less popularity and the solidity of gold winners' medals.

As Fabio Capello ponders long and hard his England

squad for the summer of 2010 in South Africa, he will also be devoting much thinking time to all of the other factors that determine success or failure on the world stage – the variety of means used to win the World Cup incorporating the bizarre, the funny and the fantastic. If he is seeking inspiration, this guide to the essential stratagems needed to win the World Cup may be just the thing.

I

Because of the Cause

IF YOU'RE GOING TO WIN THE WORLD CUP YOU DON'T HAVE
to have a demented dictator breathing down your
neck, or commentators suggesting that your players are
shooting up drugs and pairing off in homosexual rela-
tionships, or have a match-fixing court case beginning in
the middle of the tournament that concerns more than
half of your squad.

It does help, though. All of these factors have, as Fabio
Capello will know well, helped Italy to attain their four
World Cup triumphs, not least in 2006 when they became
the current holders of the trophy. For the nation of
Machiavelli, it seems essential for there to be a powerful
element of intrigue involved if winning the World Cup is
to become a going concern.

It is not only for the Italians that a powerful siege mentality or a strong cause is almost essential for a successful
tilt at the World Cup. Several other nations have thrived

on being forced to turn inwards and draw on a feeling of solidarity necessitated by external pressures, but the Italians in particular appear to require a more powerful cause than merely winning the trophy to exert a grip on a World Cup campaign and drive the team towards victory.

For each of Italy's two triumphs in the 1930s, it was the gentle pleadings of Benito Mussolini, the fascist dictator, that helped bring the trophy home. 'Win or die!' was his encouraging message by telegram to the Italian squad as they set off for France in 1938 to defend their status as world champions. Mussolini, in common with many of the great football managers, was clearly aware of the importance of ensuring that his message got across to the players in black and white and without any possibility of confusion. Whilst that barbed, brutal demand could merely have been the type of zealous rhetoric that dictators can summon at will, the players would have been keen to take him at his word rather than test whether he was merely bluffing and acting the big bully boy again.

The trophy the Italians were defending had been secured in 1934, when the World Cup had been staged in their homeland to show off 'the pulsating of the masculine energies of a bursting vitality, in this our Mussolini's Italy', as Giovanni Mauro, an Italian FIFA delegate, put it. That aside, it may have helped, on a more practical level, that Mussolini hand-picked the referees for each match in which his team played. 'How can Italy not be champions?' Mussolini had mused philosophically at the start of the tournament, presumably while casting his eyes down the list of referees assigned to the World Cup and picking out the ones that might best suit his team's progress.

'They were little crooks,' Josef Bican, the Austria forward, said of the Italians after their semi-final, won 1–0 by Italy and refereed by Ivan Eklind, the Swede, who impressed Mussolini so much that he was also given the honour of officiating at the Final between Italy and Czechoslovakia. 'They used to cheat a little,' Bican added. 'No, they used to cheat a lot. The referee even played for them. When I passed the ball out to the right wing, one of our players, Cicek, ran for it and the referee headed it back to the Italians. It was unbelievable.' Or, as Jean Langenus, a Belgian referee at the 1934 tournament put it, 'In the majority of countries, the World Championship was called a sporting fiasco because beside the desire to win, all other sporting considerations were non-existent and because, moreover, a certain spirit brooded over the whole championship. Italy wanted to win, it was natural, but they allowed it to be seen too clearly.'

For the tournament in France in 1938, a second World Cup contested by Italy in the cause of fascism, Mussolini chose for his team a tasteful strip consisting of the politically provocative black shirts, a fashion item indelibly associated with his regime. The Italians turned out in this natty little number of a change strip for the quarter-final against France at the Stade de Colombes in Paris. It had the immediate effect of bringing down upon the Italians' heads furious and near unanimous condemnation from the 60,000 crowd, both from the French themselves and from several thousand Italians who had been opponents of Mussolini's regime and who were now exiled in Paris.

The reaction of the onlookers had the unwanted effect,

for them, of unifying the Italy team, as Vittorio Pozzo, the Italy manager, had cleverly anticipated, with the Italians winning the tie 3–1 and going on to lift the trophy for a second successive time. Giuseppe Meazza, the captain, gave the fascist salute as he received the trophy and the boys dressed up nicely in sailor suits to be welcomed home by an ecstatic Mussolini, happy to have spared the team their lives in the wake of victory.

'Whether beyond or within the borders, sporting or not, we Italians . . . shook and still shake with joy when seeing in these thoroughbred athletes, that overwhelm so many noble opponents, such a symbol of the overwhelming march of Mussolini's Italians,' is how Londo Ferretti, another of Mussolini's propagandists, summed up the spectacle. England this summer might do well to consider opting for a last-minute change strip consisting of a Union Jack just to get the opposition really riled.

A more modern cause assisted the Italian team in their triumph in 2006. *Calciopoli*, the latest match-fixing scandal to hit contemporary Italian club football and described by Sepp Blatter, president of FIFA, as the worst in the history of the game, coincided with the 2006 World Cup – and the trial, involving Fiorentina, Juventus, Lazio and Milan, which began on the day before Italy's quarter-final with Ukraine, was due to conclude on the day after the World Cup Final. Thirteen of the Italian squad were drawn from the clubs involved and as soon as news of the matter broke, the *Azzurri* were besieged by crisis. There were calls for the players from those clubs to be withdrawn from the tournament – even demands that the Italian team itself should be removed from the World Cup

– and there were repeated calls for manager Marcello Lippi to resign.

Lippi was forced to mount a stubborn and public defence, through extensive press conferences, of the right of his team and players to participate in the tournament. He even received the dreaded vote of confidence from the Italian Football Federation. Massimo de Santis, one of Italy's World Cup referees, and a man subsequently convicted of involvement in match-fixing, was withdrawn from the tournament by the Italian Football Federation and the Italian players themselves felt under siege as opinion swayed back and forth on the matter.

The Italian legal authorities could not have done more to boost the Italian team's tilt at winning the trophy. Indeed, given the labyrinthine manner in which justice operates in that country, it was possible to suspect that the trial had even been timed for exactly that purpose. It was surely odd for a match-fixing trial to be played out parallel to a World Cup. Lippi said during the tournament of *Calciopoli*'s unifying effects, 'We are a family now, like never before.' A pretty dysfunctional one, perhaps, but one whose new-found sense of closeness would see it through to victory with the 58-year-old, paternalistic Lippi at its head, a man who is a master at using psychological wiles to extract the very best from his team.

Having gone to the finals in Germany boosted and unified by the match-fixing scandal, the Italians received regular top-ups to maintain their closeness and sense of a cause during the tournament. With an operatic sense of drama, Gianluca Pessotto, the sporting director of Juventus, one of the clubs under investigation (and subsequently demoted from the top division of Italian football), threw himself out of a fourth-floor window of the club's headquarters while clutching a set of rosary beads on 27 June, plumb in the middle of the World Cup. Pessotto, 35 and a former team-mate of several of the Italian players, thankfully failed in his suicide attempt, which had been sparked by his depression at the implication of his club in the *Calciopoli* scandal, although he suffered severe injuries that would hospitalise him for weeks. Alessandro Del Piero, Gianluca Zambrotta and Ciro Ferrara, the former defender who was by now a coach with Italy, flew home to visit their Juventus colleague in between the last-16 match with Australia and the quarter-final against Ukraine.

As if all that was not enough, the German hosts of the 2006 tournament, which boasted the slogan 'A Time to Make Friends' (and who characterized their hosting of the tournament as 'Operation Smile'), brought the Italians even closer together in advance of the semi-final in which the two nations were due to face each other.

'Lazy and greasy parasites and mamma's boys,' was how the Italians were succinctly described by the Hamburg-based *Der Spiegel* magazine in the build-up to the match. They were also characterized as slimy beach bums whose greatest concern was in perfecting their appearance and who had a habit of emigrating to other countries where, *Der Spiegel* suggested, they had a tendency to 'suck dry' their hosts in the manner of 'parasites'.

The magazine's front cover, entitled 'Holiday Guide to Italy', helpfully illustrated this stereotypical piece with a picture of a bowl of spaghetti with a revolver lying on top of it, which seems an odd place for any Mafioso to keep his gun. Luigi, a fictional Italian stereotype constructed by *Der Spiegel* for the purposes of its piece, was described as a type of 'overgrown baby' whose mission in life is to 'appear tired' while Mamma cooks and cleans and sews around him. After the age of 30, Luigi then seeks a beautiful young Italian wife whom he subsequently treats like a skivvy until she herself turns into an overworked, done-down Mamma while Luigi spends his days 'polishing his Fiat and talking about cars'. Italy would meet Germany by getting past Ukraine, the feature suggested, in their usual 'lazy, oily way'.

Coincidentally, a television campaign in Italy had resulted in FIFA opting to ban Torsten Frings, the Germany midfield player, from the semi-final with Italy after Sky Italia had highlighted Frings' confronting Julio Cruz in the on-field brawl that took place at the conclusion of the Germany–Argentina quarter-final. It was even suggested that, perish the thought, the video evidence on which Frings was banned had been sent to FIFA by the Italian FA.

It mattered little – the task of motivating the Italians had been done. 'No one on our side lifted a finger to make this happen,' muttered an outraged Lippi in relation to Frings' ban in advance of the semi. 'We were as incredulous as anybody else to hear about this today. It is outrageous to say that we were involved. We are happy to play any German team that they wish to field.'

Rino Gattuso was, as might be expected, more emotive than his manager about the slights visited upon his nation by the Germans. The ball-winning midfield player and a man described by Marco Materazzi, the Italy centre back, as being so volatile he was liable to 'split the atom' when he had a cause in his sights, said of *Der Spiegel*'s comments, 'I feel very angry about it. It was an insult to all the Italian people that work here. It gives me a lump in my throat, I get so angry. I still have some uncles who live here and I know how much they suffered like many others who had to leave their homes and come here to find work. This game is so much more important than any I have ever played in before because we are trying to repair the image of Italian football. I can't wait to get out there.' A more languid response was forthcoming from Alessandro Nesta, the stylish centre-back. 'The Germans criticise us but then they dress like us and eat like us. I think there's a touch of jealousy in it.'

The Italians – highly disciplined professionals and supremely aware tactically – now had another unifying cause that helped to make them supremely strong. With the world closing in with its various crises, suddenly for multi-millionaire footballers with every degree of comfort and wealth at their fingertips, it must have been rather like returning to childhood, when the football pitch offered everything to them. If that feeling had in the years since been diluted by good living and the spoils of success, then now, under these circumstances, in a hostile environment, the pitch must have seemed a welcome refuge and the game a source of comfort. Against the Germans, the Italians produced their best performance of the World Cup, proving themselves anything but lazy as they maintained a ferocious pace into extra time.

It was, ironically, the Italians' iron-hard discipline that

provided the basis for this great victory, Lippi's defence holding fast to keep their fifth clean sheet in their sixth match at the tournament. Once the 90 minutes were over, the game became a more open affair as both sides chased the winning goal and Lippi, who had been sure before the tournament that his team had the best defence in the world, now made a calculated gamble based on that belief, which had been strengthened by Italy's perform- ances up to that point. Content that his defence could deal with Germany's attack, he threw on Vincenzo Iaquinta and Alessandro Del Piero during the first half of extra time as Italy went for broke in a 4–2–4 formation that had four forwards nibbling away at the German defence. If the Germans had subconsciously been expecting Italy to revert to stereotype and sit back languorously for the draw, they were wrong.

Cannily, Lippi also had at the back of his mind that if they could not score the breakthrough goal, he had plenty of players on the pitch capable of scoring in the penalty shootout. But there was no need for his back-up plan – Germany's attacks continued to perish on the blue Italian defensive wall and Italy clinched their victory with two superb goals from Fabio Grosso and Alessandro Del Piero in the 119th and 120th minutes of the match.

The meeting with Germany was perhaps the final before the Final, with the two best teams in the competi- tion going head-to-head and giving their all for victory: the Germans were the top scorers in the tournament and the Italians its most accomplished defenders. 'How clever – they really got things right,' *Corriere della Sera*, an

Italian newspaper, commented dryly to provide the perfect coda to the stereotyping in *Der Spiegel* that had helped motivate the Italians so much in their desire to reach the Final.

'It has made us stronger,' Lippi said again of the ever-present spectre of the match-fixing trial whilst his team prepared for the Final. 'Before we came here, I warned the squad that we might face a bad atmosphere but that hasn't happened and we have shown the world that Italian football is alive and beautiful. If we had been a weak squad, *Calciopoli* would probably have wiped us out but we were very strong mentally and the lads managed to turn everything that had happened into positive energy.'

Another element in the Italians' resolve was a purely footballing one. At the 2002 World Cup, Italy had been eliminated in the first knockout round by South Korea – helped by some severely questionable refereeing – and they had then failed to make it through the group stages at the 2004 European Championships. 'We've accumulated a lot of anger after two major disappointments,' Fabio Cannavaro, the Italy captain, said. 'We put that rage to good use on the pitch and you can see that at the World Cup – we are turning that anger into something positive.'

England's record in advance of the 2010 finals is not too dissimilar to that of the Italians: elimination by Portugal on penalties in the 2006 World Cup quarter-final and failure to qualify for Euro 2008. As with Italy, who appointed a hugely experienced Champions League winner in the shape of Lippi in 2004, so England too installed as manager a man with similar experience and pedigree in Fabio Capello to take them through the two years prior to the World Cup.

It helped Italy that Lippi had created a tight-knit squad long before the World Cup began. During his first year in charge he had given out caps freely, experimenting with players, a number of whom were surprising choices for international recognition. Then, in mid-2005, the manager reversed that policy, following that period of expansion with one of contraction: he pulled up the drawbridge behind a select band of favoured players. This had the effect of unifying them in the knowledge that they were the ones who had come through the manager's selection process and who would be entrusted with World Cup work. The process of spreading the net wide had been productive – Luca Toni, now at Fiorentina, and Fabio Grosso had both caught Lippi's eye while at Sicilian club Palermo and had established their claims as internationals regardless of their modest club origins.

The tumultuous semi-final had taken a lot out of the Italians and when, in the Final, France began to get the upper hand during the second half, it was team spirit that saw the fatigued Italian side through. Almost as importantly, when their defence was breached, they had in Gianluigi Buffon a goalkeeper with a tendency to make exceptional saves look routine. When the match finished 1–1 and went to a penalty shootout, a most unusual event unfolded, with the Italian players surrounding Lippi and clamouring to be allowed the honour of taking a penalty kick. It said much about their unity of purpose.

'We are no longer just the nation of match-fixing, the

people who wash the dishes and cook the pizzas,' Umberto Zapelloni, an Italian journalist, wrote in *La Gazzetta dello Sport*, after Italy's victory, 5–3 on penalties. 'Thank you, Italy.' Gattuso was clear as to the principal guiding light that had led them to their victory. 'If the [match-fixing] scandal hadn't happened I don't think we would have won the World Cup,' he said. 'We demonstrated that with humility and the desire to be a real team you can achieve your objectives. When we've gone to a World Cup like prima donnas we've come home sooner than expected.'

Having been forced by external forces to act humbly and muck in together, the Italians' finer qualities had shone through. Nor can the team's desire to project a more acceptable image of their nation than that presented by *Calciopoli* be underestimated. 'We've shown we are great footballers, not criminals,' Alessandro Del Piero evinced. Pride had clearly been hurt and the World Cup seen as a means of mending it. In a nice gesture, Ferrara and Cannavaro took the World Cup to show the ailing Pessotto on their return to Italy.

In tandem with the heightened emotional reaction to adverse circumstances, there was sound practical sense behind the Italians' victory. They had opted for a comfortable but far from ostentatious base at the Hotel Landhaus Milser, an establishment in Duisburg that is run by Italians and possesses an Italian restaurant. The entertainment for the players was so determinedly down to earth that it consisted of nothing more than having a table-football game delivered at the beginning of June 2006 to help the boys feel the homely ambience to the

full. Not that it was anything approaching a dosshouse –
not with a choice of 50 Italian wines and pasta lovingly
stretched into perfect shape on the premises – but it was
the sort of place that a middle-aged couple, enjoying a
rare weekend away from their teenage kids, might find
sedately restful. 'Everything was done by the book,' Fabio
Cannavaro says of the organisational side of Italy's victory. 'Nothing was missing.'

It contrasted severely with England's base at Baden-
Baden, where Sven-Göran Eriksson languorously presided
over what appeared often like a bacchanalian celebration
of wealth, celebrity, shopping and bling. With the players'
wives and girlfriends so closely in attendance and sharing
so much prominence with the players in reports home, it
threw into debate just exactly who were the stars of the
England show in Germany and spawned a new acronym:
WAGS – for wives and girlfriends.

'Ours was the practical choice,' Marcello Lippi said.
'The airport, ten minutes, the training ground, ten
minutes, the city, ten minutes; a one-hour flight to all
the matches. The hotel was nice but not luxurious; it had
a garden and a small lake.' The modern footballer,
endowed with high-maintenance companions, fast cars
and access to the world's most splendiferous hotels at
the twang of a credit card, appreciates, it would seem,
something a bit more Spartan if he is to concentrate on
his work. England under Fabio Capello appear likely
to be more attuned to the necessities for competing well
in a World Cup in their planned choice of base for
the 2010 finals, the Bafokeng Sports Campus, whose
newly constructed hotel and training facilities sit in a

splendidly isolated rural location, with ready access to flights across South Africa.

Italy's World Cup victory in 1982 also owed much to a turning inwards for strength in the face of hostile external forces, on that occasion taking the form of press criticism, which perpetrated such slurs on the players as to suggest that they were taking hard drugs and that some had paired off in couples. But they were neither the first nor last to be united by a hostile domestic press but that, as they say, is another story.

Other nations have also been galvanised by a cause; not always, as in the case of the Italians, for the entirety of a tournament but at crucial junctures, when a spurt of inspiration was required from a team pulling together in harmony. At the Mexico World Cup in 1986, Argentina found themselves in a quarter-final with England for their first meeting with a British side since the Falklands conflict four years previously.

During the spring of 1982, Argentinian forces had invaded and occupied the Falkland Islands, a British overseas territory 300 miles from the coast of South America but claimed by Argentina as Las Islas Malvinas. British forces were dispatched to the South Atlantic and after a conflict lasting for two months that brought casualties on both sides, Argentina was forced to accept defeat and withdraw. The attempt to seize the islands had been one of the final throws of the dice of the generals who comprised a junta that had been in power since a military coup in 1976. This attempt at reviving support for the junta resulted in 255 British deaths and 649 on the Argentinian side, with more than half of those

18

Argentinian fatalities arising from the sinking of the cruiser *General Belgrano*. The enterprise could hardly be seen as a glorious cause, although it did spark a wave of powerful popular protest in Argentina that helped sweep away the junta.

The Mexican security forces, concerned about the prospect of warring English and Argentinian supporters, mobilised their own armed forces to deal with the situation and soldiers and sailors backed up the everyday police force as every fan was frisked on entry to the Azteca Stadium in Mexico City. Bobby Robson, the England manager, issued martial-type pre-match instructions to his players that demanded that they take out one prominent member of the opposition team. 'The nearest man goes to [Diego] Maradona and kills him,' Robson said, 'and if he doesn't, the next one does; simple as that.' The instructions clearly weren't heeded.

Maradona, for his part, was keen before the match to play down any link between the game and the Falklands issue. 'Why do you keep asking this question?' he asked journalists pressing him on it. 'We are not taking knives and guns on to the pitch.' The player had been well briefed by Carlos Bilardo, his manager, who had anticipated the Falklands issue being raised. 'I got the boys together,' Bilardo said, 'and I told them, "Tomorrow we'll have the press with us. We've got an open training session and the first thing they're going to ask you is how you feel. This is a sporting event and we only talk about football here." But we all knew what we felt.'

Nery Pumpido, the goalkeeper, still went bullishly off-message pre-match. 'To beat the English could constitute a double satisfaction for everything that happened in the Malvinas,' he said. Subsequent to Argentina's 2–1 victory, *Crónica*, an Argentinian newspaper, got the 1986 World Cup quarter-final in some sort of perspective. 'Malvinas 2 England 1! We blasted the English pirates with Maradona and a little hand. He who robs a thief has a thousand years of pardon.'

Maradona, for his part, would later admit that the Falklands had been much more of a motivation for him and his team-mates than he had maintained at the time. 'More than defeating a team it was defeating a country,' he said. 'Of course, before the match we said that a football match had nothing to do with the Malvinas War but we knew a lot of Argentinian kids had died there, shot down like little birds. This was revenge. It was like recovering a little bit of the Malvinas. In the pre-match interviews we had all said that football and politics shouldn't be confused but that was a lie. We did nothing but think about that. In a way we blamed the English players for everything that happened, for all the suffering of the Argentine people.'

A more romantic South American cause inspired Garrincha, Brazil's wayward winger, in Chile in 1962. With Pelé suffering an injury in Brazil's second match, against Czechoslovakia, that kept him out of the remainder of the tournament, Garrincha became the Brazilians' chief source of talismanic inspiration. His desire to win the cup was fuelled by his burgeoning love affair with the singer Elza Soares who, by chance, flew in to perform at a music festival in Avisa, close to Valparaiso and Brazil's training base in Viña del Mar on the Chilean coast. When

Soares visited the team's hotel mid-tournament, Garrincha promised her, 'I am going to win the cup for you.'

He fulfilled his vow. 'At Viña del Mar we lost to one man,' Bobby Charlton said of Garrincha's effect on Brazil's 3–1 win in the quarter-final with England, in which Garrincha scored his first two goals of the competition. 'Little Garrincha scored with a header. He beat a lot of our big, strapping centre-halves. He outjumped them and headed the first goal and then he bent a free-kick round the wall, which nobody really did in those days . . .'

Brazil's semi-final against the hosts saw Garrincha supersede even that performance, smacking in two stunning goals to put Brazil into a 2–0 lead in their eventual 4–2 victory. 'What planet is Garrincha from?' Chile's *Mercurio* newspaper was moved to ask about the man fast emerging as the player of the tournament.

At the final whistle in Brazil's 3–1 victory over Czechoslovakia in the Final, Soares fainted, but half an hour later she boldly made her way through the dressing room, ignored the naked athletes who shared that small space with her and made straight for the shower to embrace passionately the man who had won the World Cup for her. This was daring stuff for 1962. Soares, the woman whose face and body had inspired the Brazil winger's near sensual performances, and whose affair with the then married Garrincha would be a source of some scandal, was in no doubt of her role in bringing the trophy to Brazil. 'The 1962 World Cup was a tribute to me,' she said. 'Garrincha told me, "Thank you so much for coming here, you make me so happy. I'll play better now because of it." '

As the 2010 World Cup nears, one nation, tragically, already has a cause in its heart. When Robert Enke, the Germany goalkeeper, committed suicide by walking in front of a train travelling at 100mph in early November 2009 it united the German nation in grief. Joachim Löw, the Germany manager, declared himself 'totally empty' on hearing the news of Enke's death. The Hanover goal-keeper, 32, had been treated for depression during the previous six years and had suffered the loss of Lara, his two-year-old daughter, in 2006. Enke had nonetheless enjoyed a resurgence in his career, being voted best goal-keeper in the Bundesliga in 2008/09 by his fellow professionals and winning eight caps from his debut for Germany in 2007. He had a strong chance of representing his country as their number 1 choice at the finals in South Africa.

Tragedy can unite a set of players. Of course, by the time of the finals in South Africa, the hard edge of the grief felt by Enke's team-mates in the national side will have softened, but his memory will remain in their hearts. It may be that they will see it as honouring him to do all they can to win the tournament or that remembering him will add to their seriousness of purpose as they go about their business. It will certainly have an effect, just as all the causes before it have done.

2

Have a Mad Manager

IMAGINE YOURSELF IN THE SWEATY AND SQUEAKY SHOES OF Carlos Bilardo inside the sweltering Azteca Stadium in Mexico City during the 1986 World Cup Final. You have been slogging away as a manager for the best part of two decades, combining your work admirably with the myriad demands of being nothing less than a gynaecologist, and before that you were a committed club footballer and an Olympic football representative with the Argentina team, although never quite good enough to make the full inter-national side.

Now, having been sacked by Colombia as their manager shortly before the 1982 World Cup, you are your own country's manager, and after all those years of struggle you are on the cusp of the greatest prize possible for any football manager. Your team is on the verge of World Cup glory, winning 3–2 against a West Germany side that includes Lothar Matthäus, Klaus Allofs,

Karl-Heinz Rummenigge and Rudi Völler and managed by Franz Beckenbauer.

The final whistle sounds and your players clasp each other in emotion. Yet your immediate reaction is one of utter fury and bitter despair, and you are so insanely angry that the only way you can cope with it is to lock yourself in your hotel room, away from the partying and the celebrations. You do so only after you have addressed your gleeful players sternly in the dressing room and tried to introduce an element of sobriety to their celebrations by telling them to bear in mind that they have a World Cup to defend in four years' time and that their preparations for that must begin right away.

A World Cup-winning manager must be strong and single-minded, that's a given, but it is a huge help if he also appears to be borderline psychotic. Bilardo emphasised his credentials as a football madman by looking like one. During the Mexico tournament he could be seen constantly twitching on the touchline and smoothing down his pate, like someone who has just had a hair transplant grafted on to his head and who is anxiously checking it is still in place, while his body jerked and twisted and turned here and there, with his pop-eyes and large nose giving the impression that the pulsing, maniacal tension pounding round his head might make his face explode at any moment.

Bilardo's fury had erupted after the final whistle at the Azteca Stadium that day because his side had been 2–0 up and then conceded two German goals from corners; this was especially blameworthy in his opinion because the prevention of opposition goals from set pieces was something on which he had worked tirelessly with his players. It made little difference to him that his centre back José Luis Brown had sustained a serious shoulder injury that was hampering him in the final stages of the match, when both of the Germans' goals had arrived. The second of those, Völler's close-range header, had levelled the scores ten minutes from time but three minutes later Jorge Burruchaga, sent clear brilliantly by Diego Maradona, nicked the winner for the Argentinians. The deflation at being pulled level only heightened the feeling of release in the team at notching victory so soon afterwards, but not for Bilardo, who could only brood in solitary confinement about the loss of those two preventable goals.

Nor was this a case of the tensions of a World Cup Final overwhelming an individual. Even mid-tournament, even away from the heat and dust of the arena, Bilardo deliberately maintained a feverish state of anxiety among his players. On one occasion he discovered Jorge Valdano, his striker and a renowned intellectual and bibliophile, sitting reading a book. That would seem a fairly innocent act but it was enough to provoke a near-hysterical re-action in Bilardo.

'What are you doing reading?' Bilardo demanded of his forward.

'I need it to relax,' was Valdano's reasonable reply.

Bilardo retorted sharply, 'You don't need to relax.'

Again Valdano was reasonableness itself. 'But I get too nervous otherwise.'

Bilardo bit back at him, 'You have to be nervous.'

Valdano said, 'But I'll go mad.'

Bilardo, relentless, immediately snapped, 'You have to go mad.'

On another occasion, midway through the tournament, the Argentina manager came haring out of the team hotel, bug-eyed with anxiety. 'Jesus! Where is Jesus? Where is Jesus?' he yelled. This piece of divine madness had been inspired by one of the two Mexican police motorcycle outriders assigned to the Argentina team going by that name and the duo being considered by Bilardo and his players to be lucky talismans. On that day, the officer had not turned up at the expected time to escort the bus, sparking a panic attack in Bilardo, one fuelled by superstition at the seeming loss of a walking, talking, good-luck charm.

Manager Bilardo had transformed the Argentina camp during that World Cup into a place for people who enjoyed living on the edge of lunacy. It is not coincidental that the 1986 World Cup would turn out to be the tournament indelibly associated with Diego Maradona, a man who specialises in enjoying the vagaries of life on the edge. 'If a coach or player says they don't feel nervous,' Bilardo says, 'then they should really go and do something else because it's good to feel nerves inside. When the game starts all that goes and the player concentrates on playing and the coach on what he's doing.' Nor had Bilardo softened a jot by the time of Italia '90. 'To be honest,' he thundered at the first team meeting after Argentina's surprise defeat by Cameroon in the tournament's opening game, 'if we are going to get knocked out playing like that, then I hope our plane crashes on the way home.'

Bilardo may have given a good impression of being almost unhinged, but a certain degree of 'otherness' is essential in a World Cup-winning manager. Take Marcello Lippi, the Italy manager in 2006. At the decisive moment in the penalty shootout in the Final with France, with the Italians having just become world champions and with all of the Italian backroom staff rushing deliriously to join the players on the field, Lippi paused to return to the inside of the dugout and lift his tracksuit top and glasses case from their place on its rear shelf, like a schoolteacher gathering together his various bits and pieces on hearing the final bell of the day while his pupils bustle excitedly out of the classroom. It seemed worryingly uninvolved for someone who had just achieved immortality as a manager and was no doubt on enough of a winning bonus to ensure he might just be able to buy another tracksuit top, and even a replacement set of glasses.

A decade earlier, when Lippi had managed Juventus to victory in a penalty shootout against Ajax in the 1996 Champions League Final, his spectacles had been smashed to bits underfoot in the melee of celebrating players and backroom staff. Thinking back to that incident, he was determined this would not happen again. So as Fabio Grosso prepared to take Italy's fifth and potentially decisive penalty, Lippi removed his spectacles and carefully placed them in the pocket of his tracksuit top, certain that Grosso's kick would secure the win. He may have had only a blurred view of the full back's beautifully clipped shot sweetly kissing the back of the net but at least his glasses were safe. It does present an image of a manager able to think with cool detachment amid a situation of some turmoil, one in which other people might lose themselves.

Lippi, like Bilardo, was still thinking utterly rationally rather than emotionally at the moment of victory and could then stand back and enjoy his trademark cigar while watching the Italian players complete their lap of honour through untarnished glasses. You can't have everything, though. Lippi only managed to get through half of his celebratory cigar before the players had returned to encourage him to join in with their enthusiastic jumping and shouting. That Lippi would afterwards clearly remember that he had only progressed midway through that smoke suggests that it bothers him, even if only slightly, that he had lost a bit of control over events.

Alf Ramsey, similarly, at the greatest point in his career, remained seated on the touchline at Wembley after the final whistle in the 1966 Final. Slightly hunched over, with a distant-looking gaze, he was like a man on an isolated park bench lost in hazy contemplation of the vagaries of life, while all others let loose their feelings around him and 100,000 people roared their throats off. 'I realised I had to be sensible but inside I was completely drunk. I was dancing,' Ramsey would say of his stone-faced lack of reaction at the conclusion of the match, when his self-restraint enjoyed a knockout victory over expressiveness. His authority over the players had been constructed on his maintaining a sense of distance from them and he would still be their manager after the World Cup, so he had to uphold his bearing. His sense of duty, of what was proper for the man in charge, prevailed.

It would have been out of character for Ramsey to have leapt around at full-time and if it had not been for that stoical, steady approach, there might have been no victory

28

to celebrate. At the conclusion of the 90 minutes, with the England players reeling from having conceded a West German equaliser 15 seconds from the end to make it 2–2 and force extra time, Ramsey, unsmiling and serious of purpose, had strode towards them unhurried and unflustered, ready to impart key points to them. It was British stiff upper lip employed to best effect.

'All right. Forget what's just happened,' Ramsey said evenly and coolly to his players. 'You've been the better team. You've won the World Cup once. Now go and win it again. Look at the Germans. They're flat out. Down on the grass. They can't live with you. Not for another half-hour. Not through extra time.'

Had Ramsey said the wrong words at that time it could have had a drastic effect and might even have resulted in England losing their grasp on the match. Instead, Ramsey's detachment had enabled him to think carefully and critically. 'I realised that I must not indicate either by word or expression the least degree of sympathy for the team because they had to go on playing,' Ramsey said of his carefully chosen words and unemotional demeanour before the extra half-hour. 'I knew they could do it; they knew they could do it. But even a casual "hard luck" might have put doubt in their minds.'

When the match resumed England were refreshed and revitalised while the West Germans failed to create even one scoring chance in the additional 30 minutes. At the match's conclusion Ramsey permitted himself only a half-smile, expending his energy in ensuring that his players did not show a lack of decorum by exchanging shirts with their opponents in full sight of the crowd and in attempting to resist attempts by his players for him to be pictured alongside them with the trophy.

Ramsey remained seemingly detached even as the players implored him to embark upon a lap of honour with them – something he politely declined. His dogged, stoical and phlegmatic demeanour remained unchanged even in the light of victory. For Ramsey, being manager was a duty and that sense of service was not going to desert him after it had worked so well in leading him to football's ultimate triumph. His adoption of a remote, icy image, although fitting in with his slightly reserved character, was not done to draw attention to himself. The victory at Wembley belonged, he insisted, to the players and he was not going to do anything to impinge on their day. He saw it as being for them, not him, to bask in the adulation of the crowd. Eventually, after much persuasion, he was coerced into what for him was as flamboyant a gesture as swapping his dapper Savile Row suit for a pair of Carnaby Street bell bottoms and a frilly shirt: he quickly kissed the World Cup trophy.

Once the players had returned to the dressing room, Ramsey, as with Bilardo, proved professionally scrupulous in giving vent to his disappointment at a flaw he had noticed in his team. Bobby Charlton, focal point of the England side, was his victim, Ramsey laying into the player for giving the ball away too often, shooting too many times instead of retaining possession. Only then did Ramsey let loose and perform a tour of the dressing room to offer warm and hearty congratulations to his men, clapping them and hugging them, but his detached demeanour soon reasserted itself. As Geoff Hurst, whose hat-trick in the Final had guaranteed victory, went to leave at the end of the most glorious day of his life, his international future looked assured. 'See you soon Alf,' Hurst said chirpily. Crisply and evenly Ramsey replied, 'Perhaps, Geoffrey, perhaps.'

It seems imperative in a manager that he must be to some degree eccentric, must possess a certain amount of 'otherness', if he is to become an electrifying focal point for his players and for his country. Argentina in 1978 had César Luis Menotti, a 39-year-old self-proclaimed socialist whose trendy, playboy-style shoulder-length hair was as long as that of his players and who looked more like a lounge lizard than a hardened football manager. Menotti, who was relaxed and free with his players, chain-smoked his way through matches and espoused what he described as 'left-wing football', an expansive attacking game, at a time when Argentina was ruled by a right-wing junta that was relying on the football tournament to help shore up their rule.

By presenting an image at odds with the regime, Menotti could give the impression of being almost subversive, helping to draw his players and a country chilled by its military rulers close together, disassociating them from the regime even as it lusted after their victory in the World Cup. On the day of Argentina's Final with Holland, he ordered his players to look at the people in the stands and not at the representatives of the ruling military junta in the VIP box. 'We are not going to look at the stage-box of the authorities,' he said to the players. 'We are going to look to the terraces, to all the people, where perhaps sits the father of each of us, because there we will find the metal workers, the butchers, the bakers and the taxi drivers.' Going against the flow is essential in a World Cup-winning manager.

Democracy had returned to Argentina by the time of Bilardo's appointment. So, ironically, whereas when the country was ruled by a right-wing government the team had an alternative-style manager, now, in freer times, the team had a manager who was considerably more conservative and obsessive in approach. So much so that Menotti would not only criticise Bilardo for his style of football at both the 1986 and 1990 World Cups but would extend his jibes to his successor's taste in music.

Franz Beckenbauer, West Germany's manager in 1990, proved himself strikingly different when, at his first World Cup in charge of the team in 1986, he introduced the vogue for the manager to be standing upright on the side-lines to observe the match throughout. Every manager must dominate their particular set of players and they must have a tic, a trademark approach, that distinguishes them and that, almost paradoxically, both sets them apart and draws people to them. Italy in 1982 had the delicate, sparrow-like focal figure of Enzo Bearzot, who, on the touchline, would drape his white jacket over his shoulders as if about to embark on a leisurely evening promenade, transmitting coolness and relaxation to his players. Brazil in 1958 had as manager Vicente Feola, a very tubby gentleman so relaxed that it would sometimes appear that he had fallen asleep on the bench during training sessions.

Encouragingly for England, they now have a manager

who fits the profile. Phlegmatic and controlled, Fabio Capello shows signs of being in the Ramsey school of going against the flow. Isn't it odd that it took a man from Italy, a country with a reputation for crazy disorganisation, to impose a high degree of order on the footballing representatives of a country with a reputation for discipline and control? At the conclusion of the match with Croatia in September 2009 that sealed England's qualification, John Terry, the then England captain, appeared set to embrace Capello with a hug and then quickly thought better of it, settling for a strong, manly handshake instead, possibly with thoughts of expulsion for over-familiarity flashing through his head. In a twenty-first-century English football culture that panders to its multi-millionaires' every whim, Capello's refusal to indulge his players and bask in the shadow of their shallow celebrity sets him apart in Ramsey-like fashion and ensures he obtains respect for his singular approach to the job.

Behind the veil of madness that screened Carlos Bilardo's work at the 1986 World Cup, there was a large degree of method. In the years prior to the tournament, frustrated at seeing his players only for a few days at a time, and then only before international matches, he would travel to Europe to conduct three- or four-man training sessions with Argentina internationals based on the Continent, bringing with him videos to show them how he wished them to play. He would also stay at their homes so that he could spend as much time as possible with them, driving their spouses mad by sitting up until the early hours to talk endlessly, unstoppably, obsessively of his vision of football. This was innovative and unorthodox but it had the effect of dismantling the barrier of remoteness that traditionally hamper the efforts of those who manage international teams with players scattered among far-flung club sides. Those players who were based in Argentina would, unusually for international footballers, be summoned to working lunches at which Bilardo would outline to them the manner in which he wished his team to play.

When Bilardo did oversee full training sessions, he would introduce elements of detail that would seep into the consciousness of the players and ensure they would be in peak form on matchday, such as insisting that no player stand with his hands on his hips during training. Bilardo's logic was that if a player were to adopt such a stance during a competitive game, it would send out a message to opponents that they were tired, thus handing a psychological advantage to the other team. 'For Bilardo,' Jorge Valdano, the striker who partnered Diego Maradona, says, 'football is a sort of holy war, part of the civic mission of an army which fights for every inch of the battlefield and every second of the game.'

In January 1983 when Diego Maradona first set eyes on Bilardo, the new manager of Argentina, his immediate thought was, 'This guy's crazy, this guy's sick in the head . . .' It would, Maradona says, be something he thought time and again over the seven and a half years in which Bilardo managed the Argentina national team. Maradona, then a player with Barcelona, was that winter recovering from hepatitis in seclusion at Lloret del Mar on the Costa Brava and had just ambled on to the local

beach in preparation for a training run, when, un-
announced, Bilardo turned up, strode towards him, kissed
him and asked if Maradona could lend him a tracksuit
top so that he could accompany the player for a jog.
It was an unorthodox way for a new international
manager to introduce himself but it made an immediate
impression.

For all Bilardo's methodical style, his videos and his
lunchtime tactics talks, it was to be a gamble of monumental proportions that would see him through to the
1986 World Cup Final in the Azteca Stadium. At that
meeting in southern Spain, Bilardo offered Maradona the
captaincy of the Argentina team. The player tearfully
accepted, despite feeling 'petrified' by the offer, although
he might have been expected to be better prepared for
such a moment, given that he had collected no fewer than
200 captain's armbands in anticipation of such an honour.
Claudia, his wife, immediately scooted off to fetch them
from a bulging drawer so that Bilardo could cast his eyes
over these armbands, collected from Maradona's travels
around the world – a nice 'mad' touch that Bilardo would
surely have appreciated. Given that Bilardo and
Maradona were on the same wavelength – that is, way off
the frequencies most people use – it seems entirely unsur-
prising that the man and his manager understood each
other so well. 'I was prepared to play wherever Bilardo
wanted me,' Maradona says, adding in his usual under-
stated fashion, 'The mad guy seemed convinced and I was
going to follow him, to the death.'

From then on, Bilardo, when asked about his team for
Mexico in 1986, would say, 'Maradona and ten others'.

This was quite an investment of responsibility in the player, who had last been seen on the world stage in 1982 booting João Batista, a Brazil player, firmly in the midriff and being swiftly dismissed as Argentina made a sorry exit from the World Cup in Spain. Maradona had gone into that tournament regarded as something of an enigma at international level, one who found it difficult to cope with being crowded by defenders and who, at 21, was finding it extremely tricky to deal with the chaos that always seemed to inveigle its way into his life. He had gone through such things as a series of complicated transfer deals and niggling injuries to his powerful, five-foot-four-inch frame, which his various football clubs had bulked out on a diet of steak from the Pampas since Maradona had made his Argentinian League debut in his mid-teens.

So depressed had Maradona become by the furore surrounding his labyrinthine transfer from Argentinos Juniors to Boca Juniors a year before the 1982 finals, and so exhausted was he by the number of games he had been forced to play as his club sides cashed in on exhibiting his talent, that he had asked to be rested from international football shortly before the tournament in Spain began. At that stage, Maradona appeared on the verge of being broken by his own talents. César Luis Menotti, the Argentina manager in 1982, had refused to indulge him or give him preferential treatment, other than by allowing him to wear his favourite number 10 shirt. A lack of teamwork had let the Argentinians down at the 1982 World Cup, so Bilardo's favouring of a single, seemingly unstable prima donna looked like a crazy way to reassert that quality in his team for the 1986 finals.

Adding to all the baggage that Maradona brought with him, by 1986 he was also known by those inside the Argentinian fold to be a user of recreational drugs; and the elevation of such an unpredictable and combustible individual to the captaincy, together with his installation as Bilardo's only certain starter, had the side effect of irritating Daniel Passarella, Maradona's predecessor as captain and the man who had led Argentina to World Cup glory in 1978. So annoyed was Passarella, a more conservative figure than Maradona, with the seemingly favourable treatment being shown the younger man that in 1985 he drew a line in the sand, threatening that he would not go to Mexico with the squad unless he too was named by Bilardo as a certain starter. No such assurance was forthcoming. Bilardo was also plagued by critics outside the Argentina squad who demanded to know why he had given Maradona such elevated status. By 1985, despite having been made captain two years earlier, the player had not appeared for his national team at all in the three years after the 1982 World Cup, as Bilardo opted to experiment with Argentina-based players.

Clinching the World Cup did not dispel Bilardo's annoyance at being questioned intensely prior to the tournament about his deliberate favouring of Maradona, and decades after that tournament he would still pore over the cuttings that he kept about his person from four Argentinian newspapers that criticised his approach. Bilardo's reasoning had been simple: that forcing responsibility upon Maradona would force the player to act responsibly.

The Argentinian public were not convinced prior to the tournament. A hairy qualifying campaign had seen their team just squeeze into the finals with a last-gasp equaliser in a 2–2 draw with Peru in Buenos Aires, enabling them to avoid a play-off by the narrowest of margins. The team's subsequent results in pre-tournament friendlies were patchy. Maradona was recognised as a genius but the rest of Bilardo's team characterised as something of a faceless supporting cast. When the squad met up in May 1986 to prepare for the finals tournament, there was a feeling of persecution among them. Not only from the supporters but also from President Raúl Alfonsín, who even suggested that Bilardo ought to be replaced as manager.

'If Bilardo goes, I go,' Maradona asserted, in an interesting echo of Alf Ramsey's pledge to resign if the FA forced Nobby Stiles out of the World Cup squad on a disciplinary matter in 1966. Maradona felt that there was a 'total lack of respect' inside Argentina for the World Cup squad of 1986 prior to the tournament.

The Argentinians would be the first squad to arrive in Mexico for the World Cup, largely because they had left home in a hurry after rumours that if they lingered longer the government would intervene and remove Bilardo from his post. As a means of avoiding his seemingly imminent dismissal, Bilardo had arranged, at the drop of a hat, friendly matches in Norway, Israel and then Switzerland, far away from frenzied Argentina. They were on the road for 20 days before arriving in Mexico.

'We had to leg it out of the country,' Bilardo would remember of that time. 'Even the government was calling for my head.' Prior to departure, the manager told the members of his squad to take with them only one suit and a sheet. 'If we win the World Cup, we come back wearing the suit,' Bilardo told them. 'If we don't we will put on a white sheet and travel to Arabia instead.' That Argentina squad must be the only World Cup winners to have been forced into temporary political exile so that they could remain together as they sought to bring glory for their country.

It proved to be a boon in strengthening and uniting the players. 'Bilardo was the only one who had trusted us,' José Luis Brown said of the manager's faith in the players, who had been seen off at the airport only by their close families. 'I'd rather be understood by 30 players than 30 million people,' was how Bilardo put it. From all that, a strength and togetherness developed inside the squad. After a stormy confrontation at a team meeting shortly before the tournament, when Passarella accused Maradona of being a drug-taker and of misleading younger players, the former captain left the squad, officially through illness, and after that, according to Maradona, the remainder of the players really began to pull together.

Although well regarded as a footballer, Passarella was a bullying, confrontational individual and the last remaining link with the 1978 team. His departure was significant in that one of the problems for the squad in 1982 had been a rift between the 1978 winners and the new players and consequently they had failed to gel. Now, a new team, fresh and non-reliant on past reputations, was ready for the challenge of the 1986 World Cup. The flow of bitchiness and back-biting, the traditional blight of Argentina's World Cup squads, had been stemmed just in time, precipitated by Bilardo's stubbornness and eccentricity in naming Maradona as the only player assured of a place in his starting eleven.

Maradona was strongly motivated on a personal level by the events of 1982 and by his determination to extract what he called 'revenge' for his and his team's failure to progress at that tournament. As with many of Maradona's pronouncements, it is difficult to know exactly upon whom the revenge was to be extracted, but for Argentina it didn't matter, just as long as their great player had that powerful galvanising thought in his head to get him fired up for action.

Bilardo was emphatic as he found himself engulfed in the pre-tournament criticism. 'Let me have Maradona for 30 days and then we'll talk,' he said and his appointment of Maradona as captain worked. For all his outrageous talent, he never demanded favourable treatment, mucked in with the rest of the team and worked like a demon on the pitch. Now that Passarella was out of the way, there was a motivation to prove that his adversary had been incorrect in his assertion that Maradona would be a disruptive influence. It inspired his team-mates and made them redouble their efforts to match his work rate, in turn bolstering further the platform from which his talents could be launched to take on the world. Then, of course, his skills in themselves were awe-inspiring. 'He is the soul of our team,' Jorge Valdano said as the tournament unfolded. 'He is our great offensive key. Diego can make a balanced team into world champions. Without him, we would have to change our whole tactical scheme, perhaps have to find new players, to make up for the attacking possibilities Diego provides just by his presence.'

It was the quarter-final with England that solidified Argentina's progress and made them believe the World Cup was truly in sight. The 2–1 victory over an improving England team showcased all that was good and bad about Maradona, his 'Hand of God' goal opening the scoring and his brilliant solo run, begun from within his own half, putting Argentina 2–0 ahead. But it was the closing stages of that game that really brought Bilardo to the brink. Argentina playing a 3–5–2 formation, pioneered in international football by him, left space either side of their three central defenders and made them vulnerable to the introduction of a winger, as shown by the arrival of John Barnes with 15 minutes remaining.

It was Barnes who crossed from the left for Gary Lineker to head a goal for England in the 80th minute; and even though Bilardo was fully alive to the turbulent effect Barnes was having on his team, he refused to bring on a full back to make a back four, not even for the dying minutes, opting instead, even at such a crucial time in such a vital match, to favour principle over pragmatism. Bringing on a full back, he felt, would compromise the new system on which he had been working for four years, even if it did offer the best chance of smothering Barnes's talents.

Instead, the England winger was allowed to continue without special provision being made for him and from one Barnes cross, pinpointed to the back post, Lineker looked certain to score, until Julio Olarticoechea, the wing back, with a lunge of supreme athleticism and world-class skill, somehow nudged the ball away with his head from under the crossbar just as the England forward was considering the best way in which to celebrate the goal. Lineker remains to this day unable to understand how the Argentinian managed to do it. Bilardo's resolve, thanks to the acrobatic alacrity of Olarticoechea, won the day.

It was after this win over England, forged in steel, that strong belief in the Argentina team began to sweep their home nation – all thanks to another bloody-minded gamble from Bilardo that had only just come off for him. A World Cup-winning manager must have an indomitable faith in what he believes is right, even if others question it – and football is never like a game of chess, regardless of what the analogists may say: human error is built into even the best tactical system. Bilardo had gambled that his system would prevail more than it would fail and was prepared to stand or fall by his belief in it.

So when Arppi Filho, the dapper little Brazilian referee, blew for full-time in the 1986 World Cup Final, Bilardo was unable to celebrate. He could accept a superior team outmanoeuvring his side in open play but not losing goals from set pieces – something that offended his clear ideas on how the game should be played and which he had been drip-drip-dripping into his players through all those intense training and video sessions down the years.

On returning to the dressing room after the match, Bilardo encountered President Alfonsín, who only two months earlier had publicly expressed his dissatisfaction with the manager and who, with the nimble-footedness of a politician, now warmly congratulated him. 'Sorry Bilardo Thank You' one Argentinian supporters' banner had read high on the terraces of the Azteca that afternoon. The president too owed his football manager an apology. After carrying out some media interviews on the opposite side of the stadium to the dressing rooms, Bilardo emerged from that side of the Azteca some time after the final whistle, blinking into the light, to find himself, a newly anointed World Cup-winning manager, alone on a stretch of open ground, from where he returned to his hotel room to brood over the loss of those goals. 'I think his life is all about being obsessive in every aspect,' José Luis Brown, scorer of Argentina's first goal, says. 'Even Carlos would say that he was sorry he had missed the beautiful moments in life.'

It was less visibly lonely for Bilardo and the team when they returned to Buenos Aires to find six million people welcoming them home. Idiosyncratically, he refused to have any pictures taken of him with the World Cup trophy that he had worked so hard to hold. This was as a means of motivating himself for Italia '90 – he would, he promised himself, have his picture taken with the World Cup if Argentina were able to retain it.

Bilardo managed to guide them to the Final of the tournament in Italy but his team, riddled with injuries and self-inflicted suspensions, was a wan shadow of the 1986 version and was beaten 1–0 by West Germany. Bilardo proved too bashful to ask the Germans to allow him to be pictured with the great trophy even though he craved such a picture. In reality, behind the screen of craziness, Bilardo was really just another of those men who, although by nature quiet and thoughtful, find that their emotions become captured, twisted and mangled by the heady intoxication of being involved in the game of football being played out on the ultimate stage.

When Maradona was appointed Argentina manager in late 2008, he made Bilardo general manager. But when pressure began to mount in the autumn of 2009, with Argentina walking a qualification tightrope, Maradona began to see conspiracy theories and to regard Bilardo as an unstable background influence, especially after Bilardo announced a squad of home-based Argentina players for a friendly with Ghana in October 2009, seemingly without informing Maradona. Much political infighting ensued in the top echelons of officialdom at the Argentinian FA in the ensuing months, with Bilardo as its focal point. By late 2009 there were suggestions that Maradona's coaching staff were saying nothing more to Bilardo than hello and goodbye. Maradona himself suggested that Bilardo 'should just stay up there in his collar and tie in the directors' box'.

As in 1986, Argentina just squeezed into the 2010 finals by winning their last qualifying match 1–0, in Uruguay, after which Maradona insulted journalists furiously and crudely, live on television, leading FIFA to impose a two-month suspension on him. Amidst all this, a debate was raging over how Argentina could extract the best from Lionel Messi, their most gifted player but one regarded as an under-performer for the national team, and what his role should be at the World Cup. Argentina, it was said, now train in the afternoons because

Maradona 'doesn't do mornings'. With Maradona as the manager, backed by Bilardo, there appeared to be no shortage of the type of madness and seeming instability that saw Argentina make such a crazy success of their 1986 World Cup.

3

Avoid Great Expectations

IT DID NOT HELP AIMÉ JACQUET THAT HE HAD A TENDENCY to look like a character who could easily have been plucked from *Monsieur Hulot's Holiday*. Especially as the France manager for the 1998 World Cup was regarded prior to the tournament by most of his countrymen as someone likely to turn the nation's attempts to win the World Cup for the first time into farce. Jacquet was a former footballer who had achieved great success as a player, notably with Saint-Etienne, and who had as a manager led Bordeaux to the French League title three times, but at international level he was still widely regarded as a novice. As the 1998 World Cup approached, he had been the figurehead for the French national side for four and a half years, plenty of time to establish himself firmly as the man in charge, but even FIFA's official programme for the World Cup, normally almost obsessively neutral and respectful, described

Jacquet as 'an excellent club manager but still unproven with the national team'.

Tall and rangy, with plastic-framed, professorial spectacles, a spectacularly unfashionable greying coiffure, and a detached, dreamy, almost wistful air about him, Jacquet would amble around in football shorts when addressing his players, a style of dress that emphasised the 56-year-old's gangly, pipe-cleaner legs. He looked a tragicomic figure, a man whose seemingly melancholic demeanour was perfect for the disappointment that 'la France' felt he was sure to visit upon the nation in the summer of 1998. Not for nothing in the approach period to that World Cup did the French cruelly subvert his first name to the nickname 'Mémé', a child's expression meaning 'grandma' or 'old dear'.

By 1998, it had been fifteen years since France had first expressed an interest in hosting the World Cup and in 1993 they had finally landed the right to hold the tournament. The style in which they would do so was, of course, a primary consideration for the French. It was de rigueur that they should revamp and redesign their stadiums assiduously, with swooping, graceful curves and arcs, an effort crowned by the £267 million construction of the brand new Stade de France, a glorious 80,000-seater stadium in St Denis, in the northern outskirts of Paris, which was opened in January 1998 and described by the hosts as a cathedral for football.

The only problem was that their team wasn't given a prayer by their fellow Frenchmen – and was rated as an unholy outfit that failed to match the architecturally spectacular surroundings over which the nation had taken so much trouble. 'Nobody believed in the French team – nobody at all,' Aimé Jacquet said of that pre-tournament period. 'I mean it. I lived through hell, not only from the critics but also even from the public. There was never a quiet day, because I was getting it from all sides.'

All of this made for an almost perfect scenario for potential World Cup winners, for whom a poor credit rating pre-tournament is always a fantastic boon, particularly when they are playing at home. France in 1998 had all the advantages of being on native soil but without being burdened with the type of crackling, electric anticipation from fellow countrymen that great feats were destined to follow, simply through the mere location of the tournament. When host nations are expected to do well, it can often end in tears, as with Spain in 1982, whose supporters expected outright victory but saw their team flop so badly that their showing is still called 'the great failure'. A poor crop of Spanish players had bullied and barged their way through that World Cup, presumably in the hope that refereeing decisions would favour the home side, but even that had only taken them into the second round, where they finally bowed out.

France, then, were relieved of the burden of such expectation and there was some degree of justification behind the thinking of the French public. Their team had failed to qualify for a World Cup since 1986 – they had automatic entry as hosts in 1998 – and had developed a reputation as cavalier footballers who lacked the nerve to win decisive matches – particularly against the Germans. At the European Championships of 1992 France had arrived with a 100 per cent record in qualifying but had then performed limply at the finals. Although they had reached the semi-finals of Euro '96 in England, that had quickly been forgotten in the widespread denigration of Jacquet and his side.

Jacquet had jettisoned Eric Cantona, Jean-Pierre Papin and David Ginola early in his international managerial career. Such drastic curtailment of the international careers of those big names was radical given that many inside France viewed Jacquet as something of an interim appointment. A decade had passed since his successes at Bordeaux and after less than astounding stints as manager of Montpellier and Nancy, he had been quietly assisting Gérard Houllier with the national team, prior to Houllier quitting after the failure of France to reach the 1994 World Cup finals. Removing highly skilled but sometimes temperamental individuals from his team would, Jacquet hoped, bring the other players closer together and prevent the forming of cliques; his principal aim was to create a 'happy squad'.

The emergency surgery he had performed on his squad had the unfortunate side effect of disfiguring the team in the eyes of the paying public. They did not wish to see a side that was a triumph of substance over style. During the two years prior to the finals, Jacquet's France team did little to mollify their demanding supporters during a series of friendly matches. Jeering and whistling supporters in turn did little to help their efforts. An encounter with Scotland in November 1997 at the Stade Geoffroy Guichard in Saint-Etienne, site of Jacquet's great successes as a player and his team's last match of the pre-World Cup year, resulted in the French winning 2–1 but also being booed off the pitch – an unusual way to herald a local hero and a new year that would be crowned by hosting the World Cup.

'Whereas before we were booed for playing badly,' full back Lilian Thuram said during the approach to the finals, 'now we're booed simply for playing. It's become a habit.' It was a particularly French situation. The national team had lost only one game in 1997 – to England – and had beaten Holland, Portugal and Sweden as well as drawing with Italy and Brazil. It was a respectable run of results that would have contented supporters in most other nations; but in France, where the aesthetics must always be pleasing, the lack of polish in the performances of Jacquet's team had created general dissatisfaction.

This had grown to such a point in mid-1997 that there had been talk of Jacquet's imminent dismissal, but he said then of his continued and extensive tinkering with the team, 'What's important is that the team are ready for next year, not this year. We are still evolving. We have 12 months to get it right. Team spirit, a little luck and our potential to rise to the occasion mean we can achieve something very special when the World Cup is here.' The French public seemed less confident – they had failed to fill even modest Montpellier's stadium for the match that England won at Le Tournoi in June 1997.

The France team was regarded as overly cautious and defensive and without a proven goalscorer: all of their home victories had been achieved by the margin of a single goal. There was also displeasure at a perceived lack of effort on the part of the French players in those friendlies. For the first time in the French team's history, most of its members were playing abroad, and with major clubs in the more lucrative European leagues. This alienated them further from their public, who also believed the players to be unwilling to risk injury or even to tire themselves out when performing for the national team in friendly matches. With the 1998 World Cup on the horizon, the host nation was giving its team one great Gallic shrug.

As if to emphasise the type of flair that the team would be missing, black sheep David Ginola filmed a television commercial for L'Oréal shampoo in 1998 that had him juggling a ball and using the Stade de France as a backdrop. 'I'm not a cinema star but I care about my hair,' Ginola cooed seductively, the subtext of the setting being clearly, 'Ooh là là, just look at the type of sophistication you're missing – and a grand stadium like this is surely the natural setting for someone such as *moi* rather than the honest artisans favoured by our esteemed national team's manager.' Ginola's artistry, his copious, flowing locks and smiling, stylish, metropolitan demeanour contrasted with the 'water carrier' in the French team, as Cantona had labelled the industrious midfielder Didier Deschamps in late 1996. Deschamps had made light of Cantona's seemingly contemptuous remark but Jacquet had immediately stated that Cantona would, following his comment, never be selected for his France team.

The dogged Jacquet simply could not compete with the strong media image of players such as Cantona and Ginola. Neither glossy advertising nor outspoken comment could be seen as his forte. Instead, he found himself mocked for his rustic accent and his lack of slick communication skills – only in France could a football manager be teased for being working class. Jacquet did little to hide his lack of respect for the French sportswriters but would still become agitated when they wrote something that he considered unfair or inaccurate. A running feud developed between Jacquet and *L'Equipe*, the Paris-based daily sports paper, which characterised him as an unspectacular, provincial plodder. With the World Cup to be held in France, there was no escape for Jacquet from all this. 'They wanted to destroy me, to blacken my name,' Jacquet says. 'As there was no way to validly attack the coaching or the results, instead they went for the man. They tried to paint me as an unskilled bumpkin, not up to the job. It was contemptible.'

Even Jacquet sometimes appeared unconvinced of his team's qualities. Asked in late 1997 to name the favourites for the tournament, he suggested, 'Brazil, Italy, Germany and, of course, you've got to watch out for teams like Holland, Spain, England. France is not one of the favourites.' Italy, Germany, England and, most notably, Spain would all flounder in France.

Perhaps Jacquet, in lowering the temperature even further, was aware that if you want to win the World Cup, you ought not to worry about not having the highest-rated players or being regarded as the best in the world – especially not in your own country. The only popularity contest that really counts is the one that takes place on the final day of the tournament. Enthusiastic backing along the way, from the supporters in the stadium, is still helpful, although even that was not guaranteed in France, where appearing disinterestedly detached is as important a national sport as any other. 'The French public can be critical,' Jacquet said tentatively as the finals approached, 'but I hope they will support us in the correct way. I can't imagine that they won't get behind us. It's a massive event and national pride is at stake.'

Once the tournament got underway, of course, it could be hoped that the once-in-a-lifetime chance to host the World Cup would find those players who had been omitted from Jacquet's squad burying past differences in support of their nation's great opportunity to take advantage of being on home soil. It didn't happen. 'I thought, obviously naively,' Jacquet says, 'that from January 1998 the knives would be put away and that a sort of peace would reign. I hoped that every French man and woman would get behind the French team before the tournament began and ignore the unfounded and sterile polemics. In reality, what happened was that *Les Bleus* were forced to prove themselves on the pitch.' It is, of course, the perfect formula for World Cup success when a team is forced to find such an outlet for its frustrations.

'The business of one person is the business of all the others,' Jacquet told his team in one of his well-considered addresses to them. 'There is a winning mentality and it is about team spirit. It is about solidarity. It is about generosity.' The team, finding itself under siege from their own people, were drawn closer together in a perfect 'all for one and one for all' scenario; one that contrasted with the individualistic expressiveness of players in past, ultimately unsuccessful, French national sides.

There was still room in Jacquet's World Cup squad for Zinédine Zidane, the exquisitely talented midfield player, who was the type of overtly artistic creator who bridged past French teams with the one that was being constructed to launch a serious assault on the 1998 World Cup. Zidane, though, would have to conform to the ways of Jacquet if he was to be given the chance to express himself at the World Cup. 'He was out of the ordinary, exceptional, but he hadn't yet found a way of influencing the team to best effect,' Jacquet says of the Zidane, whom he began moulding from the moment he gave the player his France debut in 1994. 'He had the most fantastic, wonderful skills but he played football to enjoy himself – he wasn't much of a team player. When he came into the French national squad, he met other people who added a dimension to his game that made him an international footballer.'

The French cruised through the obligatory easy opening group for the hosts (copyright FIFA), beating Saudi Arabia and South Africa comfortably and squeezing a win from a tight match with Denmark. Striker Christophe Dugarry had been booed by the crowd in Marseille when coming on as a substitute for Stéphane Guivarc'h in their first match against the South Africans. When Dugarry scored the hosts' first goal five minutes after coming on, he tailored his celebrations neatly to include a grimace of displeasure at the main stand, which could have been aimed at the denizens of the press box in the Stade Vélodrome, or the fans; anyone in fact. Jacquet had also gone into this match a troubled man. The Mistral, the powerful wind that can whip the south of France, was blowing hard that day, as it had been the day before, when, in Jacquet's final training session, nothing he had planned had worked. The players had been concerned that this was a negative omen; their fears were somewhat allayed by the straightforward 3–0 victory that had been sparked by Dugarry's goal.

With so many communication difficulties between Jacquet and the press, it was inevitable that the likes of Ginola would be given free rein to stick in a sharpened stud or two. On reaching the knockout stages, France struggled to create chances against a determined Paraguay in the last 16. Ginola, on French television, gleefully told the anxious national audience at half-time that a seemingly workmanlike player such as Deschamps would never be dropped by Jacquet, simply because he was such a good friend of the manager. The message, of course, being that this was a triumph of nepotism over talents such as the one who was being forced to watch proceedings from a television studio and whose array of skills would easily have unlocked the Paraguayan defence. 'We heard everything that was being said about Aimé Jacquet as a coach, and even as a human being,' Deschamps says. 'It was hard for the squad to go through that, but we were very close and everyone was focused on going all the way.'

Another rumour had it that Dugarry was only in the team to placate his great friend, the brilliant but temperamental Zidane. Jacquet's response to such accusations was too sober and sensible for his detractors. 'There is only one boss of this team,' Jacquet said, 'and there is only one boss of any serious football team. Zinédine Zidane is a fine man and a wonderful player. He is the key to our campaign. He is the great hope of French football. But I am the boss.'

Against the Paraguayans, for whom José Luis Chilavert had performed extraordinarily in goal, an extra time golden goal, driven home from close-range by centre-back Laurent Blanc, finished the game but hardly brought the French public the encouragement that Jacquet had solved his team's goalscoring problem. Neither did the blunt, dull quarter-final with Italy which ended 0–0 with the French triumphing on penalties. 'To begin with,' Blanc says, 'no one else but the coaching staff believed we could win.'

Nor was the criticism all one way. French fans were criticised by the French players for not being genuine supporters. There were, Deschamps stated emphatically, too many collars and ties on view in the stands at the Stade de France, where the French had faced Italy and which would also be the setting for the semi-final with Croatia. Deschamps demanded that the French public dress up colourfully for that match. That would prove a serious test of the commitment of their fans, who have a tendency to sit back and demand to be entertained and whose individualism and stylised air of detachment make them feel a sense of self-consciousness about becoming caught up in being an active part of the grand spectacle of a match. The supporters saw this as common and beneath them, something you find in Britain but not in sophisticated France. But it was a clever ploy by the France captain, forcing the crowd to take a personal stake in the outcome of the match – and they did so, finally whirling themselves into close, no-holds-barred involvement with their team.

Even the French World Cup mascot, a cockerel by the name of Footix, had been finding the French public to be lukewarm in embracing the only World Cup likely to be held there in most of their lives. Régis Fassier, an actor, had been asked to fill the tournament mascot's costume during the World Cup but invitations to turn up at the various stadiums were few and far between. 'It's sad for the spectators and, personally, I'm cheesed off,' Fassier said, his giant red and gold coxcombed head under his arm. 'Professionally it's very frustrating and when you work with a character like that, eventually you become it.' He had spent the previous two years, he said, getting a feel for the costume in preparation for his turn on the world stage, only to be cold-shouldered. Jacquet must have had more than an inkling as to how Fassier felt.

The semi-final with Croatia, making their first appearance in the World Cup finals, found Jacquet's side tussling with a team that was just about their equal in terms of mental strength and technique, and it was clear midway through the first half that for the first time in the tournament France were being dominated consistently by their opponents. At half-time, with the score 0–0, Jacquet decided that powerful words were required to provide his side with a shrill wake-up call.

To British eyes, Jacquet's way of addressing his players appeared a lot less than extreme: his voice was raised a notch above the normal speaking tone but there was no shouting, no teacups were thrown, no hairdryer effect was brought into use. He looked more like a slightly miffed schoolteacher admonishing a group of suburban 13-year-olds who had become just a little bit too boisterous on a trip to a museum and who were finally silenced simply by the spectacle of their mild-mannered pedagogue losing a tiny degree of control. To the French, though, this was a severe and serious dressing-down, with none of the players daring to interject. 'We're not taking all the chances we're making,' Jacquet pleaded reasonably with them. 'Listen, guys, there is a Final on offer at the end of all this and either we react or we leave it to chance. So why are you scared of making it? Now don't let go of this opportunity.'

Almost as soon as the second half began, his ire appeared to have backfired badly as Davor Suker glided through and nudged the ball under the diving Fabien Barthez to give Croatia the lead. 'I think I was too hard on them,' Jacquet told Philippe Bergeroo, his assistant. 'Football comes down to tiny details,' Jacquet says, 'and words can have an extremely destabilising effect. But I had hardly finished my sentence when we equalised. The second half was a great moment for us. The team woke up and added a fantastic new dimension to their game.'

It also produced two French goals, but both came from Lilian Thuram, a defender, who had never previously scored any goal of any sort in a competitive match. Wasn't it a Frenchman, Napoleon, who once suggested that his generals should, above anything else, be lucky? 'This French team is equipped to score goals from anywhere because we have so many attacking options,' Jacquet said, adopting the most optimistic stance he could after his misfiring forwards had once again failed to hit the target.

Even so, the French now really did give vent to whole-hearted support of their team, with hundreds of thousands of supporters cramming the streets of Paris in celebration of the nation reaching its first World Cup Final. It was a Final in which the team would still retain the great advantage of being regarded as second-best when going into the game, even in their own Stade de France. It was a status that had sustained Jacquet's players throughout the tournament.

Their opponents in the Final were to be Brazil, touted long before the 1998 World Cup as a team destined to retain the trophy that they had won in 1994 for the fourth time. The French players were delighted to be facing the Brazilians, even though their smooth style had for decades been a principal inspiration for French footballers. Brazil had beaten Holland on penalties in the semi-final but the Dutch had completely outplayed the South Americans, leading Guus Hiddink, the Holland manager, to comment, 'Brazil, sadly, is no longer swinging and flaming. I see defenders boot the ball away shamelessly. Holland must never play like that. If we did, people would murder me and they would be right to do so.'

The reaction among the French players when watching the penalty shootout in their hotel was uncontained joy. 'We all jumped when Brazil won,' Marcel Desailly said. 'Because for us, at that moment, the Netherlands was stronger than Brazil.' The specialists had seen enough of Brazil's weaknesses to be confident about facing them, while the public were still guided by Brazil's mystical reputation.

Much of the expectation surrounding Brazil in the

1998 Final was derived from the presence of Ronaldo, but he had taken ill on the afternoon of the match and although he did play against France, his was a wan performance and France whisked the Brazilian threat almost into nothingness through playing their most inspired, creative football of the tournament, just when it mattered. Two fine headers from Zinédine Zidane in the first half left the Brazilians reeling – Jacquet had drilled into his team the weakness of the Brazilians in the air at set pieces. Laurent Blanc had also stressed the same thing to Zidane on the afternoon of the match and Zidane was aware of it himself, as indeed was anyone who had watched Junior Baiano and Aldair lumber around in the centre of the Brazilian defence throughout that tournament. 'Brazil have amnesia when the ball is in the air,' Zidane said. 'I thought, why not try getting in there?'

Once again, Jacquet's management style prevailed at half-time. Back in 1982 he had been aggrieved to see a France side containing several of his Bordeaux players 3–1 up against West Germany in the semi-final of the World Cup, only to allow their adversaries to come back to make it 3–3 and win on penalties. He had seen the after-effects on his men when they returned to their club. Now Jacquet told his team to play as if it were 0–0. 'When you have a two-goal lead it's a different kind of football,' Jacquet says. 'You have to know how to control the game, to stall, to destabilise the opponent psychologically.'

France held on to the lead throughout the second half, despite a brief sunburst of Brazilian pressure, before a flowing move concluded with Emmanuel Petit caressing the ball past Taffarel to make it 3–0. 'The team got better as the tournament progressed and we showed that we have some world-class players,' Jacquet said after the match. 'The supporters also got more confidence in us as the games went by. But we have been unfairly criticised at times and I'll never forgive those critics who were so severe on us. I hate those people. I'm determined to make them pay. They've been on my back for two years. Now I shall be on theirs.' The nation finally embraced Jacquet fully in the aftermath of the finals: his 1999 autobiography, *My Life for a Star*, sold voluminously and he received stacks of letters of apology from fans confessing that they had been among the throng who had disapproved of him prior to the tournament.

Jacquet had understood better than anyone else in France that by the late twentieth century in high-level football the team had taken over from the individual. Defenders could now match forwards for athleticism and skill, so why should they not be expected to augment the attack and score? With opposition defences more savvy, why should midfield players not take on more of the attacker's responsibilities, especially as, unlike forwards, they were not so often playing with their backs to goal, were less keenly marked and could run at opponents from deep? It was, significantly, not Zidane or Thierry Henry or Youri Djorkaeff in that France team who would be rated most highly by *L'Equipe* over the tournament but Marcel Desailly, the powerful central defender.

Back in the 1980s, when France had been admired for the *joie de vivre* that coursed through their team, it would have been unthinkable for Marius Trésor to be rated more highly than Michel Platini, Alain Giresse or Jean Tigana;

or in the 1950s, for Bob Jonquet, the centre half, to be considered a greater influence than Just Fontaine or Raymond Kopa, France's daring, dashing attackers. But the game had changed greatly. Even in the hour of Jacquet's triumph, though, much of the focus turned on the charismatic Platini, who had spearheaded the France '98 organising committee for the previous five years.

In revealing a France top underneath his suit at the end of the Final, Platini was able to carry off an act of populism that the modest Jacquet would not have contemplated, although even Platini could not escape disapproving domestic comment for sporting a football shirt under a black suit jacket – a grievous sartorial crime in the eyes of many of his fellow Frenchmen, regardless of the occasion. Platini was right behind the World Cup trophy, smiling broadly as the players collected their winners' medals at the Stade de France that July evening, and France's greatest player provided the *coup de grâce* with one of his beautifully double-edged compliments, 'Our team in the early 1980s was the better side in itself but the team of 1998 was better equipped to win the World Cup.'

Platini is perhaps how the French like to see themselves: dashing, debonair, amiable, artistic and with a certain *je ne sais quoi*. Jacquet is possibly closer to how they really are: stolid, meticulous, provincial, stoical, infused with a municipal rather than an individualistic spirit. The reflection had not been particularly flattering and so the French had railed against it until shown how winningly and handsomely effective it could be. Platini, after all, had been one of Jacquet's predecessors as national team manager and his team had failed to reach the 1990 World

Cup before flopping miserably at the 1992 European Championships in Sweden.

Paul Ince, an England player, was not impressed by the winners. 'I thought there were better teams out there,' he said, 'one of them being England.' *C'est la vie*. Jacquet, the butcher's son from the village of Sail-sur-Couzon, who had left school to work in a factory as a machine-tool operator before becoming a professional footballer, had done what had been asked of him by bringing his country the World Cup. One more barb would hardly hurt.

'They said that he was somebody from deepest rural France,' Emmanuel Petit said of the criticism that had been directed at Jacquet. 'They said that he didn't deserve to be the leader for the national team, that he came from the backwaters. So what? Do you have to come from prestigious colleges to direct a football team?' It says much about Jacquet that in the minutes after the final whistle, one of his first actions was to dash to one of the stands inside the stadium to seek out people from his home village.

Following the tournament, Jacquet stepped aside as France manager, a move he had always planned. 'I carried out my task well,' he says modestly. He took up quietly the post of national director of coaching. 'I Will Survive' had been the song championed in the dressing room by the French players, sung by them over and over again, and their manager was a survivor too, with a countryman's unflinching belief in the efficiency of his solid, hard-working ways and with the dedication to stick to them and make them work.

In 1998, France were condemned by their own people

before the tournament began, even though it was on home soil. Four years later, at the World Cup held in Japan and South Korea, Roger Lemerre's team was at its zenith and France were seen as strong contenders to retain the trophy. With them now being European Champions in tandem with being the World Cup holders, expectations ran high that they would retain the great trophy. Marcel Desailly announced that his friends and family would only be coming out to see him in the final week of the tournament, coinciding with the quarter-finals, semi-finals and Final. Let's hope they enjoyed some good sightseeing – France were eliminated at the group stage after suffering two defeats and a draw and failing to score a single goal.

A dozen years on from France 1998 and we discover a strange situation: nothing less than Aimé Jacquet disapproving of Raymond Domenech, coach of the French under-21 side during Jacquet's time as manager and now in charge of the French team that has qualified for the 2010 World Cup. 'Four years, that's enough,' Jacquet said in late 2009 of a position that Domenech had occupied since July 2004, blithely ignoring the fact that Jacquet himself had been in situ as France manager for more than four years when the 1998 World Cup began. 'After that, it's too tough,' Jacquet continued. 'There are too many factors that stop you from working correctly. That's the thing for which I blame the French Football Federation. They didn't understand the real nature of a coach's work and should have protected him, whatever he wished. It's a job you can only do for four years because you face so much exposure.' Jacquet said Domenech should stay in charge now that France had qualified for the World Cup but should accept a debate over the way his team played. 'Raymond should provide explanations on what has been happening, particularly since Euro 2008 [when France finished bottom of their group]. This is essential. It may be emotional, but we must talk football.'

Jacquet had been unimpressed with France's victory over the Republic of Ireland in the qualification play-off, which saw them progress courtesy of the controversial goal that involved a double handball from Thierry Henry in the build-up. 'France played a bad game, but I have not heard any explanation about it,' Jacquet said. 'I'm aware that if a coach gets results, he continues. But that does not stop us from talking about the team's playing style or, rather, the lack of it.'

It was criticism of exactly the type Jacquet himself had suffered prior to the 1998 tournament and that had hurt him so much. Perhaps Jacquet was merely trying to bolster his former protégé with the type of adverse comment that had served to help inspire him and his players to dig in for victory in 1998. If so, he had a gilded assistant in his task in the shape of Bixente Lizarazu, the squat full back whose attacking instincts had done much to supplement the strengths of Jacquet's midfield in 1998. Now a football analyst on the radio station RTL, Lizarazu demanded of Domenech after the final whistle of the match with Ireland, 'Can we talk about the performance?' The response from Domenech was a terse 'No, we can't.' That question and its blank response were repeated several times in the ensuing minutes before Domenech peremptorily ended the interview.

L'Equipe, the sports paper that had been left with egg

streaming down its face by Jacquet's victory in 1998, could still not help itself as it perused Domenech's efforts in the qualifying stages. 'Criticising Domenech raises the spectre of Aimé Jacquet,' it noted soberly, before adding, 'but we can't be guided by fear of ghosts. It is our duty to point out errors and areas in which the manager does not measure up.' The paper proceeded to question several aspects of Domenech's management, such as his player selection and his lack of rapport with the press, all of which echoed loudly the approach to 1998, for anyone attuned to such matters. Best of all was the revelation of a £600,000 bonus that Domenech was said to have received for guiding the team to the World Cup finals.

France are not alone in not being fancied at the bookmakers. Italy, France's triumphant opponents in 2006, were shouted down in their final 2010 World Cup qualifier: 'Go and do some work,' chanted the crowd as the Italians had to come from behind to defeat Cyprus 3–2, in a match that had become the next best thing to a friendly given that the Italians had already sealed qualification. The crowd's reaction had Marcello Lippi fuming with fury. Germany are also largely being ignored as contenders for the 2010 tournament.

In contrast, some British journalists are boasting of having put their money on England when, in 2009, they were 9–1 to win the tournament. These odds, worryingly for all with England's best interests at heart, had been reduced to 5–1 by the start of 2010. Being quoted among the select band of favourites is more often a hindrance than a help. The favourites are often the biggest flops while the instances of teams being written off, and then winning the tournament, like France in 1998, are wonderfully frequent. Diego Maradona, the Argentina captain, asserted prior to the 1986 World Cup, 'I get the feeling we are on our own.' Carlos Bilardo, his manager, agreed. 'We weren't getting any support; people didn't believe in the team, they didn't come and see them. What's more, no one understood me.' They understood everything once he had won the World Cup for them.

For England under Fabio Capello, the defeat to Ukraine once World Cup qualification had been sealed was a step in the right direction, as was losing to Brazil in the final friendly of 2009. As the delegation from the Football Association travelled to South Africa for the World Cup draw, the word from inside that body was that they were determined to play things down this time, in contrast to the trumpeted expectations of success that had accompanied previous expeditions. 'Let's go and win the World Cup!' Sven-Göran Eriksson, the then England manager had exclaimed, in a rare rabble-rousing moment, prior to the ill-fated 2006 tournament.

Yet when, in early December 2009, England were dropped into a 2010 World Cup group alongside Algeria, Slovenia and the USA, the sight of England supporters in replica shirts crowded together in bars deliriously celebrating just the draw for the group stage itself – surely a first – would have been disheartening for anyone keen for England to make a sensible tilt at winning the World Cup. There was still time for a more sombre national approach of the sort that favoured France so greatly in 1998, but as the 2010 finals approached it seemed as though nations such as France and Italy were a stride or two ahead of England in obtaining that all-important whiff of domestic disapproval.

As for Spain? Well, no one wants to be favourites. Especially when you've never won a World Cup.

4

Take Your Breaks

EVERY TIME A FRESH PIECE OF MODERN WORLD CUP subterfuge is captured from a dozen or so camera angles a lament is raised about the arrival of the dreadful and supposedly modern phenomenon of cheating. The debate spreads from the sports pages of the newspapers to the comment pages, where columnists who generally take little interest in football explain at length how the ridiculous amounts of money in today's game have created footballers who will do anything to add to their already mountainous bank balances. It wouldn't have been like this back in, say, 1930, is the implication, when many of the footballers taking part in the first World Cup were gentleman part-timers – several European national teams took weeks to reach Uruguay, the host country, travelling graciously by cruise liner – and the rewards for winning were kudos and a pleasure in representing one's country with sportsmanship and distinction. It's an attractive line of thinking – but, of course, it is entirely wrong.

Right from the off, desperate players have sought to win the World Cup by any means possible. Argentina, in 1930, were first to leave their mark on the World Cup – and on their opponents – in a truly nefarious fashion, as Wilfred Cummings, the USA team manager, recalled when capturing some of the colourful detail of Argentina's 6–1 semi-final victory over his side. 'Andy Auld had his lip ripped wide open and one of the players from across La Platte River knocked the smelling salts out of trainer [Jack] Coll's hand and into Andy's eyes, temporarily blinding one of the outstanding "little stars" of the World's Series [World Cup].' The Argentinians had started in the manner in which they meant to continue.

The first Final, between Argentina and Uruguay, was also coated in controversy. Each side wanted their own ball to be used and Francisco Varallo, an Argentina player, suggests that this led to an uneasy compromise being breached. 'The Uruguayans were sly,' he says. 'They took advantage of being the hosts. They changed the ball – used theirs, which was bigger, even though we had tossed a coin to decide which ball we had to use and we had won. Still, no excuses. Some of our players were worried about the consequences.'

Accounts of the game state that Jean Langenus, the Belgian referee, agreed that each side would see their favoured ball being used in one half of the game, leading to this being the first match ever to be dubbed 'a game of two halves' in that a different ball made each 45 minutes quite different. If Varallo is right, the Uruguayans breached even this uneasy compromise to ensure that it was their own ball that was used throughout. The Uruguayans were backed by 70,000 fired-up supporters in their Centenario Stadium and the potential reaction from those supporters to any Argentinian protest about the ball were 'the consequences' to which Varallo was referring. Uruguay, who had been 2–1 down at half-time, came back to win 4–2 and the template had been created of lacing a World Cup victory with an element of skul-duggery – supposed or otherwise – to make the winners snigger and their opponents smoulder for years to come.

Almost every winner of the World Cup has required a degree of extreme good fortune along the way. Those moments at which gamesmanship or dodgy referees or pure luck or plain cheating intervene on your behalf are essential. Even Brazil – those party-loving, smiling, samba merchants beloved by the world – have never been above the occasional piece of mendacity at what they have believed to be the appropriate moment. Yes, a Brazil squad housing the living deity that is Pelé actually bent the rules further than any banana kick. Indeed, rule bending is a tradition that the Brazilians, for all their unquestionable talent, have continued into the twenty-first century.

When Brazil qualified for the 1962 World Cup Final, in which they would face Czechoslovakia, they had a major problem. Garrincha, the winger with crooked legs who had inspired them to reach that stage of the competition, had been sent off in the semi-final with Chile and it looked certain that they would have to do without him in the deciding match of the tournament. This was a severe blow, given that he had tilted the quarter-final with

England and the semi with Chile entirely Brazil's way. 'When he stood and faced you his legs went one way and his body the other,' Mel Hopkins, the Wales left back, said of facing Garrincha. 'There's no doubt about it; he could have been declared a cripple. But my God could he play.'

Without such a player, Brazil's chances against the Czechs would be greatly reduced. All five of the other players who had been sent off in the 1962 World Cup finals had been given one-match suspensions and the Brazilians feared the same punishment was about to be meted out to their man. Making matters worse, Pelé had been injured in the second group stage game, against the Czechs, ironically, and would also be unavailable for the Final. The Brazilians' despair would soon be lifted, thanks to a solution magically presenting itself to them.

'Somehow the referee's report of the [Brazil–Chile] game just never surfaced,' Paulo Amaral, the totemic Brazil trainer, said. 'Or it was made to be that it was never written in the match report that the player with the number 7 shirt, Manuel dos Santos [Garrincha], was sent off. So Mané played in the Final but how this was done I really don't know. It wasn't even commented on. The only thing we knew was that he would be allowed to play in the Final – just like that.'

It was not quite so simple, although the mystification that beset Amaral at the time is understandable – he was clearly not 'in the know' and in those days, prior to television saturation of the World Cup finals, much more could be kept behind closed doors than now. The steps taken behind the scenes to ensure Garrincha's participation in the Final are clear, even if they were made in shadowy fashion. With FIFA's disciplinary committee preparing to sit on the morning after the Brazil–Chile semi-final and primed to take evidence from Esteban Marino, the Uruguayan linesman, and Arturo Yamazaki, the Peruvian referee, the Brazilians decided that there was only one practical solution: to remove the offending linesman, as it had been on the advice of Marino that Yamazaki had decided to dismiss Garrincha.

It might be expected that the underhand task of arranging Marino's disappearance would have been done in some hole-in-the-corner fashion by a shady operator hanging around the fringes of the Brazilian party but no, the person doing the removal work was one Mozart di Giorgio, who was not only a Brazilian football official but one who sat on the FIFA board. Di Giorgio had hit upon the splendidly inspired idea of immediately issuing the linesman, who had earlier in the 1950s refereed in Brazil, with an airline ticket for a holiday in Paris, with the only condition of this surprise treat being that he should make himself absent that very instant, that very morning, before FIFA's disciplinary committee sat down for their meeting. A suitcase full of money had reportedly been dispatched from Rio de Janeiro to Santiago to help ease matters along.

With the linesman happily removed from the scene, it was left to Yamazaki, the Peruvian referee, to explain to the remainder of the FIFA officials, blissfully unaware of the linesman's fate, why he was the only match official present to provide an account of Garrincha's dismissal. 'He had to travel,' is how Yamazaki succinctly explained the linesman's absence to them. That, apparently, in 1962, was enough to satisfy the patrician Stanley Rous, FIFA's English president, and his colleagues as to the absence of a World Cup semi-final linesman from a meeting to determine whether the tournament's star player should be allowed to participate in the Final.

Yamazaki alone would offer his version of events and he had good reason to go lightly on Garrincha: no less a figure than President Manuel Prado y Ugarteche of Peru had leaned on Yamazaki to ask the referee not to be too hard on Garrincha in his match report. Yamazaki reported that he had not seen the incident involving the Brazil winger and had had to rely on the word of his linesman before making the decision to dismiss the player. Evidence was put forward that Garrincha had retaliated under severe provocation, which was true, and that he had never previously been dismissed, which was not, but which was taken at face value. FIFA all too readily decided that Garrincha should be pardoned and allowed to play.

Given Garrincha's assessment of the Czechoslovakia team, Brazil's opponents in the Final, he would perhaps have thought that there had been little need for his football association to go to such extreme lengths to guarantee his inclusion. 'They're all big, fat guys who are no good at football.' As it transpired, Garrincha had a relatively quiet game – he was suffering from a cold on the day of the match, but the Czechs were not to know that; and their assiduous three-man marking of the winger allowed others, such as Didi and Amarildo, to wreak havoc on the Czech defence in Brazil's 3–1 victory.

74

Nor was that an isolated example of Brazilian mendacity at that World Cup in Chile. During their match with Spain, their third in the group stage, the Brazilians, in their first match since his injury, found themselves struggling badly without Pelé. The Spaniards had tight control of the game and were 1–0 up at half-time. At the beginning of the second half, Martin Verges, the Spain midfield player, was clipped by Nilton Santos inside the penalty area. It looked a certain penalty kick but Nilton Santos quickly grasped that although the referee had spotted the foul and had blown his whistle for an infringement, he was too far away to be sure where it had been committed and was now jogging in the direction of the Brazilian to see where he was stationed. Acting with alacrity, Nilton Santos surreptitiously shuffled, Charlie Chaplin-like, outside the penalty area, conning the referee into awarding a free-kick. A penalty scored by Spain at that stage would have made it most likely that Brazil would be eliminated at the group stage but after that reprieve, little Garrincha began to turn on the style and it was Spain, not Brazil, lamenting an early exit after the winger had undone the Spanish defence to help Brazil ease to a 2–1 victory.

The Brazilians were defending a World Cup trophy that they had won in brilliant style with a 5–2 victory over Sweden in the 1958 Final, although even then, their win over France in the semi-final left their reputation tarnished for anyone concerned about such niceties. With the score at 1–1, Vavá had broken the shin of Bob Jonquet, France's resolute centre half, and with substitutes not allowed at that time, that left France operating with ten men for most of the game and, from a point at which they had been matching the Brazilians, they went on the slide to a 5–2 defeat.

Four decades later, as Brazil's opening match of the 2002 World Cup was winding to a close with a 2–1 win, Rivaldo, the Brazil midfield player, crumpled to the ground after Turkey's Hakan Unsal had kicked the ball towards him while he was preparing to take a corner-kick. The ball clearly struck Rivaldo on the leg but the Brazilian's instantaneous reaction – bringing up both hands to clutch his face, falling down and lying splayed across the corner arc with one arm across his head and one over his midriff – was embarrassing to the watching world, although not, it would seem, to Rivaldo himself. Almost as extraordinarily, as a result of Rivaldo's play-acting Unsal was shown a second yellow card and dismissed by Kim Young-joo, the South Korean referee, even though a linesman had been standing almost on the shoulder of Rivaldo as the incident unfolded.

'Maybe the ball touched my leg and not my head but the other player was still wrong,' Rivaldo said, offering the world a wonderful example of a footballer's tortuous logic. 'I said sorry to him but these things happen in football.' Senol Gunes, the Turkey coach, was less than impressed. 'We took control of the game but we could not control the referee,' he said. Haluk Ulusoy, president of the Turkish Football Federation, was spectacularly un-restrained in his assessment of Kim Young-joo, who had also dismissed Turkey centre back Alpay for a foul (out-side the area) that led to Brazil's 87th-minute penalty, from which Rivaldo had won them the match. 'We gave

1,000 martyrs for Korea 50 years ago,' Ulusoy said, in reference to the fact that Turkey had supplied troops to the UN contingent during the Korean War. 'Now a single Korean has killed 70 million Turks.'

While Unsal missed Turkey's next match, Rivaldo, rather than receiving a lengthy suspension from FIFA, was free to see out Brazil's remaining fixtures, all the way to the Final and including a semi-final victory over Turkey. Not that he went entirely unpunished by FIFA, who, in light of the incriminating television evidence, punished the player with a £4,300 fine. It was a sum that, for such a well-paid footballer, equated, in man-in-the-street terms, to the amount you would expect to pay if taking some library books back six weeks late. 'I don't regret what I did,' Rivaldo said after FIFA's action. 'I don't even know why I was fined. In soccer, you have to be sly.'

It should be easy for FIFA to select the best referees globally for the World Cup. After all, while footballers are required to do the unexpected and be creative to win matches, refereeing is less about flair than consistent and steady application of the rules and control of the game. Yet FIFA has a habit of putting crackpots in charge of vital World Cup matches. One onlooker described Ali Bennaceur, the Tunisian referee who allowed the in-famous 'Hand of God' goal scored by Diego Maradona at the 1986 World Cup as 'an idiot more fit to herd camels in the desert than take charge of a World Cup game.'

The eyewitness in question was not some disgruntled England player or supporter but Bogdan Dotchev, the linesman closest to the incident, who had spotted the handball but who insisted that it was not his role to intervene and tell the referee that the ball had been handled. 'With the ref having said the goal was valid, I couldn't have waved my flag and told him the goal wasn't good – the rules were different back then,' Dotchev explained, neatly passing the buck to the referee, who shrugs off personal blame by passing back that troublesome buck in equally sleek, streamlined style. 'My assistant indicated to me that there was no foul play,' Bennaceur says, 'so I was obliged to give the goal.'

Maradona's own take on a goal that he described as 'a little of the hand of God and a little of the head of Maradona' is interesting. 'Should I have refused to accept the goal?' the Argentinian says. 'Next, you will be saying that I should ask a defender's permission before I dribble round him. You should talk to the referee, not me.' For all that Maradona is held up as a particularly notorious and audacious villain because of this blatant piece of cheating, his view on it seems to be generally in tune with those of footballers around the world.

'The highest crime in football is touching the ball with your hands,' Sepp Blatter, FIFA president, says but it was notable after Thierry Henry's infamous double handball for France against Ireland in their World Cup play-off in Paris in November 2009, which allowed William Gallas to score the goal that took France to the 2010 finals, that the Irish players, almost to a man, refused to criticise Henry for his actions.

'You can't blame Thierry Henry,' Kevin Kilbane, the Ireland midfield player, said of the Frenchman who had, apparently blamelessly, handled the ball. Damien Duff, the winger, concurred. 'I don't think you can blame

Henry,' he said, just in case anyone was in doubt. 'If it was myself or Robbie [Keane] down the other end we would have tried it.'

Giovanni Trapattoni, the Ireland manager, chose to question the process by which FIFA had appointed the match officials who had missed the incident rather than target Henry. The fault, according to the professionals, is seemingly not with the wrongdoer but with those who fail to spot the breach of the rules. This perverse logic is akin to suggesting that if your house is ransacked, the blame should be attached not to the burglar, the actual perpetrator of the deed, but to the authorities for not happening to have police officers strolling past the premises at the time of the crime. FIFA, of course, when it came to seeking to punish Henry for the game of football's 'highest crime' simply sat on their own hands and did nothing, even though at the 1994 World Cup Mauro Tassotti of Italy had been suspended after they had consulted video evidence of his foul on Spain's Luis Enrique, and even though they had fined Rivaldo in 2002 after looking at the film of his feigning injury against Turkey.

The England team in the dressing room at the Azteca Stadium in 1986, realising that they had been cheated by Maradona, had immediately asked FA officials if they could have the match with Argentina replayed. But once the dust had settled a few days later, a couple of prominent members in the England party, perhaps indiscreetly, admitted that if one of the England players had managed to mask a handball as cunningly as Maradona had, they would have happily taken the resultant goal. As Maradona put it, 'I don't think it's cheating; it's cunning.

Is it cheating to handle the ball? Oh no, no, no. It's not cheating. It's craftiness.'

Not all of the English players that day were so sanguine. 'It still rankles with me that he has never really admitted to what he did,' Terry Butcher, the centre back, says. 'He's never really put both hands up – the hands of God – and said, "Yes, it was the wrong thing to do." An English player would have done that. It tarnishes the image to me.' By one of football's strange coincidences, when Maradona was appointed manager of Argentina in late 2008, his first match was a friendly with Scotland, who at the time had Butcher as their assistant manager.

Brought up to date with Butcher's lingering resentment, Maradona responded, 'England won a World Cup with a goal, and it was plain to see by everyone, that never crossed the line. So I don't think it's fair that anyone should judge me, when stuff like that went on.' As he spoke, eyes bulging, he spread his palms wider and wider, like a fisherman exaggerating the size of a catch, to emphasise the distance that Geoff Hurst's famous shot in 1966 had rebounded off the crossbar and in front of the line. By the time Maradona had finished emoting, Hurst's rebound was halfway to the edge of the 6-yard box.

The difference was that Hurst's goal was not a deliberate and calculated piece of cheating, as in the case of Maradona, but a lucky bounce going in England's favour. The goal was given thanks to Gottfried Dienst, an eccentric Swiss, who had the appearance of a zany classical music conductor and whose refereeing style in the 1966 World Cup Final was, to say the least, unusual, and which was complemented perfectly by that of Tofik Bahkramov.

Widely described as a 'Russian linesman', Bahkramov was, unbeknownst to almost everyone inside Wembley, an Azerbaijani who had fought on the front line against the Germans during the Second World War and who was operating by 1966 under the catch-all identity of the Soviet Union.

As England players claimed Hurst's shot to have gone in and the Germans insisted it to have not, Dienst scurried over to consult the equally eccentric Bakhramov, a tall, rake-thin individual, with a wild mane of unkempt grey hair, toothbrush moustache, wide-eyed expression and a thin white belt holding up his black shorts. Bakhramov grasped the chance to advise Dienst that he ought to award the goal and for Bakhramov this was an opportunity to extract revenge on the Germans for which he had been waiting more than 20 years. Asked a long time later why he had decided to give such a marginal decision in England's favour, he would habitually respond with a one-word answer, 'Stalingrad'.

Hurst would admit many years later that it seems more likely than not that the ball bounced in front of the line. 'I had a bit of sympathy for the Germans,' he says. 'They genuinely believed the ball had not crossed the line and they may be right. I can no more claim with certainty that the ball did cross the line than they can claim that it didn't. Having listened to all the arguments over the decades and watched the replay hundreds of times on TV, I have to admit that it looks as though the ball didn't cross the line.'

Few World Cup incidents have provoked so much debate. 'It was not a goal because the ball bounced down and hit the line,' Franz Beckenbauer, the West Germany player, insists sternly. 'That's no goal, you know. The whole ball has to be behind the line. That's the rule.' Yet even the losers on this occasion – Beckenbauer included – admit that while they are of the belief that it was a phantom goal, it had a less dramatic bearing on the result of the match than has often been suggested. Wolfgang Weber, another West Germany player that July day, suggests, 'Too much has been said about the third goal. England have entered the annals of football history as worthy world champions.'

For all the Germans' generosity, that goal, which made it 3–2 to England, was still key to victory. Certainly England were the better team on the day, especially so during that extra time period, and when Hurst got England's fourth, he did so by galloping through to score against a German defence left threadbare in desperate pursuit of an equaliser. Of course, what goes around comes around. Back in 1954 West Germany owed their first ever World Cup crown to a British official who ruled out an 87th-minute goal from Ferenc Puskas of Hungary during the Final. 'I got an "equaliser" right at the death,' Puskas said, 'but that Welsh linesman Griffiths disallowed it for offside, even though the English ref, Bill Ling, had given it. We were already back at the centre-circle by the time he flagged. I'll never forgive him for that.'

Mervyn Griffiths was an eccentrically pugnacious and stern Welsh match official whose lineage would include the comically strict Clive Thomas who, during a final group game at the 1978 finals, allowed Brazil to take a corner close to the end of their match with Sweden only to blow for full-time just as Zico was heading the ball into the Swedish net, thus pushing the Brazilians into second place and a testing confrontation with Argentina, the hosts, in the next stage. It was an encounter that would prove, ultimately, and perhaps unfairly, fatal to Brazil's hopes of winning that year.

But Maradona's 'Hand of God' goal was not just a consummate piece of 'craftiness'. It also had a tremendous psychological effect on the England players. After all, it could not truly be said of Maradona's Argentina – unlike England in 1966 – that they seemed destined to win their 1986 quarter-final with England. His handball temporarily destabilised the English defence and Peter Shilton, the England goalkeeper, suggests that it upset his concentration so badly that it affected his goalkeeping when Maradona cut through to score his second three minutes later.

Adept pieces of psychology can also swing a World Cup – think of Marco Materazzi's goading of Zinédine Zidane in 2006. Jack Taylor, the English referee, awarded Holland a penalty kick in the opening minute of their 1974 Final with West Germany after Uli Hoeness had whisked Johan Cruyff's legs away from underneath him. It was a decision that was entirely correct, but as Taylor waited for Johan Neeskens to take the penalty for the Dutch, Beckenbauer, the West Germany captain, sniped at the referee. 'Of course you are an Englishman,' he said, subtly bringing into play the suggestion, albeit not made directly, that Taylor, because of recent historical enmity, might be inclined to favour the Germans' opponents.

Taylor insists that he was not seeking to even things up

when he awarded West Germany their own penalty and a chance to equalise in the 25th minute, but when Bernd Hölzenbein, the West Germany winger, threw himself down convincingly in the penalty area, with Wim Jansen, the Holland midfield player, in close attendance, it would have been tremendously courageous not to have given the award of a penalty. Taylor did so. 'I sensed the referee would blow his whistle again if one of us went down in the penalty area,' Gerd Müller, the West Germany striker, suggests, 'and that's the way it was. It definitely wasn't a penalty; he [Hölzenbein] went down very easily.'

Beckenbauer confirms that the opportunity for the West Germany equaliser arose through chicanery. 'He ran against the player's leg and immediately went down,' he says of Hölzenbein. 'That was his speciality.' Sepp Maier is another West German World Cup winner with no evidence to offer in Hölzenbein's defence. 'I have to say it was no penalty. Those who knew Hölzenbein knew very well. Hölzenbein simply flew over.' The comments of his former team-mates have incensed Hölzenbein and caused considerable friction between them, while Taylor remains convinced that he did the right thing in giving the penalty. Paul Breitner, the German who put the penalty away, recalls that he sensed immediately that the game had turned hugely in his side's favour after an opening 25 minutes that had been dominated by the Dutch. The Germans duly powered on to victory.

Britain retains a worldwide reputation for fair play that owes much to the England team's World Cup history lacking the blemishes of others. Cheating remains anathema to the public, regardless of footballers' seemingly double standards with regard to it – as evidenced by the wave of revulsion that swept not just the Republic of Ireland but Britain too after Henry's handball – but accepting a piece of good fortune falling your way is a different matter. It is a rare winner of the World Cup that gets by without a little lucky nudge in the right direction.

5

Don't Worry About Penalties

WORLD CUP PENALTY SHOOTOUTS ARE A BLACK AND white issue. A figure in those colours, the national team strip of Germany, is the recurring motif in that aspect of the game and the Germans' efficiency from the small, round, white spot, 12 yards from goal, has done little to deflect from unfortunate national stereotypes, given that penalty shootouts are less about joy and creation than nervelessness almost to the point of unfeelingness.

Not content with winning every World Cup penalty shootout in which they have ever been involved – yes, that's *every* World Cup penalty shootout in which they have ever been involved – it was even a German who invented this tortuous spectacle four decades ago and when the Germans won their third World Cup, cunningly disguised as West Germany, in 1990, they won not only one match but half the tournament by scoring penalty kicks. This came just at a time when the world was pondering the problems of an increasingly automated, computerised, alienated way of life. George Orwell suggested in *1984*, his fictional account of a nightmarish totalitarian world, that a vision of the future would be a boot stamping on a human face – for ever. At the 1990 World Cup, a vision of the tournament's future appeared to be a German taking a penalty – and scoring unerringly every time.

It seems perverse that the Final of the world's greatest football competition should ever be settled in such a way; it is a bit like having Kraftwerk providing the music at a wedding reception. On the two occasions on which penalty shootouts have settled the Final – Brazil beating Italy in 1994 and Italy defeating France in 2006 – the lasting memories are not particularly of the winning penalty kick, which says much about this method of settling matches. Instead, the enduring image of 1994 is of Italy's Roberto Baggio, one of the tournament's most pleasingly creative forces, standing downcast, hands on hips, after sending his penalty in the shootout high over the Brazilian crossbar.

Memories of 2006 are more closely bound with the dramatic dismissal of Zinédine Zidane in extra time than with the means by which Italy were made winners. World Cup shootouts make the wrong moments from their finals remain memorable. Or, as Woody Paige of the *Denver Post* put it in disbelieving, football-agnostic style after the USA had hosted that first goalless World Cup final in 1994, won 3–2 on penalties by Brazil, 'The two greatest teams on the globe can't score one stinking goal! And finally they have a shootout, soccer kicks at 12 paces, to decide the champion. That's not boring; that's dumb. Why not flip a coin, just as they did before the game?'

It is a terrible, random way of separating two teams that have proved themselves not only the best in the world but the equal of the other over 120 minutes of taut, tense play. If a World Cup Final is to end in a draw, there must be a better way of settling the issue of who is to be declared world champions. It would surely not be too hard to arrange a replay two or three days later – the Final of the last penalty-shootout-free World Cup, in 1978, would have been replayed two days after the original match if it had been drawn – and FIFA would not have too much of a problem selling tickets and television rights for such an event.

If a replay were to be required in a match prior to the Final, the logistics are simple: if time were pressing before the next round of competition, the replay could be held the day after the original match, which is not as odd as it might initially seem. With every competing nation having a squad of 23 at the finals, a fresh team could be fielded even if the players who had participated in the original match were deemed too leg-weary to play within 24 hours. The prospect of having their onward progress determined by the reserves might help prod managers to go for broke rather than settle for penalties.

The only people likely to protest about the removal of penalty shootouts from World Cup tournaments would be the Germans, who have taken penalties to their hearts. Even successive FIFA presidents have admitted that this is an unsatisfactory method for deciding memorable matches. After England and West Germany had drawn 1–1 in their colourful semi-final in 1990, only to be separated by penalty kicks, João Havelange, the FIFA president, promised to look into another means of concluding a tied match in time for the 1994 World Cup, but nothing was done. Appropriately, that tournament began with a spectacular penalty-based farce: Diana Ross, the singer, missed a 'penalty' in ludicrous fashion during the opening ceremony, sending the ball wide of a goalpost only for the makeshift goals at which she had aimed from a few yards away still to collapse on cue as they had been meant to do in tandem with her shot hitting the net. The tournament ended in a similarly unsatisfactory fashion, with Baggio's miss.

One brave voice has been heard from inside FIFA railing against this ludicrous means of concluding a match and that outspoken dissenter, who sees shootouts as being a blot on the World Cup landscape, is not some maverick willing to jeopardise his career by speaking out against accepted practice but none other than Sepp Blatter, the president of FIFA. 'We have four years or so, so I think we have time,' Blatter suggested steadily, wisely, reasonably, with the measured tones of a patient visionary, in 2006, as he took a quick glance towards the then fairly distant finals in South Africa, before hurling some ideas for the replacement of penalties into the ether like the jolly creative cavalier that he is.

'Maybe to replay the match if it's the Final; you can't do that through the tournament because of lack of time. Maybe to take players away and play golden goal. When it comes to the World Cup Final it is passion, and when it goes to extra time it is a drama, but when it comes to penalty kicks it is a tragedy. Football is a team sport and penalties is not a team, it is the individual.' Yet with the 2010 World Cup on the cusp of its kick-off, Sepp has been strangely quiet on the issue. Shootouts remain integral to the World Cup and even England, for whom they have become a *bête noire* during the past two decades, will have to be prepared to cope.

If winning the World Cup is the ultimate test of a team holding its nerve, then the penalty shootout is the element that twists and squeezes those nerve ends, like a particularly sadistic torturer, once they have been shredded to bits by weeks of taut competition. Prior to the 1982 World Cup, which saw the tournament's first shootout (although shootouts had been used in qualification four years previously), it had been rare for teams to be so tightly locked together that a deciding element was required. The last time had been in the 1954 and 1958 World Cups, when five play-offs were used to separate teams level on points after the group stages; although if goal difference had been used, only one of those play-offs (the USSR v England in 1958) would have been necessary. There had not been a replayed knockout World Cup match since 1934 – when Italy faced Spain two days running – so it seems puzzling that, in 1970, FIFA should suddenly decide that shootouts should be incorporated in their rules.

It is fitting that the first World Cup finals penalty shootout, in the 1982 semi-finals, should involve the cadaverous spectacle of an almost spectacularly cynical

West German side. The Germans were fortunate to make it as far as a shootout in that they had been 3–1 down to France early in extra time and also given that during the match Harald Schumacher, the West Germany goalkeeper, had brought Patrick Battiston, the France forward, to within an inch of his life with an assault of quite terrifying ferocity that took out the Frenchman and knocked him unconscious as he coursed through on goal.

Schumacher should have been dismissed instantly but was not even booked and so was free to face the French in the shootout. It fell to Alain Giresse, a France midfield player, to take the first penalty in a World Cup shootout and he describes a difficult experience. 'It was only 30 or 40 metres that I had to walk to take the penalty but to me it felt like kilometres. My nerves were on edge and I was emotionally shattered. I tried not to look at the goalkeeper but that was really hard. I really didn't want to look at him considering what he had done to us during the game.' Giresse's penalty, despite the testing circumstances, was perfect: he hit a low, right-footed shot into the left-hand corner, sending Schumacher the wrong way.

Undeterred, the West Germans went on to win the shootout even though Uli Stielike goes down as a national disgrace, given that he actually saw his penalty saved in the 5–4 shootout win that saw the Germans progress to the Final. Not only have the Germans triumphed in every other World Cup shootout that they have faced since then, but not one German has missed a shootout penalty – a level of efficiency that is not so much inhuman as suspiciously robotic. Steely Stielike's reward for missing on that humid night in Seville was the cold shoulder from his colleagues; he spent the rest of the shootout sitting on the ground with his head between his legs.

German success in winning that shootout – and all those that were to follow for them – appeared to be derived from what the Germans themselves describe as 'Prussian self-discipline', Prussia being the large, sprawling, militaristic northern state of the German Empire that preceded and hugely influenced modern Germany, and which has given us the fearsome black eagle on a white background that decorates the strip of the modern German team. 'We felt the cold of Germany's calculating game,' Michel Hidalgo, the France manager, said of that 1982 semi-final. 'We have been eliminated brutally. I would say, scientifically.'

The Germans' penalty shootout victory was also a shocking way to conclude a semi-final that had been blessed with some wonderfully creative French football and it seems apposite that their winning on penalties was inextricably bound up with Schumacher's cruelty towards a fellow professional. 'These days it would have been a straight red card,' Michel Platini says of Schumacher's brutality. 'West Germany would have been down to ten men and we'd have surely gone through to the World Cup Final.' Instead, Schumacher, who had doled out furious, simmering aggression towards the French all evening, was free to defy the French in the shootout; one in which poor Battiston, the forward, might have scored.

In his absence, when defender Maxime Bossis saw his

penalty saved by Schumacher, it allowed striker Horst Hrubesch to give the Germans victory. Bossis was, in the moment, so traumatised that he clutched hold of his shorts and pulled them up to reveal his undershorts; a bit like a terrorized, disorientated five-year-old, lost on the first day of school. 'There's no compassion among professionals,' Schumacher said, on hearing that Battiston, who was stretchered off to hospital after Schumacher's near-fatal mid-air challenge on him, had lost two teeth. 'Tell him I'll pay for the crowns.'

The next day on which there was a World Cup penalty shootout, 21 June 1986, West Germany – who else? – celebrated by beating hosts Mexico 4–1 on spot-kicks after a grinding 0–0 draw in a quarter-final for which the siesta could have been invented. A much more inspired quarter-final match earlier the same day, between Brazil and France, also ended in a draw and the penalty shootout again took its toll on two of the World Cup's more colourful and artistic participants.

'Don't you think that as you're both forwards, it stands to reason that you know how to take a penalty?' Henri Michel, the France coach, angrily upbraided Bruno Bellone and Yannick Stopyra after they had reacted with dismay at being nominated to take kicks in the penalty shootout with Brazil. Michel had noticed Stopyra and Bellone walking away with their legs shaking, although both did score from their kicks. Michel Platini and Sócrates, on the other hand, two of the outstanding creators on the field that day, both missed their kicks. 'I was destroyed – in a pitiful state,' Platini said.

A third quarter-final also went to penalties during the

1986 tournament in which Belgium beat Spain 5–4, and only Maradona's 'Hand of God' arguably came between England and Argentina having to settle matters from 12 yards as well.

At the 1990 World Cup finals the Germans surpassed even themselves, with their path to their third successive Final measured precisely in neat, 12-yard segments. Fittingly, it is Karl Wald, a referee from Frankfurt, who takes the credit for the invention of the penalty shootout and its incorporation into FIFA's statutes four decades ago. 'The penalty shootout is a high-tension case,' he says, 'and I am very proud that there are the rules that I proposed in 1970, still in their original form.' Yes, well done, Karl.

Franz Beckenbauer, the Germany manager, was convinced in 1990, unlike in 1986, that his team could go all the way. 'Can you believe we reached the Final of the World Cup with these players?' he had asked incredulously after taking his team to the Final of the competition in Mexico. The 1990 German model was, in his opinion, much improved, and it motored along powerfully on a midfield engine that included such talents as Thomas Hässler, who had just been bought by Juventus for £6 million, and Lothar Matthäus, already a *Scudetto* winner in Italy with Internazionale. The availability of such players, who combined refinement with strength, power and athleticism, convinced Beckenbauer that his team had the invention and drive to win the nation a third World Cup.

So it seemed as they cleared a path through the group stage, playing some stunning football in demolitions of

Yugoslavia and the United Arab Emirates. The Germans' 3–5–2 system worked to their strengths; the extra man in midfield bulking out the portion of the park that contained their deadliest weapons. Even after an injury to Hässler in the group stages, the Germans could call on Pierre Littbarski, the one-time wunderkind of German football, who had had to be fined by Cologne in his younger days for dribbling too much and failing to pass the ball to his team-mates. His emergency re-emergence at the 1990 finals showed that he had harnessed with maturity his talents for the benefit of the team, while still adding a welcome element of unpredictability to the West German side, a human touch in a team with iron in its soul.

West Germany were by far the most exciting of all the teams in the opening round of the 1990 tournament: powerful, fast, dynamic, overwhelming the opposition through an irresistible combination of speed, slickness and skill, like a diamond-headed drill capable of cutting through any resistance. The best German teams are always notable for players such as Beckenbauer and Matthäus, supreme athletes, who streak forward from deep – players with an air of haughtiness and impatience about them, efficient to a tee. Players who put the accent on finely honed, technical skills that provide them with a complete mastery of every aspect of the basics of the game, making a fine art of craftsmanship rather than a desire to show off or to elaborate.

Those familiar characteristics were writ large in the West Germany team of 1990 but they had also been upgraded to meet the demands of modern football. Where

Beckenbauer had once strolled imperiously, now, in the 1990s, Matthäus moved with more pace, to fit in with a game whose pulse had quickened. He displayed a voracious hunger to transport himself from back to front and had an unusual talent for hitting a moving ball from outside the penalty area with the same accuracy as a stationary one, with the deadly variation of being able to finish by using either foot equally strongly. When not scoring, Matthäus would be pinging passes from the centre of the field to the right or to the left.

The Germans, explosive in the early stages of the competition, defeated Holland in a thrillingly open match in the last-16 knockout stage and had had an average of 16 attempts at goal in each in their opening four games. Beckenbauer had stated that the winner of the competition would emerge from the match between the Germans and the Dutch, so it would have been fitting had he then decided to allow his team to play even more freely, given that they were now, in his opinion, the predestined winners.

'There's always a time in life when it all comes right,' Matthäus said with winning modesty, 'when you seem to have reached a level that at other times seemed unthinkable. Well, perhaps that moment has arrived for me. Football is all about attacking the opposition before they do the same to you.' In a tournament marked by caution and appeasement, the Germans' outright aggression had been channelled into an attractive form. 'My team likes to play under pressure,' the straight-backed Beckenbauer said approvingly.

Yet after their momentous win over the Dutch, cracks

would begin to appear in the German façade. They did outplay Czechoslovakia in the quarter-final and the Czechs did desperately clear a series of on-target efforts off the line and enjoy assistance from the woodwork in preventing German goals, but it required a penalty-kick, and one acquired in dubious circumstances, to give the Germans the sole goal in the match. Jürgen Klinsmann slipped between Frantisek Straka and Jozef Chovanec and then surged for the turf as if he wanted to burrow through it. Helmut Kohl, the Austrian referee, immediately pointed to the spot and Matthäus sent Jan Stejskal the wrong way with his penalty.

It was still not good enough for the exacting standards set the German team by Beckenbauer, their stern manager. 'We played badly,' he said. 'Our team had players who kept the ball to themselves as long as they liked; the players were not agreed on their actions; they did not play very well in front of goal.' Czechoslovakia, on their knees by the end of their pounding at the hands of the Germans, and still smarting from their defeat, must have been relieved not to have met the Kaiser's team on a day when they lived up to his idea of efficiency.

For all their image of Teutonic invincibility, petty jealousies and disputes always tend to surface at some point inside any German World Cup squad. Back in 1986, Uli Stein, the West Germany squad goalkeeper, had memorably announced early on in the tournament that Beckenbauer was a 'soup buffoon – with a team playing like a bunch of cucumbers'. This showed imaginative lampooning that had more in common with satire than a dutifully dull, cliché-toting, professional footballer and was issued by a Stein who had become frustrated at Beckenbauer (who had appeared in television commercials for soup) selecting Harald Schumacher as his first-choice goalkeeper. Stein was quickly dispatched home, regardless of his gaudy wit.

In advance of the 1990 semi-final with England, the West Germany team chef was arguing with the team doctor about the players' diet – these were the early days of northern European players' food consumption coming under more scrutiny. The chef was determined that the players continue to eat the sizeable portions of meat that had sustained them throughout the tournament and the doctor was convinced that they should switch to a more pasta-based diet to restore energy levels after draining matches in the Italian heat.

Germany's strikers were also nibbling away at each other's egos. Rudi Völler had missed the quarter-final with Czechoslovakia through suspension and had suggested that Jürgen Klinsmann had been less than willing to help Karl-Heinz Riedle, Völler's young replacement. 'Was he really watching the game?' was Klinsmann's stingingly witty reply to Völler's bitching as Rudi and 'Klinsi' prepared to renew their partnership in the semi-final.

The Germans, explosive and adventurous early on, now began to fall more into line with a tournament that was characterised by the number of times in the knockout rounds – four – that penalty shootouts became the means to separate teams, more than in any other World Cup. There was good reason for this. The pass back to the goalkeeper had not yet been made illegal; to be onside, an attacking player still had to have two of the defending team fully between him and the goal, while the tackle from behind would not be clamped down on by FIFA until the 1994 World Cup. All of that allowed plenty of scope for any team keen on killing a game and, in that dreaded phrase, to play for penalties. This had become a tactic that not only gave inferior teams a chance of winning because they didn't have to create anything from open play, but also afforded losing managers a chance to save face by going out on what was often described as a 'lottery'.

The preponderance of penalties at the 1990 World Cup saw outstanding players miss from the spot in shootouts, again highlighting how far removed this spectacle was from the flowing movement of the world's favourite game. In fact, so sterile were so many of the games in the 1990 finals – a tournament that had the lowest goals-per-game ratio of any World Cup and saw a then record 16 dismissals – that it threw up the prospect of a team proceeding to the final fuelled entirely by penalties. 'We might finish up winning the World Cup without winning a game,' Jack Charlton, the phlegmatic Ireland manager, said. 'I don't care.' After drawing against England, Egypt and Holland in the group stages, his side had just defeated Romania on penalties in the first knockout round, after a 0–0 draw. Kevin Sheedy, a midfield player, neatly summed up the subtleties of emerging victorious from a match in that way when he explained the technique and thought that he had put into taking the first kick in the shootout: 'I'm going to bash it right over his head' was, he said, going through his mind as he faced Silviu Lung, the Romania goalkeeper.

Gary Lineker saw England through to the semi-finals by scoring two penalties in the quarter-final with Cameroon and his subsequent comments, in tandem with those of Sheedy, suggest that British and Irish players were willing to give penalty taking only so much thought and no more. 'The thing I didn't plan for was having a second penalty,' Lineker said. 'I thought, Now what do I do? Having practised just the one all the time, I couldn't hit the same one again, so I thought I'd just hit it down the middle. Thankfully, he dived out of the way.'

Penalties had become an over-valued currency that was devaluing the spectacle of the game at World Cup level. 'Stuart Pearce was our penalty taker before the tournament started,' Bobby Robson, the England manager, said, 'and Gary Lineker actually came to me and asked whether I would mind if he took the penalties. I liked the fact that he wanted to take them. I remember asking why and he said, "Well, I could win the Golden Boot and it might just boost my earnings." I quite liked that.' The fact that Lineker had been top scorer at the World Cup four years previously was possibly lost on Robson!

For the first time, both semi-finals would be settled on spot-kicks. Down in Naples, Italy would lose out to Argentina in this way, Aldo Serena having saved the vital penalty for the Italians and describing it, years later, as the 'cross that I still carry around with me'. Sergio Goycochea, the Argentina goalkeeper, who had flouted the rules by rushing from his line to save from Roberto Donadoni and Serena, further highlighted the random nature of penalty shootouts. 'I thought very little,' he said of his approach to the shootout with the Italians. 'The goalkeeper is always the most tranquil person in this situation. The responsibility is on the person kicking the ball. Diego [Maradona] gave me some tips on how the Italians take penalties because he plays in the league with them. I choose a place I am going to go, wait until the last second, and when the ball is kicked, I go to that place and hope the ball is kicked there.' Of ten penalties taken against him in the quarter-final and semi-final shootouts, Goycochea conceded just five.

The following day, 4 July 1990, England pushed West Germany to the brink of elimination only to join the Italians in losing out on penalty kicks. 'Maybe we were just able to control our nerves a little bit better,' Jürgen Klinsmann said (although his nerves were not directly tested in the penalty shootout). Peter Shilton, the England goalkeeper, had done exceptionally well against the West Germans in terms of anticipating the direction of their penalties but such was their assiduousness in penalty taking that he still missed each one of their spot-kicks by mere inches. 'It was my first World Cup and my first shootout,' Bodo Illgner, the West Germany goalkeeper, said, 'but I felt I had nothing to lose. I just concentrated on looking and feeling confident when the England players came to their kicks.' Pearce, conversely, who had fiddled with the ball on the penalty spot, had looked less than assured before his kick.

'It is the regulation,' Beckenbauer said, doing his best not to disassociate the Germans from their reputation as sticklers for order, regardless of how meaningless and absurd that was. 'That is how it is. There is no alternative.' Bobby Robson disagreed. 'Football is supposed to be about endurance and temperament and fighting spirit. We graced a World Cup semi-final, which we did not consider we lost, but you have to accept the penalties rule. Not only did we feel we could beat Argentina in the Final but we owe them one from four years ago. Nobody has been able to beat us. That makes everybody feel good about themselves but [Paul] Gascoigne is broken-hearted and neither [Stuart] Pearce nor [Chris] Waddle [who missed England's penalties against the West Germans] is feeling too clever. The way we played was heart-warming but the finish was so disappointing.' Matthäus had made straight for Waddle after the shootout to tell the Englishman, 'That was a terrible way to decide things.' Geoff Hurst, the winner in 1966, watching back in London, summed up the horror of losing on penalties when he cast his eyes over Waddle and Pearce after their misses from the spot. 'Oh God! Look at those faces . . .'

Not content with having eliminated England in such cruel fashion, West Germany went on to become the first team to win a World Cup Final with a penalty kick. Their dour, dull war of attrition with Argentina in the Stadio Olimpico in Rome – the first Final in which one of the participants failed to score – was settled six minutes from time when Rudi Völler took a tumble in the box and Andreas Brehme stroked the ball low past Goycochea for the only goal of the game, the German craftily changing from his usual left-footed stroking of the ball to hitting it with his right.

Carlos Menem, the president of Argentina, accused

Edgardo Codesal, the Mexican referee, of armed robbery after the Final, in which Codesal dismissed two Argentina players and whose award of the penalty with which the World Cup was won had been incorrect – something with which even the Germans agreed. 'It was certainly not a clear penalty and Rudi said as much straight afterwards too,' Klinsmann admitted. 'The clear penalty was just before that actually, from the Argentinian goalkeeper on Klaus Augenthaler. I think the referee was saying, "I missed the call right before", so he called it in that moment.' Complaining of the 'evil black hand of the referee', Diego Maradona lamented losing in such a fashion. 'I will have to tell my daughter that the mafia also exists in soccer.'

A 1997 survey carried out by the FA's Technical Department and Liverpool's John Moores University found that 88 per cent of penalties in normal play were scored but that that percentage was reduced to a 79 per cent conversion rate in penalty shootouts. It also revealed that in a shootout players were more likely to shoot low towards the net, even though the same statistics showed that a goalkeeper was more likely to save a penalty that was kept close to the ground than one aimed higher. The unmistakable conclusion is that, hard as it is to take a penalty during 90 or 120 minutes, a ratchet effect sees the intensity increase a couple of notches in the deadly shootout situation.

'You can never replicate shootouts,' Bobby Robson said, 'because it is not possible to put 20,000 people behind a goal on the training ground to recreate the atmosphere, noise, tension and pressure of the real thing.'

England's problems with penalties have recurred in the two decades since their involvement in that first shootout, under Robson. Glenn Hoddle, England manager in the second half of the 1990s, had felt there was little point in practising penalties and England were accordingly eliminated by Argentina in the 1998 finals. In 2006, Sven-Göran Eriksson did his best to simulate the sensations of a shootout by making the players huddle together in the centre circle and walk to the penalty area on their own before taking their practice kick in training; all to no avail.

Yet it is possible to turn around a poor record in taking penalties. Italy had never won a penalty shootout before the 2006 finals and that seemed to account for their hurling themselves furiously down on the Germany goal during the dying moments of extra time in their semi-final to win by those two goals in the final two minutes. Encouragingly for England, when the Italians did face a penalty shootout, against France in the Final, they proved impeccable in their approach to it – not least because the entire team was demanding that they be allowed to take a kick, such was their desire to do well for each other and their confidence in their ability to stay steady through that test of nerve. It was quite a sight – the manager fending off players desperate to subject themselves to this drastic ordeal. Lippi, in the end, had to turn players away rather than persuade them to take a penalty, as is often the case with World Cup managers and their players.

'In Berlin, all the players wanted to take a penalty,' Lippi said. 'Even Buffon said to me, "If you need me, I'll take one, boss." When I saw that, I was convinced we would win but we did not prepare in any special way for the penalties. We didn't practise them. Choosing the penalty-takers was the easiest thing I had to do during the entire tournament. Simply because all the players were so sure we were going to win that they were all trying to catch my eye and gesture to me, saying, "Let me take one, let me take one!" A shootout says a lot about a team's mentality; its self-belief.'

Three years previously, when Juventus and Milan had been forced to settle their Champions League Final at Old Trafford on penalties, Lippi had found his players slinking off when it came time for him to select his takers. 'Am I to take them on my own, then, lads?' he had asked himself on that occasion – and Juventus duly lost.

Lippi's sole dilemma in 2006 was deciding the order of the takers and he opted to round off the five selected with Fabio Grosso. He chose Grosso, potentially, to settle the issue because he had won the last-gasp penalty against Australia that had seen the Italians into the quarter-finals and because Grosso had scored the late, late goal against the Germans that had helped to ease Italy into the Final itself. It does not make particular sense, given the difference between those two instances in a game and taking a penalty in a shootout, but confidence is an instinctive rather than a rational entity. The positive feeling that was coursing through Lippi and his team was reflected in their scoring all five of their kicks, with Grosso, as predicted, taking advantage of the one French miss to clinch the trophy.

That boundless confidence of the Italian team simply glows when set alongside the wan explanation from

Sven-Göran Eriksson for England's exit from the 2006 finals. 'We were just not good enough at converting our penalties – that's it,' is how Eriksson glibly, passively, resignedly, explained it away. 'You can never be sure about penalties but I never imagined we'd take them as badly as we did,' Eriksson elaborated. 'It wasn't tiredness, it was nerves. Taking a penalty for England at the World Cup is not like taking a penalty in the Premier League. The pressures on the Portuguese players were not even close to what the England players felt.' Ricardo, the Portugal goalkeeper, said, 'I could see in the eyes of the English players that they were not OK. The goal was shrinking for them. I just had to prolong their suffering.'

The England players had practised penalties every day for the six weeks in which they had been together for the World Cup finals but still missed three out of four in Gelsenkirchen at the conclusion of that meeting with the Portuguese. The Portuguese had taken the opposite tack to England and it had worked for them. 'We haven't practised penalties,' Luis Figo, the Portugal captain, had said two days before the match. 'We still have Friday if the coach wants to practise but so far, we didn't. It's a question of nerve. And we hope to have more nerve than England.' So it proved.

Fabio Capello got down to work early to bolster confidence for this, the ultimate test of World Cup will. 'Yes, a penalty shootout is a terrible moment,' he says, 'but I lost a [1970 European Cup-Winners' Cup] semi-final on the toss of a coin. I look at penalty shootouts as an opportunity. You have a chance. The best players can still win.' With this aspect of the game seemingly all about marrying basic technique with a superior positive attitude, England may have to hand finally the physician to mend the Achilles heel that has nagged away at them for so many years.

So, relax, don't worry about penalties. Even against the Germans. Well, maybe not against the Germans, but against just about everyone else.

6

Don't Impress the Press

CULINARY MATTERS WERE UPPERMOST IN ENZO BEARZOT'S mind as the Italy manager set off for Spain with his squad for the 1982 World Cup. 'I don't want the tomatoes,' Bearzot said with serious emphasis. Unlike most of those who are leaving home for several weeks in mid-summer and who are concerned about the standard of food that will be available to them on arrival in their temporary quarters, he was preoccupied with what might await his party on their return. It may, superficially, have seemed harsh to single out in this way the tomato, a fruit that is among the most favoured in Italy and a staple of multifarious fantastic recipes, something reflected in the Italians' name for it: the *pomodoro* or 'golden apple'. But Bearzot was not thinking of sophisticated cuisine but of the tomato in its raw, not to say, rotten state, and in its form as the missile most favoured by discontented Italian football supporters when greeting failed international football teams at the airport on their return from unsuccessful World Cups.

The build-up to the 1982 World Cup had been decidedly different for the Italians. Since the Second World War, each Italian team had been lauded by its own people before every tournament, cheered off as winners-in-waiting, such was the belief in innate Italian superiority on the football field. Some had returned with honour, such as the 1970 team that played admirably well in Mexico but who concluded the tournament as patsies for Pelé's Brazil. Others, such as the 1966 team, had returned to participate, passively, in the sport of hurling . . . the tomato.

For all the emotion, positive and negative, expended by Italians on the World Cup, the nation had still reached 1982 without producing a winner in the post-war period – during which the influence of the World Cup had really begun to be felt. The first tournament of the 1980s proved to be a departure, then, the first to find an Italy team viewed as no-hopers as they departed for a World Cup, with Italians resigned to the idea that their team would be returning home early and empty handed. Such was the lack of enthusiasm for the team inside Italy that it looked as if Bearzot's wish to avoid the tomatoes might be granted. A team from whom failure on a grand scale is expected can hardly be said to have let down their supporters if they simply fulfil the serious lack of expectation surrounding them.

The Italians were regarded as a flawed squad. They had faltered in the final qualifying matches, finishing only as runners-up to Yugoslavia, having lost to a mediocre

Denmark side, and had only squeezed a 1–0 victory over Luxembourg out of their final group game. They had then suffered pre-tournament friendly defeats to France and East Germany and all of these unimpressive results had formed, collectively, the impression in Italian minds of their team's lack of quality. 'I would prefer a fine defeat rather than a flawed win,' Bearzot had said soon after his appointment in 1975, an opinion that flew in the face of all Italian orthodoxy and immediately marked him down as a dangerous maverick.

Enthusiasm among the general public was further dampened by the withdrawal through injury of smooth-moving striker Roberto Bettega from the Italy squad for the finals, and the inclusion of Paolo Rossi, who had been suspended for two years after alleged involvement in a match-fixing scandal, and who was consequently short of match practice, having only returned to action shortly before the end of the 1981/82 season. Marco Tardelli, one of Bearzot's first-choice midfield players, was struggling for form, so hopes were heaped on Giancarlo Antognoni, the midfield player, one of those golden boys of Italian football who come along every now and then and upon whom crazy expectations are heaped. His preparations had been hampered somewhat by suffering a fractured skull in a league match, an injury that had left him in a coma for two days and that had almost claimed his life, but he was still in Bearzot's squad.

The general lack of faith in the Italian team encouraged the Italian press to be scathing in its criticism in advance of the tournament, something that would prove of enormous value to this team. Most members of the press are, by necessity, kept unaware of the nuances of form, mood and fitness inside a World Cup squad and are entirely unreasonable in allowing for the fine line between success and failure at international level. The pressures of finding an interesting story and of deadlines do not always conspire to allow cool and considered judgement. So being written off by the press at the beginning of a World Cup is not only a good idea but also a valuable source of fuel for a team who, in time-honoured fashion, can pin adverse comment on the dressing room wall as a source of motivation. For Italy in 1982, the influence of the press would perhaps be the most important on any football team in history and the critical jousting with words in which the Italian press indulged prior to the tournament would eventually look like a series of puff pieces in comparison to the ink that was spilled once the team's World Cup was underway in Spain.

The Italian press, with its squadron of daily sports papers, is perhaps the world's most intense, but other nations are not spared. 'You'd all like to see me fired, I know,' was Sir Alf Ramsey's disarmingly direct suggestion to a critical press as England embarked on their defence of the World Cup in Mexico in 1970. It seems an extraordinary situation to be in for a World Cup-winning manager but Ramsey's dedication to winning the World Cup for England did not extend to making extra efforts to accommodate journalists and his lack of a media-friendly persona had begun to work against him, even though England had maintained a record of extraordinary and consistent success in the years leading up to the 1970 World Cup. Funnily enough, the West German press were simultaneously excoriating Helmut Schön, their own manager, by asking, 'Why don't we have a Ramsey?' Perhaps the two nations should have swapped managers for a bit, just to give everyone a breather.

It is almost a condition of winning the World Cup that a team has to be regarded before the tournament as not being good enough to do so and the harsher and more vicious the criticism the better. The media pundit, Jimmy Hill, breezily dismissed England's chances of victory in the early summer of 1966 with his own particular brand of absolute certainty: 'It's not Alf's fault – nobody could win the World Cup with those players,' he said of Ramsey's men. So let's dust Jimmy down, get that St George's flag bow tie spinning again and have him give Capello's England more of the same before the 2010 tournament. It's his patriotic, national duty and, if given a platform to bluster, Jimmy can go at it all day.

Twenty years later, at Italia '90, England manager Bobby Robson was moved to suggest, 'If there was a war on, you'd shoot them,' in reference to the English media who had criticised his team fiercely before that tournament and in its opening stages. 'Bring them home,' ranted the *Sun* in a bellicose fashion, as if Robson's players were troops dispatched to a futile, faraway, unpopular war, after England's scrappy opening 1–1 draw with Ireland. 'A sense of shame fills the heart of every right-thinking Englishman this morning. How could our lads play like that? How could they let us down so badly? It was truly the most appalling performance by an England team in living memory. We're a carbuncle.' Robson's team went on to reach the semi-finals, where they played magnificently against West Germany, only to lose after the dreaded penalty shootout; they were agonisingly close to meeting a well-below-par Argentina in the World Cup Final.

The more straightforward England football managers such as Robson often issue a clarion call to the press, asking why they don't simply get behind the team at a World Cup. The press who cover the England team, after all, are almost entirely British, so why not root for the team on whom they are seemingly united in following? This is to misunderstand newspapers, and how some, but not all, are ready to switch in an instant to reflect what they feel is the national mood rather than seeking something close to an objective truth. Ridiculous, playground-type fun at others' expense and sometimes lunatic headlines is what the high-circulation titles, in particular, are after; asking for restraint from them is like seeking deep and serious meaning from the goings-on at a toddler's birthday party.

England, and Bobby Robson in particular, had been seen off to the 1990 World Cup with a spectacularly bad press. Robson was said to be indecisive and too loyal to players such as Peter Shilton, the 40-year-old goalkeeper who was said to be over the hill, and winger John Barnes. Robson was warm and pleasant but insecure, with mood swings that would see him become absolutely furious, only to revert swiftly to his more relaxed, amiable self. He was said to be wary of the more individually talented players, the great debate prior to the 1990 finals being Robson's seeming unwillingness to give Paul Gascoigne his head. The press pummelled the England manager for his habitual spoonerisms and comical penchant for mistaken identity – he once spent a conversation with Bryan Robson referring to his namesake as Bobby and himself as Bryan. He was also excoriated for his failure to play Steve Bull, a striker as British as brown sauce, but who, just like that delicacy, was surely out of place at an international feast.

'Dear Bobby, we are still in the World Cup. Can you please tell us how?' wrote a quizzical John Sadler of the *Sun* after a win over Belgium had enabled England to reach the quarter-finals. When England defeated Cameroon and took a step further, to become the first British team to reach the semi-finals of a World Cup on foreign soil, the reward for Robson and his team was further incredulousness. 'England staggered to victory . . . looking the least likely of World Cup semi-finalists,' wrote David Miller in *The Times*. 'It is up to Italy and West Germany to give the World Cup real style. Neither England nor Cameroon looked capable of being a match for the Germans as they disputed the right to a semi-final place. England's performance was no better than average . . . England's random organisation here truly saw the chickens coming home to roost for Bobby Robson.'

England eventually finished fourth at Italia '90, losing the third-place play-off 2–1 against the hosts. In 2006, the Italians themselves faced sudden sharp press criticism, which began as they reached the quarter-finals. 'During the past year the press have been raving about our performances,' Marcello Lippi said, 'and now they are criticising us just because of the last couple of matches. I don't understand how their minds can change so quickly.' The Italians went on to win the war of words by lifting the trophy.

The press had also caused serious trouble for an Italian team, not to mention sparking off something close to an international incident, at the World Cup of 1962. FIFA's decision to award that World Cup to Chile had provided a momentous boost to a poverty-stricken country that had been badly and tragically shaken by earthquakes two years prior to the tournament. Two million homes had been destroyed and 5,700 people killed in that disaster and the Chilean authorities hoped that the World Cup would help revive morale in their nation.

Some outsiders were still less than enthusiastic about the decision to award the tournament to Chile, seeing it as a backwards step into a backwater. 'Malnutrition, illiteracy, alcoholism, poverty . . . these people are backward,' Corrado Pizzinelli, an Italian journalist with *La Nazione*, had offered loftily, while Antonio Ghirelli, one of his colleagues, offered a more lyrical picture postcard of the host country. 'Chile is a small, proud and poor country,' he wrote, 'and it has agreed to organise this World Cup in the same way as Mussolini agreed to send our air force to London (they didn't arrive). The capital city has 700 hotel beds. The phones don't work. Taxis are as rare as faithful husbands. A cable to Europe costs an arm and a leg. A letter takes five days to turn up.'

Their words helped spark the 'Battle of Santiago', a match that saw hacking, spitting, punching and bodies sprawled on the turf as the players of Italy and Chile came together in their group game. 'I wasn't reffing a football

match. I was acting as an umpire on military man-
oeuvres,' Ken Aston, the English referee, said of
officiating in a game that saw him dismiss two of the
Italians, almost as token gestures in a match continually
and severely disfigured by the on-the-field violence.

'The press has a lot of influence, even on governments.
And it goes without saying they can influence a coach's
mind,' Carlos Bilardo, manager of Argentina in 1986,
says. He underwent severe criticism from the Argentinian
press prior to his team's successful 1986 World Cup but
fell back on experience from his other career to rationalise
how to deal with such adverse comment. Dr Desoldati, a
cardiologist and the head surgeon at Alvear Hospital,
Buenos Aires, had stressed to the young gynaecologist
Bilardo that he could take opinions from fellow doctors
but that the final diagnosis must be his own. This he
applied to his work with the national football team,
listening to the opinions of fans and journalists, and
taking them on board, but always trusting to his own
instincts and judgement before making any decisions.

When the Italian team, already bathed in press criticism, dipped into the 1982 tournament in Spain with an
opening 0–0 draw with Poland, in which Rossi looked a
mere forgery of the man who had done much to light up
the 1978 World Cup in Argentina, the Italian press suggested that Bearzot ought to drop him for the following
two group matches. When the manager failed to do so,
the sulphuric level of feeling against Bearzot in the press
burned even more furiously. His managerial time was seen
by the press to be coming to an end and the competition
among the writers was to see which one could most

spectacularly bring him down. Not only did the Italy squad bristle at being under attack from their own press representatives but it was compounded by the players feeling a stifling sense of claustrophobia at their head-quarters in Galicia in northern Spain. They were kept tightly under guard in their hotel and training camp by the security-conscious Spanish authorities, who were jumpy about the possibility of terrorist attacks by ETA, the Basque separatist organisation, even though ETA had said it would not interfere with the World Cup.

It was not only the Italian press that were commenting adversely on the team. When the Italians made their unimpressive start to the tournament, the Argentina man-ager César Luis Menotti, ready to comment on anyone and anything, said, 'Such huge sums of money are at stake that the Italian players have lost the will to play.' In the early 1980s Italy had the most lucrative football league in Europe: Zbigniew Boniek of Poland and Michel Platini of France, two of the brightest stars of the 1982 World Cup, had already been signed up to leave their respective home-lands and join Juventus in the aftermath of the tournament. Denis Law, the former Manchester United, Torino and Scotland striker, and by 1982 a media pundit in Britain, piled in with his own emphatic criticism of Bearzot keeping faith in Rossi. 'You can't be out of the game for two years and then come back in a tournament like the World Cup,' was the Lawman's summing up in passing judgement.

Bearzot patiently begged to differ with the consensus of critical opinion. 'Italy has been very unlucky recently,' he said after the match with Poland. 'We score few goals although we create great opportunities and nobody can be blamed. They never endangered Zoff. Then we pulled ourselves together and we almost won. Don't forget we hit the woodwork and had the only scoring chances of the game.' Privately, the Italy manager knew he had forced himself into a corner by bringing Rossi with him. He knew it was a huge gamble but rather than mollify the media by excluding Rossi from his squad, he included the player because he knew that, on form and at his best, he was untouchable.

There was, in the Italians' group, with matches played in the cities of Vigo and La Coruña, a feeling of being on the fringes of the tournament and the lack of goalscoring and explosive football from the teams involved helped provide the atmosphere of a sideshow. Italy went 1–0 up on Peru early in their second match but then reverted to type, retreating into defence to hold their lead even when Peru were reduced to ten men just before half-time after Jaime Duarte, the Peru right back, had been removed from the action to undergo treatment for an eye injury. The single-goal lead having been preserved by the interval, Rossi was replaced by Franco Causio, a 33-year-old midfield player from Udinese. Once again, Rossi had looked pallid and lacking in energy, bringing further press condemnation down upon Bearzot's head, not only for fielding him but for even including him in the Italy squad, the criticism growing in intensity after the packed Italian midfield had been unable to prevent the Peruvians getting an equalising goal.

Another 1–1 draw, with Cameroon in their third group match, saw Italy through to the second round but only because they had scored two goals to Cameroon's one – both having finished the group on the same goal difference of zero. Rossi had finally shown signs of life in this match, veering out to the left wing to cross for Francesco Graziani to score the Italian goal. Within a minute of that, though, Grégoire Mbida had equalised and the local Spanish fans began to roar on the Africans, who were participating in their first World Cup, as the Cameroonians went close several times to a second goal that would have been a knockout blow to the Italians. There were hints in the Italian papers that there could have been something amiss. The wife of the manager of Cameroon was reputed to have flown home with a bag full of foreign currency, raising ugly suspicions of bribery and corruption, a familiar spectre in Italian football.

Press grumbling exploded into the best arm-waving outrage that mere ink can buy with the headline accusation that the Italian players would each now enjoy a £30,000 bonus for reaching the second round. The suggestion that the players would receive such rewards for scoring only two goals and participating in three luridly unexceptional draws was seen as a public outrage and demands were made that the money be diverted instead to the country's deserving poor rather than to undeserving, pampered, under-performing prima donnas. Rossi was once again singled out for particularly stinging criticism.

It was all too much for the prima donnas in question who, furious at their poor critical write-ups, voted 18–4 to observe a *silenzio stampa*. No further communication with the press would be forthcoming for the remainder of the tournament and the press would not be allowed to venture inside the team's training facilities. From then on, the Italy squad had decided, they would do all their communicating through their actions on the field of play and almost instantaneously, freed of concern about critical comment, the Italians became a team transformed.

'We had read, in the press, tales about us that just were not true,' Bruno Conti, the Italy winger, recalls. 'The most horrible was that Rossi was "with" Cabrini and that players were seen in bars or shooting up drugs.' One press 'report' had suggested that Rossi and Cabrini were 'living like man and wife'. 'This didn't go with what we were trying to do or represent,' Conti continues, 'so we got together and created a news blackout.'

It initially made little impact on some members of the press. 'They are our worst team ever – just hopeless. Who cares if they don't speak?' one Roman journalist exclaimed after the Italy team had announced their decision not to communicate with the media.

It had by then been nearly a year since the Italians had managed to score more than one goal in an international match, and that had been in a friendly against Bulgaria. No previous World Cup winners had ever failed to win at least two of their opening three matches, whatever the tournament format. One slip-up is almost obligatory for World Cup winners, but none had enjoyed a record so mediocre as to draw all three games and scrape through only on goal difference.

It made matters even trickier that, through having finished second to Poland in their group, the Italians would now face Argentina and Brazil in the next stage. FIFA, with 24 finalists at the World Cup for the first time, had

Left: The ball used in the first World Cup Final in 1930. The hosts Uruguay employed the first underhand tactics to ensure that their ball, not Argentina's, was given priority.

'Win or die!' were Mussolini's instructions to the Italian team. They lived out his fantasies with this salute (**below**) in 1934 and by adopting these rather fetching sailor outfits (**right**) four years later.

Left: The Hungarian team in 1954. The magnificent Magyars became the first 'beautiful losers' in a World Cup Final when an unheralded West Germany consigned them to a defeat from which Hungarian football has never fully recovered.

Above: Home advantage – and a military dictatorship – definitely helped Argentina in 1978. What would have happened if Holland had dared to win?

César Luis Menotti's playboy image (**left**) made him a perfect role model for the players. Another one of his masterstrokes was to suggest that star striker Mario Kempes (**right**) shaved off his moustache.

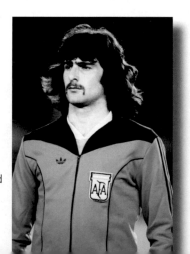

Above: For Argentina's next World Cup triumph, in 1986, Carlos Bilardo's extraordinary decision to appoint Diego Maradona as his captain three years ahead of the finals proved a decisive factor.

Left: The pair's relationship suffered in the run-up to the 2010 finals, but is Maradona a mad enough manager to win the World Cup?

Above: Vicente Feola (*centre*, with Pelé on his left) was an unlikely figure of a Brazilian manager, but he led the *seleçao* to victory in 1958. Pelé (**right**) later became more interested in endorsing products and pontificating about the Brazil team.

Left: In Chile in 1962, Garrincha was sent off in the semi-final but was 'miraculously' not suspended for the Final.

Above: Brazil, 1970. Arguably the greatest ever World Cup winners, but it is often forgotten that they had their own pre-tournament crisis and change of manager.

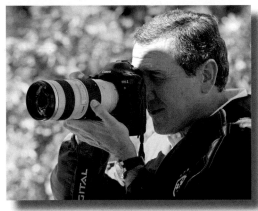

Right: It would be 24 years before Carlos Alberto Parreira's eye for detail and emphasis on defensive organisation brought Brazil its next success.

Left: The one rogue element in 1994, Romário (*centre*), provided the goals. His captain, Dunga, lifting the famous trophy here, will look to strike a pragmatic balance between defence and attack as manager in 2010. It worked for 'Big Phil' Scolari (**right**) in 2002.

Above: A champagne-stained shirt for one of the World Cup's most sartorially neat managers, Enzo Bearzot, at the end of the 1982 Final was an insignificant matter in comparison to the hail of tomatoes he had dreaded if his Italy team had flopped.

Above: The World Cup is the prize on the table as Bearzot (*front right*), goalkeeper Dino Zoff (*front left*), midfielder Franco Causio (*back left*) and Sandro Pertini, the popular president of Italy (*back right*), enjoy a game of cards on the flight home from Spain. Bearzot was the only person in Italy who supported the recall of Paolo Rossi (**right**) in 1982, according to the striker, but the manager was rewarded with the goals that won the World Cup.

Above: The Italian squad were again beset by a scandal, *Calciopoli*, in 2006. Here captain Fabio Cannavaro expresses the team's support for Juventus sporting director Gianluca Pessotto, who had failed in a suicide bid in the middle of the World Cup.

Above: The decision of the German press to stereotype the Italians was all the motivation the *Azzurri* needed to beat the hosts in the semi-finals.

Right: Vittorio Pozzo, the only manager to win the World Cup twice. Marcello Lippi is aiming to repeat the feat in 2010.

Left: Lippi was calmness personified during the 2006 penalty shootout. His main concern was not to damage his glasses and then have a nice, quiet cigar.

Above: Italy's other winning tactic in 2006 appeared to be not wearing any shorts. (*Left to right*) Andrea Pirlo, Fabio Cannavaro, Rino Gattuso, Gianluca Zambrotta and Manuele Blasi (who did not make the finals squad) model for Dolce & Gabbana before the tournament.

Right: Gattuso continues the tactic after the final whistle in Berlin.

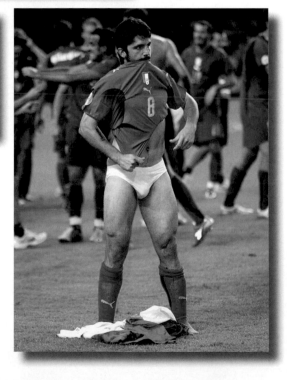

concocted a new, weird system of corralling four teams into semi-finals by having four groups of three in the second stage of the tournament. It was a set-up unique to that World Cup, and it appeared to have done little to favour the Italians. Argentina had lost to Belgium in their opening match, but had then pulled Hungary and El Salvador apart and were claiming that theirs was a side technically improved on the spirited winners of the 1978 tournament. Brazil were already seen as champions-elect, such had been their flair in putting ten goals past New Zealand, Scotland and the Soviet Union down in the steaming hot south of Spain. This was a group under which the earth was expected to shake.

Italy does not do grey – the country's life and its people tend to oscillate either from magnificent brightness to darkest gloom. With half of the Spanish tournament lived out in bathos, the Italians suddenly exploded into colour and, for them, a dreary tournament now began to open up like a flower in bloom.

César Luis Menotti, the Argentina manager, was in agreement with the Italian camp when it came to the esteem in which he held journalists. 'Not only do they know nothing about football,' he said before his team met the Italians, 'but if you were to shut them up in a room by themselves, they couldn't even write home a letter to mother.' Still, the Argentinian was as capable as any pressman of getting his predictions wrong. 'Italy's strength is in defence,' Menotti said. 'They don't have good forwards. Paolo Rossi is not capable of going full out for 90 minutes.'

When Argentina gambolled out to face Italy, the

European nation the closest in style to them, at the Sarrià Stadium in Barcelona, they were caught cold by an Italian side easing into a classic high-powered, counter-attacking game and whose strength was as great in midfield as in its, admittedly superb, defence. During the first half the Italians treated Diego Maradona, Ramón Díaz and Mario Kempes, the Argentina forwards, with arresting toughness, as might be expected in something resembling a transatlantic derby, while the Italian midfield was carefully twisting itself into shape to spring swiftly forward.

A blunted Argentina were sliced through twice in the second half by an Italy whose team spirit had been soldered together perfectly by the burning anger behind their united front against the press. Both goals were appropriately collective efforts. Conti and Antognoni spirited the ball through the Argentina defence for Tardelli to place it in the net and then Francesco Graziani, Rossi and Conti cleared the way for Antonio Cabrini to scoop the second. The Italian press, who had assembled like vultures to pick over the carcass of their seemingly dying team, were left scrabbling around in search of long-forgotten superlatives to describe this pulverisation of the World Cup holders – and just when the press needed player quotes the most, there would be none available to them. Goalkeeper Dino Zoff was the only member of the squad who they had collectively agreed would communicate occasionally with journalists but so dull were Dino's mumblings that it only emphasised how much the reporters were missing from the other, livelier players.

It contrasted severely with previous tournaments, such as the 1974 World Cup in West Germany, when familiar journalists had been greeted like long-lost friends and freely admitted to sit with the Italian players in card schools at their sumptuous headquarters at the Mon Repos hotel, close to Ludwigsburg. 'It's definitely a burden,' Sandro Mazzola confided laconically on being among a tight group of favourites for the World Cup, as he turned away from his game and lolled, tracksuited, in his chair, 'because then, whatever you do, everybody wants more from you.' Italy had gone into the 1974 finals without having conceded a goal in 12 games – a period that included two wins over England, with Fabio Capello scoring in both games – and were highly favoured to go all the way by an enthusiastic press. It would all end horribly for those press-friendly individuals and Ferruccio Valcareggi, the Italy manager, would be taken by surprise when immigrant Italian workers pelted their team coach with rocks after their meek early exit.

In 1982, as the team were holed up in their headquarters, the Italians' lack of contact with the press and their desire to prove they were no write-offs assisted them in concentrating on the task in hand. It helped them that FIFA's oddly constructed three-team group gave them six days of rest before they played Brazil, while the two South American sides would each play their two strength-sapping games inside three-day periods.

In contrast to Italy, the Brazilians were hugely press-friendly; the world's football writers had been near unanimous in their acclaim for the South Americans' style in zipping through their group and their wondrous, attacking football made the press rave about them in the same terms as those they had used for the team of 1970.

Where Italy had kept their game with Argentina tight to the point where it had often descended into street-corner-type scuffles, the Brazilians had played openly against the Argentinians, inviting their fellow South Americans to come out and show what they could do and to see if Brazil could do better. The Brazilians came good on their promise yet again, sweeping to a fine 3–1 victory. Guess which of Italy and Brazil the world's press still liked best?

It would, though, be the Italians who forced the issue as to whether that Brazil team might be undone by their own fancy football. With the score at 1–1 in their match, a slack pass in front of goal from Toninho Cerezo saw Rossi pounce for a second time in the match and his slick shot from the edge of the penalty area curved away from Waldir Peres in the Brazil goal. Falcão levelled the match at 2–2 but it was Rossi, now looking fresh and fit, who pinged in the winner. Finally, the Italians were scoring goals, being inventive and showing that they were far from being a shambles. 'Our true aim is total football,' Bearzot said softly while showering the Brazil team in compliments that they could take with them as souvenirs of Spain for the journey home.

Those two matches against the South Americans had had an utterly transformative effect on Italy's World Cup; they were encounters in which they had combined tight marking, intimidation, swift counter-attacking, rapacious wing play and precise goalscoring. For all that Brazil were an excellent side and easier on the eye for casual World Cup viewers, they lacked the all-round competence of that Italy team. Key to the Italian victory was their effective defence, which included the tight, borderline-illegal man-marking of Claudio Gentile, the elegant sweeping of Gaetano Scirea and the fulsome play of the right back Fulvio Collovati. Then there was Antonio Cabrini, the kingpin in this Italian team's most fluent version of *catenaccio*, a lively full back ready to spring into attack and link with the darting, unerringly fine Conti, a winger who could score and create in equal measure and on whose crossing Rossi thrived.

An absence of contact with sweaty scribes appeared to have acted with the efficacy of a stress-releasing spa holiday in the Swiss Alps. For the press, in contrast, previously so dismissive of the Italy players, the opposite effect had taken hold. Now desperate to rub shoulders and resume their relationship, some looked on the brink of madness as they found themselves, like the spurned party in a particularly intense and combustible relationship, forced in desperation to gaze longingly at the wordless players through the perimeter fence of their hotel on the outskirts of Barcelona. It was an unrequited love, with the players entirely unwilling to go back on their mutual pact even though the press would now clearly be prepared to be so much more compliant. In a nation with several daily sports newspapers, this was a desperate situation for the sportswriters. 'It was the malicious lies told about our bonuses that made us finally decide no longer to speak with the press,' was Rossi's succinct explanation.

To make matters worse, the Italian Football Federation confirmed that the press stories about the bonuses had been wrong. The figure that had been the subject of so much speculation in the press was not for having qualified from the opening round but the sum up for grabs if Italy were to win the World Cup.

Those Italian journalists who, seeing upcoming matches against Argentina and Brazil, had been waiting to chisel out some tightly wrought words to stab at the hearts of Bearzot and his team – on what they had been sure was their imminent World Cup immolation – must have been astonished at the sudden change in his side.

The Italy manager was a tall, slim, pipe-smoking, relaxed and urbane figure, whose appearance radiated calm; he wore shades and sported a lightweight summer suit with thin blue and white stripes and light blue shirts with smart, button-down collars. He was still on speaking terms – if only just – with the press, even if his players were not. 'Firstly, I have to say that Brazil played the most beautiful football of the World Cup,' Bearzot said after his team's momentous victory over the South Americans. 'I am sorry for them but Italy deserved to qualify.' The manager pointed out that, for all the descriptions of Italy as a defensive team, the Brazilian penalty area had been crammed with the entire Brazil team to defend the corner-kick from which Italy had scored their third goal. After the Brazil match, even Bearzot briefly lost his temper with the press; it was as if the emotion and vindication of that great victory had meant he felt justified in no longer containing his frustration with them.

A semi-final with Poland only underlined how different Italy were from the side the Poles had met three and a half weeks earlier. Two close-range goals from Rossi sent the Italians into a Final with West Germany, who had become the European champions in the tournament hosted by

Italy in 1980 and who were undefeated by a fellow nation from their own continent since 1978. 'I don't want anything said that would inflame or depress the public to an excessive degree,' Bearzot said before the match, his worldly wise demeanour and calm underlining the benefits of having only himself, rather than excitable young players, as the conduit between the team and the sportswriters. 'I do not want the Italian people prepared for a big victory on Sunday because failure would then be regarded as a disaster. I definitely don't want the tomatoes.'

Bearzot had little need to worry. After a slowish first half against West Germany, during which Cabrini sent a penalty kick slithering past the post, the Italians overwhelmed their opponents during the second 45 minutes for a worthy 3–1 victory. Paul Breitner, the West Germany full back, would pay the Italians the highest compliment by saying that this was an Italian side with the type of team spirit, work ethic and selflessness more usually found in a German team. It was also an attack-minded side even if one built on a concrete defence: Scirea, the sweeper, created Tardelli's famous goal in the Final and Gentile did the same for Rossi. Conti, Antognoni and Tardelli, the midfield players, were brimming with imagination and know-how and the indispensable talent not only to do creative things but to do them at such a speed that the opposition could not keep pace.

The Italian press would create their own twist in the tale – one designed to fit subsequent events – by saying that they had been extra-critical of the team to try to gee them up, get them moving, to make the players prove whether or not their critics were correct to be so hard on them. A more fitting conclusion was provided by the Italy manager who, after the Final, addressed the journalists who had called for his sacking prior to the tournament. 'And what do you think now?' Bearzot asked of them. For once, a football man and not the press had had the last word.

7

Take Your Time

WINNING THE WORLD CUP HAS A LOT IN COMMON WITH developing a holiday suntan. Don't do the equivalent of roasting on a poolside lounger all day when you first arrive and ending up crippled by third-degree burns for the remainder of your stay. Instead, increase your resistance to the harmful effects caused by exposure to the world's media, fanatical supporters and desperate opponents by building very slowly towards success.

Even a defeat at the group stage can be a terrific thing. In one of the most historic of all World Cup matches, West Germany lost to East Germany in the opening segment of the 1974 World Cup. The victory was hailed stirringly across Eastern Europe and the Soviet Union as a triumph for communism over capitalism at a time when the Cold War was still chilling the world – as good a boost for morale as a fine May Day parade of armaments down Tverskaya Street in Moscow.

East Germany's win may have been a tremendous propaganda victory – not least because Helmut Schön, the West Germany manager, had defected from the east in 1950 – but its greatest practical effect was to galvanise a West Germany squad that had been, until then, disunited. By the time West Germany were winning the World Cup in Munich, their eastern brethren were back home thumping the tops of their rickety, old Soviet-built televisions in an attempt to get a good picture for the Final. 'That defeat to East Germany woke us up,' Franz Beckenbauer says, 'and we finally started to work together as a team.'

Italy, as we have seen, diced with elimination at the earliest stage in 1982, drawing all three of their group stage matches and looking like pallid, lethargic, unenergetic, condemned men. They scraped, by their fingertips, into the last 16 and if the surviving teams had been ranked at that point, Italy would have been bottom of the table. Once the next round began, though, every team was, in effect, starting afresh and the Italians were able to build from the ground up, as it were.

England, in 1966, did just enough to get through each of their first four matches until finally turning on the style for the semi and the Final. After Argentina's 6–0 win against Serbia in their second group game in 2006, the world hailed the 24-pass, nine-man move that had concluded with Esteban Cambiasso scoring the second goal and the Argentinians, even that early, were quickly acclaimed as the team of the tournament. Things could not get any better than that for them – and they duly went out in the quarter-finals to their no more than average German hosts.

'Self-belief grows gradually with each game and that strengthens the team's character and personality,' Marcello Lippi, manager of the Italy side that won the World Cup in 2006, says. His team had been only just starting to think about getting into their stride while the Argentinians were demolishing Serbia & Montenegro, and it would be a week later, in Italy's third group match, against the Czech Republic, that the Italians would finally begin to make a slow and calculated acceleration towards the ultimate reward.

'There was a turning point after the game with the USA and before facing Czech Republic,' Lippi says. 'That was when we realised we had a great chance of going all the way to the Final because France's results meant that [if Italy beat the Czechs] we'd be up against Australia in the last 16 and then Ukraine or Switzerland. We knew then that we couldn't waste the opportunity before us. It was clearly not the same as coming up against France, Spain, Brazil or one of the other top teams. Not that it would be easy, but we'd avoid the big names. The players and all the rest of us were well aware of that situation when we took on Czech Republic, and that was reflected in our performance. We displayed tremendous hunger and will to win . . . we were determined to win the group and make the most of the great opportunity before us.' A short, calculated spurt at exactly the right time ensured the Italians of downhill momentum towards the Final.

At the 1954 World Cup in Switzerland, West Germany did not so much make slow progress at the start of the tournament as appear to have stopped dead in their tracks. Following a victory over Turkey in their opening match, the Germans came face to face with Hungary, a team that had entered that World Cup as perhaps the strongest favourites in the tournament's history. Not only had the Hungarians been crowned Olympic champions in 1952 but they had not been beaten in more than four years and were inspired by Ferenc Puskas, 'the Galloping Major', one of the greatest of all international forwards.

This was a Hungary team that, in 1953, had become the first country from outside the British Isles to defeat England at home – and they had done so in sumptuous style, with an emphatic 6–3 victory that owed much to a sophisticated approach that had England defenders stumbling around their own penalty area in an almost somnambulant fashion as they sought a way out of their waking nightmare. The Hungarians showed that their victory had been no fluke in a World Cup warm-up match in May 1954, thrashing England 7–1 in Budapest.

West Germany, in contrast, had been barred, in disgrace, from participation in the 1950 World Cup – the first to take place after Adolf Hitler's Thousand Year Reich had closed down well ahead of schedule – and were something of an unknown quantity at the 1954 tournament. A Germany team had finished third in the 1934 World Cup but that had been held in Benito Mussolini's Italy, where his fellow fascists might have expected a few favours from the dictator's hand-picked referees, with third place a most suitable conclusion for them, in that they avoided a confrontation with their confrères in the Final.

The Germans' only other World Cup appearance, in France in 1938, had been considerably less successful.

Following the Anschluss, under which Hitler had co-opted Austria into becoming part of greater Germany, a number of Austrian players were brought into the German squad by order of the Reich. 'Me: lonely and deserted on the edge of a steep rock,' Sepp Herberger, Germany's newly appointed 41-year-old manager, had said wistfully after his coaching staff had deserted. Orders that Hitler's greater Germany team be adjusted for each match to include five or six of the Austrians had been too much for them. Germany, with a swastika woven tastefully into the team badge on their jerseys, used the Nazi salute at the finals but despite that show of power they were swiftly eliminated, after a replay, by Switzerland, in their first game, a straightforward knockout system being employed from start to finish in that tournament.

Following elimination, Herberger was less introspective and more condemnatory. 'The Austrians have to learn a lot: during a game, they prefer to give in rather than fighting for victory,' he said, in one of the most dangerously incautious post-match interviews in football history, given that the Führer himself was an Austrian, although, perhaps fortunately for Herberger, not particularly interested in the game of football.

Herberger survived and remained national team manager as the 1954 World Cup began, but his players now represented a fresh but shrunken German entity – minus not only Austria but also the newly communist eastern chunk of the fatherland which had been carved up by the Soviet Union at the end of the Second World War. West Germany arrived at the tournament representing a beaten-down and shamed people still struggling to recover from the self-inflicted damage of the conflict and Herberger's team had made hard work of scraping past Norway and the short-lived Saarland in qualification for the finals. All of that was still incidental to the main theme: Hungary were expected to sweep all other nations aside and be crowned world champions. That theme of Hungary gliding majestically down on the World Cup appeared not so much a good, calculated guess but utterly inevitable when they thrashed the West Germans 8–3 in each side's second match. Instead, that defeat would prove the springboard for the losers to trump the men who had so gladly humiliated them.

'With 16 teams, Switzerland 1954 was the first truly representative World Cup' would later be FIFA's official line on that tournament, but even though world football's governing body appeared to have arrived at the perfect number of finalists, there had still been room for a unique and seemingly minor idiosyncrasy peculiar to that tournament that went a long way towards an explanation for that result and, ultimately, helped the West Germans to snatch the World Cup from the seemingly more deserving hands of the Hungarians. The opening stage had been divided into four groups, each comprising four nations, but instead of each nation playing each other once, as would later become the norm, two of the countries in each group were seeded and would face only those that were unseeded. Turkey and Hungary were the seeds in Pool 2, with South Korea and West Germany unseeded.

It meant that Herberger, going into the match with Hungary, calculated that with defeat being almost inevitable and goal difference not yet a factor at the World Cup, his team would be scheduled to face Turkey for a second time, in a play-off to see who finished as runners-up to Hungary. Rather than run his first eleven into the ground against the Hungarians, he opted to send out a largely second-string side and keep his best men fresh for the play-off with the Turks, three days later. Herberger was a pragmatist who pioneered pithy truisms that would remain long in circulation. 'If you don't shoot, you won't score,' was one of his favourites. Even he, though, who viewed football realistically rather than romantically, would not have expected the resultant onslaught from the Hungarians, who were 7–1 ahead until the West Germans notched two late goals. The match ended 8–3. 'I believe we would have lost today, even with our strongest team,' Herberger said, mustering a defence of his team selection, as criticism rained down on his head.

Only four of the West Germans who had faced Hungary were selected for the match with the Turks, which West Germany won 7–2, before beating Yugoslavia 2–0 in the quarter-finals and Austria 6–1 in the semis, winning a place in the Final with, inevitably, Hungary. The Hungarians, in common with any team in such a situation, were now brimming with confidence about facing a side that they had whipped so easily earlier in the tournament. Herberger, using a wonderful piece of reverse psychology, did nothing to dissuade them from such thoughts. 'It would be the greatest upset of the World Championship,' he said on the eve of the Final about the prospect of his team overcoming the Hungarians. 'But we don't believe it and we are making ready to hail as champions tomorrow that marvellous goalscoring machine which is the great Hungarian team.'

The Hungarians accepted such flattering praise only too willingly, in the opinion of some West German players, who believed that the earlier result had created a huge sense of complacency in the minds of the Hungarians with regard to their repeat opponents. 'Suddenly you win against a team as strong as Austria and are in the Final,' Horst Eckel, the West Germany midfield player, says. 'We were so happy and everyone said, "Ah ha, the Germans are strong too." Only one team didn't understand this and that was Hungary.' Gyula Grosics, the Hungary goalkeeper, confesses his surprise at finding the West Germans blocking his path to a winner's medal. 'Three matches earlier we had beaten the Germans 8–3 and, to be honest, after that match I couldn't have imagined that we'd come across the West German team again in the Final.'

A great weight of expectation hung on the Hungarians. There was political pressure from the leaders of their communist state to earn a victory for national prestige and after having scored a phenomenal 25 goals in their four games en route to the Final, Gusztav Sebes' team were expected to cruise through another encounter with the team they had annihilated earlier in the tournament.

'Our greatest enemy is not so much physical fatigue as nervous tension,' Sebes said, before unveiling his own pithy adage: 'I had never suspected that the World Cup would be such a test of nerves.' Those nerves were on edge when, the night before the Final, the Hungarians were subject to hearing the contestants in Switzerland's national brass-band competition battle it out, with the entrants parading up and down until the early hours of the morning outside the Hungarians' hotel. On the day of the Final, when the players went to their rooms for an early-afternoon nap, the din started up once again.

On arrival at the Wankdorf Stadium in Berne for the Final, the Hungarians discovered that it was already packed to capacity and had been sealed off by the Swiss police to prevent anyone else entering the ground. The team coach carrying the West German squad had arrived earlier and their players were already inside the stadium, relaxed and carrying on with their pre-match preparations. The Hungarians were made to leave their bus and force their way through the throng outside to plead with officials to allow them into the stadium. Sebes would later claim that he had been assaulted by a policeman, using the butt of his rifle, as he attempted to explain that this was the Hungary team, without whom there would be no match.

One special consequence of the first meeting between Hungary and West Germany hung over the Final: an injury to Puskas, inflicted upon him by Werner Liebrich, that had forced the Hungary captain to miss his team's subsequent two matches and left in doubt his participation in the Final. It had been Liebrich's third serious attempt at doling out a whack to remember to Puskas during the initial match but he had finally got his man. The repeated fouling from the powerful Liebrich had even drawn words of outrage from the West German press, who already had enough to write home about, given the size and seeming significance of the defeat. 'It wasn't that the German match was especially tough – in fact it was more like a friendly, they showed such little resistance,' Puskas said of the two teams' encounter at the group stage, 'but Liebrich caught me from behind, my leg went and I had to be taken off.'

It seemed to matter little when Hungary went 2–0 ahead inside the opening ten minutes, through Puskas and Zoltan Czibor. But as the match developed they discovered that this was a different West Germany to that which had lost 8–3, although it was not entirely a team full of different faces: six of the players who had participated in the match in Basle a fortnight earlier would take the field in Berne and the defence remained pretty much intact; Werner Kohlmeyer and Jupp Posipal, the two full backs, retained their places in the team, as did centre half Liebrich. However, the Germans hit back, hard.

'We sat back and tried to keep the ball in midfield to neutralise the game and tire the Germans out,' Puskas recalled. It did not work; the West Germans' resolve had only been strengthened by going 2–0 down and by half-time they were level. Six minutes from the end, Helmut Rahn put West Germany 3–2 ahead and that is how it remained. 'Games last for 90 minutes,' was Herberger's addition to his growing volume of pithy footballing witticisms in the wake of the match. Puskas echoed the West Germany manager's sentiments. 'We lost because we forgot that a match lasts for 90 minutes. We deserved what we got. We should never have relaxed after going two up; we should have pressed on, looking for the third to kill the game off.'

The injury that Puskas had sustained in the original match between the two nations had had more of an effect on his team-mates than on the player himself. Some believed that Puskas was still unfit as a legacy of Liebrich's foul and that, with victory all but assured over a team they had trounced earlier, Sebes had included him in sentimental fashion so that Puskas would go down in history as one of the 11 that had won the World Cup. Puskas did open the scoring in the Final and had another goal disallowed in the last few minutes but, in between, when Hungary needed his inspiration to combat West Germany's determination, it didn't help that several players had doubts in their minds over the staying power of their captain.

'On the day, they beat us and in doing so perhaps revealed a deep self-conceit in the team that had never shown itself before,' Gyula Grosics, the Hungary goalkeeper, said. 'After we got the second goal in the eighth minute, we thought it was all over. That match was lost by us, not won by the Germans. It was the saddest day in the history of Hungarian football. It shattered the myth – our legendary status – and neither the experts nor the general public at home could bear it.'

It was a seismic moment in world football: the arrival of West Germany as a hugely potent force in the game. Their players would admit that the Hungarians were the most purely talented team in the tournament but German stoicism in building slowly from that near-standing start had, in classic tortoise and hare fashion, seen them overhaul the supposed champions elect.

The Germans had prepared assiduously, training four times a day under the methodical Herberger. They had also been the first team to wear screw-in studs, supplied to them by Adi Dassler, founder of the Adidas football-boot-making company and, in the wake of the Final, hailed inside West Germany as 'the shoe-maker of the nation'. His new invention had been a huge help to the West Germans showing sure-footedness in the Final, which was played out on a rain-sodden pitch. A Germany team that had visited England in 1901 'seemed to have a good idea of the game but, being imperfectly shod, could not keep their feet', according to the *Manchester Guardian*. As the second half of the twentieth century got underway, such amateurish images had been banished for ever with the establishment of a well-heeled West Germany as world football's über-professionals.

The repercussions of the result were radical. West Germany's victory created such euphoria inside their own country that it is often credited as the source of their post-war economic miracle, whereby West Germany was quickly turned into the wealthiest, most efficient and dynamic nation in Europe. 'We are somebody again,' became a common, Herberger-like catchphrase among Germans as they experienced this boost to their collective self-confidence in the aftermath of the Final. Across in Hungary, the reaction was diametrically different. Hundreds of thousands of people poured into the streets in the hours after the match and, inflamed bitterly by the reversal of fortune that had hit their team, began to vent their opposition to their communist rulers. 'The atmosphere was so bitter it could be felt months later,' Grosics recalled. 'In those demonstrations, I believe, lay the seeds of the 1956 uprising.'

Dubbed in West Germany as 'the Miracle of Berne', the

win entered German mythology almost as soon as the final whistle blew. Herberger was attributed with near-mystical powers with regard to foreseeing the effect of a hefty defeat from the Hungarians at the group stage. 'Sepp Herberger knew he could qualify for the quarter-finals even while losing to Hungary,' Helmut Schön, who would become Herberger's assistant shortly after the 1954 finals, said. 'So he deliberately did not field his strongest side [in the first game] against the Hungarians. It was a shrewd move because it meant that, whereas he knew the exact formation and strengths of the Hungarians, the formation of the German team in the Final would be new to Sebes.'

That is a neat and alluring explanation but doesn't really fit with Herberger's pragmatic outlook. It seems more likely that he had been attempting merely to ensure his team's survival in the tournament and to maintain the prospect of making stealthy, cat-like, progress through it, to as distant a point as possible. It was a modest ambition that brought immodest rewards for him and his nation.

8

Wallow in a Crisis

THE MANAGER HAD LOCKED HIMSELF AWAY IN HIS ROOM and when he did emerge it was to inform his players that the public would be well within their rights to spit at them in the street. This was life inside the West Germany training camp prior to the 1974 World Cup, when a dispute over bonus payments had the manager, Helmut Schön, threatening to jettison his entire squad of stars, including Gerd Müller and Franz Beckenbauer, and replace them with reserves. A last-gasp settlement was reached but failed to pep up the team. Their flaccid performances in the early stages of the tournament prompted dissatisfied supporters to make known their feelings towards the players, leading Beckenbauer to spit towards the Hamburg crowd during West Germany's second match, with Australia. The fans had treated him with scorn by chanting for Uwe Seeler, the local hero and a distinguished international of the recent past, and the win over Australia was a soggy performance to match the West Germans' opening one, against Chile.

'I am sorry,' Beckenbauer said afterwards. 'I blew a fuse! I was rude but I had been provoked.' The Kaiser was known for strolling imperiously through football matches and through life, so when he resorted to the actions of a street-corner thug it was as good a signifier as any that the West German squad really was beset by turmoil, even if the people in the stands and on the terraces were not fully aware of just how deep the problems ran.

A crisis or a whiff of scandal can do much to pull a team together and transport it to the ultimate victory in football. In 1982, Paolo Rossi entered the World Cup under a cloud after having been implicated in the *Totonero* match-fixing scandal that had resulted in him receiving a lengthy ban from football. He would always deny the charges and his initial three-year ban was reduced to two years, allowing him to return to club football with Juventus very shortly before the finals. Opposition supporters in Italy would catcall the Juventus striker as 'prison trash' prior to the 1982 tournament and when he began it, his performances in Italy's first three games were ineffective.

Yet Rossi's two-year absence had proved a boon – and without it, Italy's chances of winning that World Cup would have been reduced considerably. The wiry little player had always had a physique that verged on the frail and suspect knees had plagued him severely, even since his teens. Having been involuntarily rested from the strenuous physical demands of competition in Serie A for two years, by 1982 he was quite possibly in the strongest and most

143

resilient shape of his entire career. The opening three games, in which he had failed to hit the net, had served the purpose of getting him match fit. Once the fiercest stage of the competition arrived, he found searing form, and the six goals that made him the tournament's top scorer were indispensable in Italy winning the competition.

Scandal has never been far away from all of Italy's World Cup triumphs. The 1938 tournament, held in France, was illuminated by the talents of Leônidas da Silva, nicknamed the 'Black Diamond' or the 'Rubber Man', who collected goals almost as easily as nicknames and who had hit five of the seven that would make him the tournament's top scorer by the time the Brazilians were preparing to meet Italy in the semi-finals. 'He was a rigorously Brazilian player,' Nelson Rodrigues, the Brazilian playwright, would say of Leônidas. 'He had the fantasy, improvisation and the sensuality of the best Brazilian players.'

As such, his presence seemed assured for the semi-final. Not so: Ademar Pimenta, the Brazil manager, curiously decided to leave Leônidas out of the match with Italy. 'I am resting him for the Final,' Pimenta said, which seemed a strange tactic to adopt upon coming face to face with the defending world champions. The Italians duly won 2–1 and went on to triumph over Hungary to retain the trophy. Rumours would surface that henchmen of Benito Mussolini, the Italian dictator, had 'persuaded' Pimenta to follow his particular course of action in sidelining Leônidas for the match.

A mid-tournament crisis engulfed England, in 1966, centring on the studiously aggressive Nobby Stiles, who was an unlikely-looking hard man in that he was slight of build, weighed in at less than 11 stone, stood five feet six inches in height and was a bespectacled individual off the field who was nicknamed Clouseau in recognition of his various mishaps. But once he had his contact lenses in place for each 90 minutes, he would be transformed, like a Clark Kent with goggle eyes, into a demon enforcer at the rear of the England midfield.

During England's third game at the group stage, with France, Stiles, by his own admission, exceeded even his usual enthusiasms. The England man described his wild cawing away of the legs of Jacky Simon, the France centre forward, as 'the tackle from hell'. Simon had, in the French way, artistically flicked the ball away first time and was turning to stay with the play when he was hit by a wrecking ball of a tackle from Stiles that left the Frenchman crumpled in a heap on the halfway line at Wembley in front of the Royal Box and in fine view of the various assembled dignitaries therein, most notably the *éminences grises* of the FA.

In the wake of the match, Stiles was buffeted by near-universal condemnation in the British press for his tackle. More critically for Stiles and England, those at the FA demanded privately of Ramsey that he remove Stiles from his squad for the remainder of the tournament. Attitudes to discipline in English football then were that a player should not represent the country if there was a suspension hanging over his head and they were effectively saying that even though Stiles's offence had gone unpunished by the referee, it was so grave that he ought to be suspended by England.

This was a crisis indeed: the manager had no one else who could match, in his specialist role, the inimitable Stiles. 'If he goes, so do I,' Ramsey sharply told the FA's international committee. 'You will be looking for a new manager.' With their ultimatum having been thrown back in their faces, they relented and Stiles's ongoing interventions in England's subsequent three matches would be crucial in winning them the trophy. 'Charlton, Moore, Hurst . . .' Antonio Rattín, the captain of Argentina, said, on recalling the England team that he encountered in the quarter-finals. 'Then there was that madman who played with the contact lenses . . . Stiles . . . the little bald guy. He got stuck in.'

The great Brazil side of 1970 had their own pre-tournament crisis when João Saldanha, the manager who had supervised their jet-winged qualification, sought to change tack drastically with the team shortly before the finals. Saldanha was a man who would not duck criticism from journalists and supporters – it was they who had to duck when Saldanha came after them, fists flying, to dole out retribution. When fellow professionals weighed in with caustic comments, Saldanha rightly gave them the higher level of respect that they deserved as more knowledgeable commentators, choosing to seek out the most serious offenders with a loaded gun. Even more controversially, in the spring of 1970 Saldanha made it clear that he was planning to drop Pelé, just as the Brazilians' preparations for the tournament intensified. Although a Pelé-inspired Brazil had proved far superior to their South American counterparts during the qualifying competition, Saldanha was concerned about the physical threat offered by the European teams at the Mexican finals – where Brazil had been drawn in a group with Czechoslovakia, England and Romania – and had begun to change the emphasis in his team to a muscularity to match such opponents.

When Saldanha was summarily sacked shortly before the finals, two prominent Brazilian managers turned the job down, deciding that they did not need the hassle that went with the post, and so Mario Zagallo, a quiet, hard-working, unassuming man, without the flamboyancy that Brazilians liked to see associated with their team, took over, stating modestly that he saw it as a matter of national duty. Amid all this flux, and with Zagallo third choice for the post, it looked questionable as to whether Brazil could restore their reputation worldwide after the terrible disappointment of their 1966 World Cup effort in England. Still, Zagallo plodded along happily and methodically, and, under his charge, Brazil emerged, swinging and flaming, with Pelé at the heart of the team, to earn undying admiration for their infectiously bright and enterprising style of play.

With Saldanha removed and harmony restored, Zagallo's 1970 team coursed through the tournament with seven fine victories, throwing up memorable moments in each of their matches. Franz Beckenbauer, the West Germany captain, enjoyed those finals too. 'The games in Mexico were colourful, the country laughed, and the football danced,' he says of the 1970 World Cup.

When it came time for Beckenbauer's own country to host the finals, four years later, things were slightly different. 'All I ever hear from you is money, money, money!

That is bad form,' was the pre-tournament address from Helmut Schön, the 58-year-old West Germany manager, to Beckenbauer, Horst-Dieter Hottges, Günter Netzer and Wolfgang Overath, the players' delegation who were demanding increased financial bonuses as the tournament approached. Schön had been on the verge of not only sending the players home but decamping himself from the isolated Malente Sports School, 50 miles north-east of Hamburg, where his squad was based for pre-tournament preparations. Eventually, a bonus figure was agreed, satisfactory to the players, for each one to receive in the event of them winning the World Cup.

The emphasis on personal enrichment showed how much West Germany as a nation had changed in the two decades since Sepp Herberger's team had toppled Hungary from their pedestal in the 1954 Final. His humble collection of hard workers had been replaced by a set of players made hugely wealthy since the introduction of a professional football league in West Germany during the mid-1960s and reflected a country at the peak of its powers, reborn in the aftermath of the Second World War. Outsized figures of the West Germany players had been hung from buildings across the country to celebrate the finals and to represent them as the dominant force in the tournament, but the players' reputations were shrinking with each passing game of the opening phase.

Gerd Müller, whose ten goals had made him the tournament's leading scorer in 1970, was the key striker in a West German national team that had played beautifully in winning the 1972 European Championships, but he also found life stifling at a tournament that should have been a celebration of all that was good in a revitalised Germany. Instead, after the mediocre displays over callow opposition in Chile and Australia, the West Germans were trumped by their East German counterparts in what would be the only meeting of those two countries in the four decades that Germany was divided politically. The East Germans' surprise 1–0 victory enabled the communists to claim the moral high ground, in contrast to their seemingly spoilt counterparts. 'My players will get no bonus money at all,' Georg Buschner, the East Germany manager, said sanctimoniously, providing a brief masterclass in inverted snobbery, 'not even if we win the competition. We are amateurs. Financial reward is out of the question.'

A lack of cohesion on the field during the West Germans' opening three matches had been a direct reflection of the rifts in their dressing room. One cause of ongoing discontent was the lack of clarity over whether Wolfgang Overath or Günter Netzer was to be the nominated playmaker. Another was that life at Malente, their base, was so regulated and tedious that they complained of it having the feel of a barracks. Eventually the players would break loose and enjoy a couple of wild cigar and champagne parties, with local girls brought in to get things swinging – all to Schön's extreme distaste.

The players knew their own performances were unconvincing. Full back Paul Breitner, who had opened the scoring for his country with a 30-yard shot past Chile goalkeeper Leopoldo Vallejos in the opening game, states that he was only able to score from such a distance because, in his opinion, Vallejos was 'half-asleep' and only woke up once the ball had gone speeding into his net. An ever-swelling chorus of whistles had flowed reedily from the crowd during that match in Berlin as the West Germans stuttered through the game.

At the conclusion of the match with East Germany, Breitner and his team-mates had again been engulfed in booing and jeering from their own supporters as a reaction to Jürgen Sparwasser scoring the only goal of the game close to its conclusion. T-shirts had been on sale from the start of the tournament emblazoned with the slogan 'Germany – world champions' in anticipation of the ultimate success at tournament's end. After the East's victory, sceptical supporters were wondering to which Germany the slogan referred.

That defeat was a 'rude awakening' for West Germany, according to Overath, one that forced the players to reassess fully their attitude. The team had only a short time before been negotiating 'like megalomaniacs', Breitner says, over the amount of money they would each be paid if they won the tournament and now they were facing up to the prospect of outright humiliation if they failed to up their game for the next, even more demanding phase. One benefit of their poor early form and of losing to East Germany was, conveniently, to give the West Germans a more straightforward passage to the Final. As in 1954, when Herberger's team had benefited from FIFA tinkering with the format for the World Cup, so their successors would too.

The 1974 finals saw the introduction for the first time of a second group phase, consisting of two groups of four, rather than the tournament metamorphosing into a knockout competition after the initial four groups of four. This allowed FIFA to squeeze in a lucrative extra batch of games and, appropriately, benefited the capitalists among the two Germanys. Had West Germany beaten their eastern neighbours they would have gone on to share a group with Holland, Brazil and Argentina; instead, their defeat had left them facing Poland, Sweden and Yugoslavia. Schön chose to take some consolation in the fact that his team's poverty of performance in the opening stage had at least deflated expectation of them. 'I am glad we are no longer the favourites,' he had commented after the match with Australia.

As the West Germans faced up to the next phase, more emergency talks took place between the players and Schön, a tall, elegant gentleman with a kindly disposition and a love of the theatre, antique furniture, classical music and opera and a man who felt that the modern players were too well-rewarded and that their riches diluted the pleasure that they could take from the game itself. 'Money never came into it for me,' he would say of his own playing days. With Beckenbauer as the conduit, the more powerful players told the manager in no uncertain terms that he had to make major changes to the team. 'We told Schön he had to do something or we'd be out of the competition,' Müller says.

In effect, Schön was muscled aside and Beckenbauer began running the team, informing the manager that wing play was expendable and that the key from now on would be to deploy players wide in midfield who would busy themselves, when not attacking, by darting back to help

151

out the defence. Rainer Bonhof came into the side, where he instantly provided greater power in midfield, and Bernd Cullmann was jettisoned, not to be seen again at that World Cup.

The team that faced Yugoslavia in the first game of the second phase showed four changes from that which had lost to East Germany and Overath was now fully assured of his place in midfield to the exclusion of the talented but mercurial Netzer, whom Müller and Beckenbauer had had cause to criticise and chivvy during matches. Netzer's response, which contained a knowing understanding of his popularity within the squad, was that there was little that he could do with the ball if the rest of the team refused to give it to him. He had displeased Schön by joining Real Madrid in 1973 rather than remaining in West Germany for the year before the World Cup and now Santiago Bernabéu, the Real president, was in Netzer's homeland hawking him around German clubs in the hope of offloading a player who had proved a disappointment in Spain.

Overath too had his moments of unpopularity; his name having been booed by the Berlin crowd when the names of the West German team were read out before the match with Chile. But the team's performance now went from 50 per cent efficiency to 90 per cent, according to Breitner, as the Yugoslavs were beaten 2–0. 'It is dangerous to celebrate the day before the evening is over,' Schön said cautiously after this win.

Schön, reportedly confined to bed with circulatory trouble following the match with the Yugoslavs – although perhaps more through a desire to escape the external and internal pressures of the World Cup – issued a statement that was supposed to refute the idea that Beckenbauer had taken over from him but which confirmed that the Kaiser had a role surpassing that of a mere player in Schön's set-up. 'Naturally I have for a long time been discussing with Franz everything concerning selection and tactics. But I am the manager and I give the orders.' Within hours things would become even worse for Schön when he received the news that his poodle had died.

Sweden offered strong resistance in the second match but eventually went down 4–2 to the West Germans, who were then presented with another high hurdle in their final match of the second phase, in being confronted by a fine Poland team who had won all five of their matches up to that point. Fortune intervened in the Germans' favour against a team that Breitner rates as being the best in that competition, when a snap thunderstorm and torrential rain half an hour before kick-off turned the Frankfurt pitch into a swamp, leading to the bizarre sight of the local fire brigade being brought in to pump water off its surface. For all their flair, Breitner suggests, Poland had three or four 'fair-weather' footballers in their team, and on a foul night for football, the West Germans squeezed past them 1–0.

The Final with Holland presented the West Germans with a crisis in its opening minute. Berti Vogts' man-marking of Johan Cruyff went slightly awry, given that the little German lost the Dutchman the first time he got the ball, and Uli Hoeness became the first West German to make his mark on the match by conceding the penalty from which Johan Neeskens opened the scoring. Holland, in common with the Hungarians of 1954, had blazed a trail to the Final, scoring 14 goals and conceding just one (and that was an own goal). Possibly even more importantly, they had looked to most observers to be by far the most impressive side in the competition, playing with a level of creativity and flair that put them on a level with the Brazilians of 1970. That opening goal, which resulted from the Dutch enjoying unbroken possession from the instant they kicked off the match, seemed to encapsulate their superiority over a West Germany who had shown only the occasional flash of style in reaching the Final. As the game settled early on into an orgy of Dutch domination, West Germany were, Breitner felt, like a boxer on the ropes, and that Holland team had everything in their armoury to finish them off, even very early in the match. The West Germans looked in danger of a severe thrashing.

But it did not happen. As Johnny Rep, the Holland forward, memorably suggested, the Dutch forgot to score the second goal, and their temporary amnesia allowed the West Germans to survive their biggest on-pitch crisis of the tournament. 'The biggest mistake was that we wanted to demonstrate how good we were,' Ruud Krol, the Holland centre back, said. 'We forgot to make more goals.' Sepp Maier, the West Germany goalkeeper, thought that the Dutch had become big-headed after receiving so much good press for the style with which they had lit up the tournament and that they believed that they would go on to score several more goals. Rep admits that their primary aim early in the match had been to make the West Germans look ridiculous rather than to seize the initiative and really make their early dominance count.

'We were satisfied to have the ball,' Arie Haan, the Holland midfield player, says of his team's showboating. 'They scored two counter goals because we didn't press enough and in the second half we didn't have the luck.' It was fatal for the Dutch to believe that they were on easy street. As Cruyff had suggested pre-tournament, 'The Dutch are best when we have to fight together against the others and not with ourselves.' The feeling of relaxation early on in that match, that perhaps the struggle was already over, did them little good. For all their beauty, this was also a Dutch team vulnerable to any team able to soak up punishment on the ropes without hitting the canvas. 'We have the team for attacking,' Krol said, 'but this is a problem sometimes because sometimes we are too much attacking and we take the big risks.'

Breitner, who equalised for the West Germans, is crisply emphatic on the reasons for his side's 2–1 victory. 'Our two goals in the first half, my penalty after 25 minutes and Gerd Müller's goal just before half-time,' he says, 'were a logical consequence of the Dutch team's carelessness and arrogance.' This neat subverting of stereotypes, with the Dutch seen as strutting egotists toppled by their own hubris, is hugely humorous. The thinking behind it even persists to this day in the idea that the Dutch would have been the more worthy champions; an idea put forward keenly even by the players who failed to turn the theory into practice on the day. 'Wherever you go in the world, a fan will know the names of that Holland team,' Haan says. 'We did something beautiful.' Cruyff is among other Dutch players who believe that finishing second in that World Cup is not something to lose sleep over, given that they provided the world with so many wonderful memories; true, but also loftily presumptuous in its way. The German mentality, whereby you have to prove you are the best by winning, seems rather more humble.

German players, Schön would suggest once the dust had settled, take a perverse delight in making the most of the niggling pressures and tensions that unsettle others. While the Dutch were basking loftily in the acclaim that had built around them with each passing game in that tournament, it was the West Germans who had got their heads down and used the frictions caused by their series of crises as a source of power to win them the trophy.

9

Play for the Team

THE AUDACITY OF MICHEL PLATINI HAD TO BE ADMIRED when he visited Brazil in 1997 and deigned to sum up the impact that nation's team had made in winning the World Cup three years previously. The Frenchman, normally a master of diplomatic small talk and an amiable, jolly presence on official occasions, said that he felt moved to congratulate Brazil on winning the 1994 tournament 'with the poorest Brazil team anyone could remember'. It was a joke that was less risqué than it seemed, given that it found a degree of resonance within that country, where the methods used to secure a first World Cup in 24 years were still regarded as debatable. Wilson Piazza, the centre back in Brazil's 1970 World Cup-winning team, has suggested that most Brazilians would have trouble bringing to mind the names of the winners in 1994, in contrast to those of 1970, although that seemed a risky personal assertion given that Piazza is not usually the first name to trip off the tongue when conjuring up memories of the giants of 1970.

Brazil's win in 1994 was impressive enough to inspire the 14-year-old Ronaldinho to set aside all other ambitions and aim for World Cup glory, but the manner in which it was achieved was regarded almost as a betrayal of the nation's heritage by some within the nation. Carlos Alberto, captain in 1970, described the 1994 winners as not having purveyed genuine Brazilian football. Yet Carlos Alberto Parreira, the manager of Brazil in 1994, had turned up for duty at that World Cup insisting that Brazil would do just that and play 'like Brazilians'. 'It is our instinct,' he said, 'and the only way that we will once more be successful. We want to go back to our roots, to the flat back four, zonal marking and attacking football. That is how our players have played since they were boys. You cannot put Brazilian players in a straitjacket. Brazilians play best when you leave them free.'

It was just what the world wanted to hear – and then Parreira seemed to go and do just the opposite. This was as stiff and disciplined a Brazilian team as it was possible to see: eight rigorously dutiful players in defence and midfield, drilled in cautious, largely risk-free football, whose main task was to stiffen the game and see what happened as and when it was possible to deliver the ball to Bebeto and Romário, the small, nippy strikers, the latter of whom was the only wild card in the team. Romário, a native of Rio, would seek out the action in the most crowded part of the pitch like the back-streetwise city boy he was. Instead of shying away from the penalty area, he would, like an eager pickpocket, view it as the place where he could do his work most effectively.

Brazil in 1994 were criticised for being too serious, too organised, and the perceived lack of flair in Parreira's team put pressure on the manager – for the whole three years before the tournament. Not the team, then, to provide football to match the sunburst-yellow of their shirts. Romário, consistent in behaviour only in his unwillingness to be chained to any disciplined routine on or off the field, would frustrate his managers throughout his career, marching to his own drum – usually one beating out a heavy nightclub rhythm into the early hours, often shortly before the start of that day's training.

'I am prepared to die for that glory that is Brazilian football,' Romário said with self-sacrifice and with the gravitas of a statesman, on touching down in the USA for the finals. They were choice words given that the five-foot-six-inches-tall, self-styled 'street cat' had always previously demanded enormous leeway and large doses of self-indulgence from his managers in return for the donation of his talents. 'I accept my responsibility and declare that this World Cup is my life,' he went on. 'Whatever happens in the next four weeks will shape my life. This will be my great year.'

For all Romário's stirring words about what he was planning to do, Parreira was happy just to see the player there at all. There was a heart-in-mouth moment for the manager when, shortly before the team was due to leave Brazil, Romário had gone missing, only to be discovered playing beach football with his friends. Even then the beginning of Romário's journey to the USA had been a bit less dignified than the fine words that he had used on landing there. Embarking upon the aeroplane to the USA, the squad's loose cannon had kicked up a storm over the seat that he had been allocated. The manager had placed Romário in a seat between fellow strikers Müller and Bebeto, to try to promote harmony among them. But Romário wished to sit with his pals, not least because he believed that Müller had no right to be on the plane. Romário had helpfully advised Parreira that the manager ought to include Edmundo, Romário's friend, and a man not known for his calming influence, in the squad at the expense of Müller, who, Romário said, was good at club level but not up to scratch for international football. Besides all that, Romário, 28, had wanted a window seat.

When Pelé had said, on the matter of Edmundo, that Romário ought to allow the Brazil manager to make decisions with regard to the team, Romário had described Pelé as 'mentally retarded', adding in reasonable mitigation, 'He shouldn't have criticised me. The Brazil team of today is not a Pelé team. It has nothing to do with Pelé.' This formidable lack of self-restraint had almost led to Romário's exclusion from the World Cup – he had missed most of Brazil's qualifying matches after publicly and caustically offering Parreira 'advice' on his team selections and was only recalled to the team for their final qualifying match, with Uruguay, in which he scored twice to take Brazil to the finals. As with many of the greats, exaggeration was another powerful weapon in Romário's armoury. 'I have scored against every team, every country, every defender in the world,' he said.

For Parreira, an intelligent 51-year-old who painted seascape watercolours as a means of relaxing, this was clearly going to be a long World Cup. He had been subject to constant criticism at home for fielding teams as colourless as his paintings were bright and for being too reliant on European-based players – there would be eight of them in his first starting line-up in that World Cup, against Russia. It was also, strange as it may seem, widely felt that this was Brazil's last chance to win another World Cup, given that they had been seemingly superseded by every other major nation, most painfully Argentina, in the years since triumphing in Mexico in 1970 and had tried a variety of means to attain success, only to crash, sometimes quite spectacularly, out of every tournament without reaching the Final.

With victory the most important thing, Parreira, rationalist that he was, had decided to construct the team that the nation wanted – even if the nation did not quite realise it. His was the identikit World Cup-winning team, one bulked out by able-bodied workers, who, like a human pyramid, could afford, through balanced discipline, to carry one rogue element – in this case Romário – who, by virtue of his prime, free-standing station atop the construction, would attract most of the attention.

The analysis of Marcello Lippi, Italy's winning manager in 2006, would have found a degree of resonance with Parreira. 'I tried to give the Italian players the same conviction that I had within myself,' Lippi says, 'which was the conviction that I believed strongly, 100 per cent, that in Italy we had the potential to create a World Cup-winning team. I am not convinced of having brought

161

together with me to Germany the technically best players that were available. But I was firmly convinced I had called on the ones that could create a team, and that they could play with one another to the best of their abilities. In this day and age you win if you become a team. It doesn't necessarily mean that you've got to have the best football players in the country. It's possible that the best, all together, don't become a team. It's like a mosaic: you have to put all the pieces together. I did have big players, top players, but their greatest skill is to have been able to put their ability at the service of the others.'

Italy's 2006 World Cup team would pace itself carefully and cautiously through games before exploding colourfully into life when the time was right, as in the semi-final with Germany, in which the two teams sparred gamely before Lippi, sensing German weakness, threw on attackers for the concluding stage of the match and was rewarded with the two late match-winning goals. This is how a World Cup must be won in modern times, when teams are so tightly matched for technical skills and fitness. A team such as Italy may not quite capture the imagination of those outside their own country in the same way as other champions of the past because, unless watched closely, their short bursts of requisite brilliance can easily be missed. Such a unit can also swoop towards the World Cup almost under the radar, with other teams exerting themselves in a more eye-catching way but failing to measure their efforts properly across the entire tournament.

The emphasis on tight-knit teamwork saw players such as Valdo and Edmundo left behind when Parreira ventured forth to the USA. It is why David Ginola and Eric Cantona were immersing themselves in their multifarious other activities as France strode to victory in 1998. When England's silky striker Jimmy Greaves was injured early in the 1966 tournament, it was expected he would be restored to the team when fit. Instead, Alf Ramsey persevered with the seemingly more workmanlike Geoff Hurst – so ordinary that he is still the only man to have scored a hat-trick in a World Cup Final.

Italy lost Alessandro Nesta, a proven world-class performer, at the start of the tournament in 2006 and brought in Marco Materazzi, a centre back who had failed miserably in the seemingly simple task of holding down a place at Everton, but who would perform powerfully and score the Italians' equalising goal in the Final. Italy in 2006 seem more synonymous with Materazzi and Fabio Cannavaro, the diligent centre backs, and Rino Gattuso, the holding midfield player, than with the gilded Francesco Totti or even Andrea Pirlo. In a team comprised of a particularly doughy consistency, the more tasty ingredients were introduced only sparingly. For example, Alessandro Del Piero, the brilliant attacker, was sprinkled on that tournament in cameo appearances, arriving for instance as a late substitute to provide the vital spurt that enabled the Italians to accelerate to victory over the Germans. A balance has to be struck between flair and dependability, and where the seasoned drinker might order a Scotch and ginger ale and ask the waiter to go easy on the ginger ale, a successful World Cup manager tends to the opposite extreme, watering down and even dousing the fieriness in his team. When Lippi talks about his 2006 winners, he speaks of 'positive energy' and an unquenchable team spirit, not of carnival-type colour.

Germany have reached seven World Cup Finals, and won three of them by going about their business with what appeared to be a cold contempt for anything that might be mistaken for gaudiness. 'Our secret, as it always is for the German team, was to be incredibly fit and well-organised,' Rudi Völler, the Germany manager, said proudly of his side getting to the 2002 Final. 'We did not always play marvellous football in Japan and Korea but we had an incredible goalkeeper in Oliver Kahn, who kept five clean sheets out of seven, and Michael Ballack, who always scored at the right time.' Or, as Franz Beckenbauer put it, 'Apart from Kahn, you could put that lot in a bag and beat it with a stick and whoever got hit would deserve it.' They still came within a whisker of winning the trophy.

Brazil cannot afford the luxury of mediocrity. When they take the stage for their first match in a World Cup, the world expects them to make a good tournament even better. If it has been poor until then, Brazil's moral duty is to give it a lift. But after the Brazilians had faced Russia in San Francisco in 1994, they instead spread mystification among those who had seen them play. Certainly they had been good but they had not showcased any cartwheeling skills, flips or a breathtaking introduction of a new dimension to the game. The world was disappointed – it had expected more from them – and, like a teacher disappointed in a less than brilliant showing from a favoured star pupil, sucked on its teeth in a state of frustration, hurt, bafflement and confusion, hoping only that this had been an aberration and that normal service would quickly be resumed.

Romário had darted and dashed here and there against Russia like a hyperactive toddler but his performance did little to light a fire under his team, and nor was the overall middling nature of Brazil's showing illuminated by the spectacular in either of the two goals scored. One was a close-range poke from Romário; the other a penalty kick from Raí after Romário had been sent thudding to earth inside the box. Parreira, afterwards, seemed to suggest that even he would like to see what his team might do with the shackles off but that it was more than his job was worth. 'There were expectations not only from the Brazilian people but all those who know what Brazil can do,' he said. 'If we had played with our chest open and our whole heart, who knows what would have happened?'

No nation is invested with more responsibility to entertain on a regal scale than the Brazilians and Parreira, like any wise politician, was happy to play along with the idea while working with the realities of the modern game by taking a more measured approach. A heartily physical Cameroon side were their second opponents at the group stage and amid the whipping studs and beefy bodychecks, the Brazilians stayed steady, gliding to victory with a practised ease. Goals from Romário and Bebeto were separated by a scoring header from centre back Márcio Santos. It had been accomplished, efficient stuff, this brushing off of a team determined to hustle them out of their stride, but the world was still awaiting the vital spark that would see Brazil really catch fire. It would be a long wait. This was a team designed to nudge its way steadily to victory through rationed displays of superior technique.

Parreira's assistant, Mario Zagallo, acknowledged this global craving for wild, inflammatory stuff as he provided his boss with a break from finding a new way of telling the press what they wanted to hear. 'We will attack our opponents in the traditional Brazilian way,' Zagallo maintained fiercely, as he took over public relations duties before the third group match with Sweden. 'But you have to remember that other teams always make a bigger effort when they play Brazil. They seem to find greater motivation.' The Swedes lived up to Zagallo's expectations, buffeting the Brazilians with attack after attack inside Detroit's stifling, roof-enclosed Pontiac Silverdome and went 1–0 ahead through Kennet Andersson before Romário went rolling through on goal, repelling three challenges and sending a shot snaking past Thomas Ravelli in the Swedish goal to secure a draw.

Adding to the disappointment at Brazil's performances was that a framework had been put in place for them to thrive as entertainers at the 1994 tournament. FIFA had decided that matches must be played in midday heat and humidity unfamiliar to most of the world's footballers and this was to Brazil's advantage in that it made it a tournament for technically accomplished teams rather than those that played a kick-and-rush percentage-type game. Another new FIFA ruling beneficial to Brazil that was zealously espoused by referees from the start of the tournament was that players tackling from behind with no hope of winning the ball were to be dismissed. The offside rule had been altered in the early 1990s so that the attacking player now had only to be level with the second last defender; not only that, but in marginal cases match officials were obliged to give the benefit of the doubt to the attacker. This was also the first World Cup at which the pass back to the goalkeeper had been ruled out as a means of time-wasting on the part of the less enterprising teams. All of these rule alterations seemed designed to bring brio to Brazil, yet Parreira's team stuck stubbornly to their careful, watchful game.

Part of the reason for Parreira's caution might have been Romário himself: if the manager was going to accommodate a player of such invention and skill but one not known for his willingness to track back or adhere particularly closely to any tactical scheme, the insurance policy was to construct a near impermeable barrier behind him so that the striker could not inflict too much damage on his own team. Mauro Silva was a powerful force in the Brazil midfield but not blessed with extravagant skills. Raí, the playmaker, was almost static and subdued in comparison with the type of inventive blur of arms and legs and feints and dummies of Brazilian legend. The midfield man had been searching for form as the World Cup dawned and was damned with faint praise when his manager explained his inclusion in the team. 'It's much easier to get him back to his best than find someone else with similar characteristics.' Even then, Raí's contribution to the team in the early matches was so muted that he was dropped after the group stage to make way for the even less flamboyant Mazinho.

The emphasis on leaving nothing to chance was

reflected in Brazil's hotel being sealed off from the world, including player's agents and relatives. Parreira's players were also forbidden to criticise their manager. 'Brazil is its own worst enemy,' Parreira said. 'One of our biggest challenges is to achieve unity among the players.' With 24 years of failure bearing down on his shoulders, Parreira would conduct press conferences twice a day to satisfy the media, but that did not prevent the omnipresent Pelé from suggesting repeatedly during the tournament that Parreira ought to be dismissed. 'Brazil couldn't play any worse,' Pelé had pronounced after the group game with Sweden. 'You have to follow your own way,' Parreira suggested. 'You can't pay attention to all the things you hear.'

It did not help Parreira that his managerial experience seemed limited – previously, he had been manager of Kuwait at the 1982 World Cup and the United Arab Emirates at the 1990 tournament. He looked destined to be one of those well-travelled, well-paid Brazilians hired to coach nations who were always likely to be among the extras at any World Cup but who still wanted to look good for the few frames in which they appeared. He had been among the Brazilian backroom staff at the 1970 tournament – but as a fitness coach. So tired did he become of the endless questioning of his abilities that Parreira insisted that he would retire after the World Cup in the USA even if Brazil won it. His pronouncements tended to oscillate between requisite Brazilian extravagance and weary caution. 'Technically I consider our team to be the best in the world right now,' he had said before the tournament began, before reaching for the brake with, 'We don't have the superstars we had before but the

Left: Karl Wald, the inventor of the penalty shootout. Yes, he is German.

Below: France were the first team to suffer the heartbreak of losing on spot-kicks, in the infamous 1982 World Cup semi-final.

Left: Uli Stielike, here being consoled by Pierre Littbarski, missed that night, but remains the only German ever to have missed from twelve yards in a World Cup shootout.

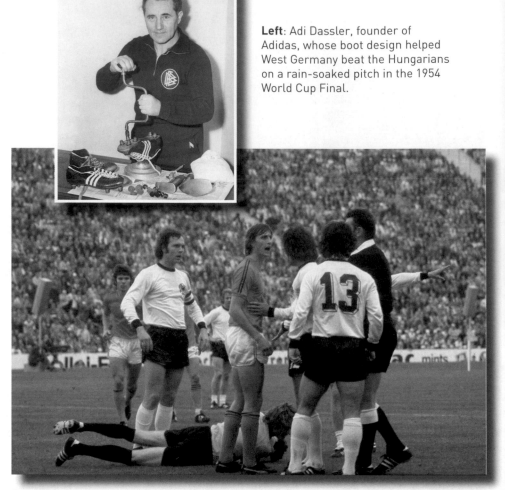

Left: Adi Dassler, founder of Adidas, whose boot design helped West Germany beat the Hungarians on a rain-soaked pitch in the 1954 World Cup Final.

Above: Franz Beckenbauer (*second left, standing next to Johan Cruyff*) ensured that he had the ear of Jack Taylor after the English referee had awarded Holland a penalty (**below**) in the opening minute of the 1974 Final.

It was Bernd Hölzenbein's apparent dive (**left**) that won the Germans parity – and arguably the World Cup – midway through the first-half. Jürgen Klinsmann (**below**) continued his nation's fine tradition of acrobatics in 1990, especially against Czechoslovakia in the quarter-finals.

Above: Cheating, or rather simulation, knows no national borders. Rivaldo's antics in South Korea were one of several less spectacular moments in Brazil's World Cup history – but still helped them win.

Above and left: Footix, the mascot for the 1998 World Cup, adopted a variety of versatile and expressive poses as he went all around France trying to drum up enthusiasm for the tournament only to be met by practised *ennui* from the French public. Régis Fassier, the actor in the costume, who had put everything he had into the role, soon got cheesed off.

Below: The French fans eventually got behind their team, but the slow build-up helped take the pressure off the host nation.

You know he's worth it! David Ginola (**above left**) did all he could to belittle the France of Zinédine Zidane and co, while manager Aimé Jacquet (**above right**) was singled out by the press and ridiculed for his provincial accent and working-class background.

Above: President Jacques Chirac did not lose the opportunity to cash in some credit. Michael Platini, on his left, managed to get away with the couture calamity of a France football shirt underneath his suit.

Left: Belo Horizonte, 1950: England 0 USA 1. A result best avoided in 2010, but an early loss can be the making of a World Cup winner.

Below: Referee Ali Bennaceur's view of the 'Hand of God'. The Tunisian referee was called 'An idiot more fit to herd camels in the desert than take charge of a World Cup game' by none other than his Bulgarian linesman Bogdan Dotchev (**inset**), here on the right, with Bennaceur (*centre*) and Costa Rican linesman Berny Ulloa Morera.

Above: Injury had deprived England of Bryan Robson earlier in that 1986 tournament against Morocco. Ray Wilkins, seen comforting 'Captain Marvel' here, was sent off in that match, but England arguably became stronger after the twin setbacks. It was still not enough to win the World Cup.

Above and right: Factors behind 1966: Nobby Stiles, whom Alf Ramsey laid his job on the line for; the wet Wembley pitch; an injury to Jimmy Greaves (*on the left*).

Below: It was another linesman who made the decisive call, however, thanks to his antipathy towards the Germans. (**Left**) Tofik Bakhramov appears to be wondering whether he should be somewhere else as he checks his watch at the coin toss with (*left to right*) West Germany captain Uwe Seeler, referee Gottfried Dienst, the other linesman Karol Galba and England captain Bobby Moore. (**Right**) Bakhramov readies himself to give Dienst his verdict on Geoff Hurst's controversial second goal.

Left: Alf Ramsey's calm, detached manner is reflected in that of Fabio Capello, seen here (**below**, front row, far left), in his one previous World Cup appearance, with Italy in 1974.

Right: The word 'WIN' appears to be missing from this banner, but the England fans are as optimistic as ever.

Below: England were hoping that Wayne Rooney, sent off for this stamp on Ricardo Carvalho as England lost to Portugal in the 2006 finals, will come roaring back four years later to inspire a momentous World Cup victory. It worked for Maradona in 1986 after this red card against Brazil in 1982.

standard is good.' More often he would speak of the 'maturity' of his team, of its 'mental discipline'.

There was still no slipping of the mask when Brazil faced up to the USA in their first knockout tie, midway through the tournament. Even in the midst of a tournament, these Brazilians were basking in near anonymity. 'I know who Pelé is,' Mike Sorber, one of the USA players, said, 'but these guys Romário, Bebeto and Raí, I never came up against their names. If you don't know the hoopla behind a guy, he's just another person, like you.' Alexi Lalas, the USA centre back, chimed in with, 'People tell me they're great but I don't know any of the guys on their team. They're not my idols.' Facelessness seemed the reward for the 1994 Brazilians' subverting of personality to the team ethic.

Again the Brazilians looked hidebound, cautious, as they carefully manoeuvred their way past the type of team from whom they might have been expected to take half a dozen goals. They could still have done without the distraction of Leonardo, the midfielder pressed into service as an enterprising full back, being dismissed for elbowing Tab Ramos shortly after half-time, an offence so grievous that the player would subsequently be suspended by FIFA for the remainder of the tournament. Still, with just over 15 minutes remaining, Romário, who had earlier hit a post and had had a shot cleared off the line, drew three men to him and nicked the ball to Bebeto to nudge it into the net.

Back in 1988, Brazil had bid to host the 1994 tournament but had lacked the financial backing to bring solidity to their bid, something that was not an obstacle for the USA. By going easy on the hosts, whose population had finally become enthused by this alien game thanks to their own team's progress, Brazil made sure they did not bring down on their heads unpopularity with the locals for the remainder of their sojourn in the north of the American continent.

The Brazilians had strolled about and stroked the ball around against the USA but in the quarter-final with Holland, confronted by a talented team and in a match with a fierce competitive edge, Parreira's team finally emerged from their shells, showing that they had the fire within them to meet a forceful challenge from near-equals and that it had, after all, been worth conserving energy in the opening four games. Brazil thoroughly outperformed the Dutch, Romário and Bebeto putting them 2–0 ahead and a powerful, long-distance shot from Branco, in for the suspended Leonardo, sealing the 3–2 win after the Dutch had fought back tenaciously to equalise.

'Defence is the key to success,' Tommy Svensson, the Swedish coach, insisted before his team's semi-final with the Brazilians. 'I don't speak only about our four players at the back – our midfield is very hard to play against.' He might have found comfort in his own words as half-time came with the score 0–0, but, after an hour the gulf between the teams became evident as Parreira's team finally came to the boil. Brazil had had a host of shots on target, the Swedes just one, but it took until ten minutes from time for the decisive act in the game: Romário climbing into the air and hanging there for a few seconds before heading Jorginho's cross low past Ravelli.

As the tournament drew towards its conclusion, Brazil, harnessed by Parreira's methods, were much like

blinkered thoroughbreds who could still not help themselves in breaking free and playing fine football even
within Parreira's disciplined system. The Brazilian feel
was still there, even if muffled by the layers of constraint.
'It was difficult even to walk through the Swedish penalty
area,' Parreira said, 'but really, we outplayed them in
every aspect of the game. The only difficulty was to get
the ball into their net. We had 29 shots in all and nine of
them were real situations in front of goal. We took only
one chance but one is enough.' After 24 years it opened
the way again to a Final between Brazil and Italy.

For all that improved athleticism and better tactical
awareness on the part of opponents made caution necessary, Brazil were trying to get the better of no one more
than themselves. 'Do you expect me to win the World Cup
with a disorganised Brazil?' Parreira said shortly before
the Final. 'We still apply the main principles of the
Brazilian way, with a flat back four, zonal marking and
the emphasis on possession of the ball.' Zagallo cut to the
quick: 'The teams that tried to play 1970 football here –
Argentina and Colombia – have gone home early. It is
more important than it used to be to know how to play
when the other team has the ball. A team that attacks
indiscriminately, as Brazil have done in the past, or knows
only how to defend, is not going to win the World Cup.'

When the cautious, cagey Final ended 0–0 after 120
minutes and Parreira began to prepare for penalties, he
found that the set of players who had finished the game
only featured four players he had rehearsed in the art of
taking a shootout kick. Romário had not been among
that steady-Eddie five, but as Parreira scanned the players

around him to find one with the mettle for this nerve-racking test, Romário indicated with a flick of the head that he was the man the manager sought.

After Márcio Santos, Parreira's most reliable man in practice, had missed Brazil's opening penalty, it was Romário who settled the team's nerves by scoring their next one and setting the team up to triumph in the shootout. The maverick had proved to be one of Parreira's most reliable men; it was almost as if Romário had finally been overcome by the atmosphere around the Brazil team and by Parreira's tournament slogan of 'Maximum efficiency: zero error' and had become a team player – or at least as much of one as he was ever going to be. His penalty clipped the post on its way into the net and Brazil, with even the wildest element in the team tamed to a degree, were on their way to the World Cup.

Dunga, the defensive midfielder who was symbolic of the new efficient Brazil, scored the decisive penalty before Roberto Baggio's heartbreaking miss. As manager of the Brazil team in 2010, Dunga will be happy to purvey much of the same team ethic, and pragmatism, in South Africa.

10

Don't Worry About the Brazilians

SUPERLATIVES HAVE RAINED DOWN SO REGULARLY ON
Brazil throughout the nation's World Cup history that
they might easily have all been used up by the beginning
of the twenty-first century. As Brazil approached their
seventeenth successive World Cup in 2002, though, there
was a clamour within that country insisting that that side
had exceeded every one of their predecessors. Those players heading for Japan and South Korea were widely
agreed to be the worst side ever assembled in the nation's
illustrious footballing history.

Brazil had used 63 different players and three different
managers in qualifying for the 2002 tournament, which
had concluded with them only just scraping into the finals
in their last qualification game to preserve their record of
being the only country to have participated in every
World Cup finals tournament. They had lost six times in
the qualification matches and, it seemed, had done so to

most of South America, notching defeats to Argentina, Bolivia, Chile, Ecuador, Paraguay and Uruguay. The greatest number of defeats sustained during a qualification campaign by any previous Brazil side had been a mere one. Luiz Felipe Scolari, the latest manager, appointed in the middle of 2001 to get Brazil to the finals, had succeeded in that task – if only just – but as the actual tournament approached, he was being lambasted for what was seen as his dogged, defensive approach.

For all that Brazil are perceived worldwide as carefree, loose-limbed, easy-going, instinctively brilliant footballers who bring enormous joy to the game, there is an arrogance at the core of followers of the Brazilian national team. If you don't believe this, try mingling at a World Cup with those incredibly telegenic Brazilians and you will gather plenty of evidence of it. They believe, almost always, that they are the best in the world and, unlike other nations, who need to win the World Cup to demonstrate to themselves and others that they are the best at any particular time, the Brazilians' belief is that they are indisputably so, under all circumstances, and that winning the trophy is merely a rubber-stamped endorsement of that.

So it was hard for Brazilians to cope with having a team in 2002 that they had branded as failures even before a ball had been kicked in the tournament. This was a new feeling for Brazilians (at least in 1994 there had been optimism that the team would come good) – that of awaiting the seemingly inevitable crash landing of their representatives. On all previous occasions on which the Brazilians had failed to win the trophy, the feeling inside that nation had not been that they had lost out to better teams but that they had been undone by their own folly in terms of team selection and approach. This theory is backed up by the fact that when the Brazilians do lose out in World Cups, their opponents are frequently assisted by the Brazilians shooting themselves, as it were, in the foot. Given the teeming stream of talented players that Brazil perennially produces, those supremely self-confident supporters could very well be correct.

So there is little need to worry about the Brazilians in World Cups. If they get things right, they will almost always win it; if not, sit back and watch them unravel.

The final nuts and bolts were still being hammered into the brand-new Maracanã Stadium even as the 1950 World Cup, held in Brazil, was getting underway. Rain poured through the roof of its VIP section and the press box during the opening matches but few Brazilians doubted that the 200,000-capacity bowl would be complete for the Final and that, similarly, Brazil would follow closely the tournament's unwritten but understood script and lift the World Cup in its final match. An unusual World Cup format meant that there was no designated Final; instead four nations would contest a group in the second stage with the group winner to be declared world champions. As it transpired, the last match to be played, between Brazil and Uruguay, would be the decider and so was, effectively, the Final.

The prolific Rio-born composer and football fanatic Lamartine Babo dashed off a banner-waving anthem called 'March of the Brazilian Team', which hailed the prospect of Brazil lifting the trophy. The Brazilian press, in the hours prior to the match, published souvenir editions featuring pictures of the Brazil team and headlined 'world champions', as if the encounter with Uruguay was a mere formality. This Brazil team had been playing what was described as 'the football of the future' and had scored 21 goals in five matches. Even a draw would be enough for Brazil to win the World Cup and that may have helped a complacent atmosphere to build around the team. Their base at the São Januário stadium in central Rio had a carnival atmosphere on the morning of the match, with numerous guests mingling with the players, including politicians with an eye on nearing elections. The players became drawn into small talk, photo opportunities and providing autographs.

Angelo Mendes de Moraes, the mayor of Rio de Janeiro, strode to a microphone to complete the pre-match formalities as the Brazilian and Uruguayan players stood on the pitch, awaiting kick-off. 'You, players, will soon be hailed as champions by millions of your compatriots,' De Moraes, a politician who put the pomp in pompous, told the Brazil team as the Uruguayans listened disbelievingly. 'You Brazilians have no rivals in the entire hemisphere. You will overcome any opponent. I salute you already as the winners.' Flávio Costa, the Brazil manager, had been a lone voice struggling to be heard above the clamour as he anticipated this final match with some apprehension. 'The Uruguayan team has always disturbed the slumbers of Brazilian footballers,' he warned. 'I'm afraid that my players will take the field as though they already had the championship shield sewn on their jerseys. It isn't an exhibition game. It is a match like any other – only harder than all the others.'

Brazil were being hailed as World Cup winners all day . . . until 11 minutes from time in that final match when Alcide Ghiggia raced into the Brazilian penalty area to make the score 2–1 to Uruguay and take the trophy south – even though the Brazilians failed to present it to them in the aftermath of the match. The all-engulfing sense of anti-climax that reverberated through Brazil was so profound that even the Brazilians' opponents themselves took it to heart.

'We had ruined everything and what had we got?' Obdulio Varela, the Uruguay centre half and captain, said of the victory over Brazil, which had owed much to a sterling performance on his part. 'We got a title but what was it in relation to this sadness? If I could play the match again I would score against us.'

The over-confidence surrounding Brazilian anticipation of victory meant that when Uruguay's Juan Schiaffino equalised Friaça's opener in some style midway through the second half, the Maracanã was suddenly plunged into silence. Up until then Uruguay had played very well without scoring. Now that they had put the ball in the net, it made real the prospect that Brazil's smaller neighbours might just be about to spoil the party; and the chilling fear that spread through the crowd infused the Brazilian players and instilled enough extra confidence in the Uruguayans for them to make that final spurt for the trophy.

This was such a disaster that Nelson Rodrigues,

177

the Brazilian playwright, described it as 'our Hiroshima', the horrors of which were still fresh in the minds of people the world over. That defeat hung over Brazilians for decades afterwards and saw members of the 1950 Brazil team hounded in the streets long after they had ceased playing professionally. 'Under Brazilian law the maximum sentence is 30 years but my imprisonment has been for 50,' Moacyr Barbosa, the Brazil goalkeeper in 1950, commented with sadness, shortly before his death in 2000. He had been blamed for conceding Brazil's second goal in their cataclysmic defeat. 'He is the man who made all of Brazil cry,' a woman once said in earshot of him while pointing him out in the street in the 1970s.

It had been the first time Pelé had seen his father cry and he vowed, at that moment, to help win the World Cup for Brazil, doing so in some style in 1958 and making his contribution in 1962 too, even though his participation was ended by an injury early in that tournament. Those successive victories made Brazil favourites to win in 1966 but they made the mistake of relying heavily on players who had brought them the two previous triumphs. 'Brazil are no danger. They're too old,' Alf Ramsey briskly told his England players when dismissing the South Americans after watching them early in the tournament. In their opening match with Bulgaria, Brazil had included five players who had been in the winning team eight years previously. Ramsey was quickly proved correct.

Pelé was kicked hard and had to hobble around with a huge bandage on his thigh during a second straight 3–1 defeat, to Portugal at Goodison Park, that eliminated Brazil at the opening group stage for the only time in World Cup history. But the heavy treatment doled out to Pelé was a distraction and masked the team's lack of freshness and strength in depth. The real reasons for their early elimination were the inclusion of players such as a well-out-of-sorts Garrincha, a lack of internal harmony in the squad and waning authority on the part of Vicente Feola, who had brought Brazil their first World Cup victory in 1958. Over-confidence in Brazil at the prospect of a third successive World Cup triumph had been accompanied by a fitful attempt at preparation. Throw in some lamentable goalkeeping and strange team selections and Brazil had not failed to neglect anything that might bring them tumbling off their pedestal.

No such mistakes would be made in 1970, when Brazil's preparation, team selection and play were almost flawless; so when they arrived in West Germany for the 1974 World Cup finals, the world was expecting more of the same, but other than sporting the classic yellow and blue strip, this team appeared determined to blot out all memory of their predecessors. 'This is the fittest Brazilian team ever,' Mario Zagallo, the manager, said proudly, as Professor Cláudio Coutinho fronted a team of four physical training instructors who had been drafted in to get the players into peak condition. Six million dollars had been spent on their preparation, which included billeting the 22 players in a PE school in the mountains close to Rio for four months before the tournament began. Their Brazilian chef had for three months been gradually introducing West German ingredients and cooking fats to their meals and the team's hotels in West Germany had been selected in 1972 and paid for entirely in advance.

Yet in the group stage Brazil were unable to score against either a Yugoslavia side that might have won if they had been playing the team in front of them rather than the name; or a Scotland team whose ramshackle, quickly thrown-together couple of weeks of World Cup preparation had been distinguished only by some quite spectacular drunkenness on the parts of Billy Bremner and Jimmy Johnstone.

The severe emphasis on physical preparation, on developing a robustness to mimic the Europeans, had robbed the Brazilians of their winning personality; and worked only insofar as it put central defenders Luís Pereira and Marinho Peres in the unusual position of being the most lauded among their team. 'Brazil have learned to defend in the European way but they have lost their individuality,' Rinus Michels, the Holland manager, said before their vital second-group-stage encounter with the Brazilians.

The shadow cast over Brazil by Pelé in the post-1970 epoch was a long one and it fell as early as 1974 when, although still playing for Santos at club level and only 33 years of age, he opted not to play in the World Cup. Zagallo, a former team-mate, admitted that Pelé would have strolled into his squad and said in his own defence that months of persuasion had failed to make the great man change his mind about playing in West Germany.

Brazilian journalists muttered among themselves about the inferiority of Pelé's young and inexperienced successors at that tournament, so when Pelé himself turned up at that World Cup, the pressure on the group who had come along after him began to build even more intensely. Even at that early stage in his commercial career, Pelé was reputed to have contracts with approximately 50 companies to front their products and, as a trade-off for pushing their stuff, he would make public appearances at which he would always be available for a quick quote on the Brazil team. This would become a regular theme down the years and in 1974 Pelé's role as a roving ambassador for Pepsi-Cola saw him sit down over two days in Frankfurt for 24 one-to-one individual interviews with lucky representatives of the world's press.

Even though this was early in his career, as the great judge of all things Brazilian, Pelé had clearly eased himself comfortably into the role. As Zagallo, with mounting defensiveness, defiantly promised a hard-as-concrete reception for Holland's gilded forwards in their crucial match with Brazil and defiantly insisted, against the flow, that his team could stop the seemingly inevitable progress of the Dutch to the 1974 final, Pelé calmly put his former colleague and manager's struggles into deadly perspective. 'Always Zagallo has seemed afraid of something,' he said, with that husky, rich-as-coffee drawl as he damned his former international team-mate and manager slowly and coolly. 'Perhaps that is why he turned to spiritualism for reassurance. Certainly in football he seeks security above all. He was not a player of genius but he did the running and work of three men. As a manager, he cannot abandon the values he had as a player . . . We have Edu, an attacking left winger capable of swinging a whole game over to aggression, one who could be the key to reviving the traditional adventure in our team, but Zagallo prefers Dirceu, who tries to play as he did. Even if Brazil reach the final, I fear that they will play cautiously until the end.'

It was wonderful stuff. Pelé, as an all-seeing, omnipotent, living deity – much like Johan Cruyff, whose pronouncements at Barcelona were in a similar vein – would always lie beyond criticism because of his achievements on the field. No one questioned whether the opinions of a great player, but one who never dirtied his hands in management, might not be a bit like Pepsi-Cola itself – mildly refreshing but, overall, with a rather frothy, fizzy and insubstantial aftertaste.

Zagallo had promised before the match with the Dutch that Cruyff and his compatriots should not view the Brazilian penalty area as a type of children's playground, which, he suggested, had been the case in some of the previous games in which the Dutch had participated. His team was as good as his word. A violent encounter included a right hook from Marinho that knocked Johan Neeskens out cold as the Dutch, on a rainy night in Dortmund, still proceeded fluently to the Final with a 2–0 win. 'Brazil lost far more than their title,' Rinus Michels, the Holland manager, said, only slightly enigmatically, after the match. Zagallo's compatriots appeared to agree: the manager's house in Brazil was stoned after Brazil's exit, an expression of anger as much at the style of play he had forced upon the team at that World Cup as on the exit itself.

'Don't concede goals, don't let the other team play and

only attack when certain,' had been Zagallo's less than expansive approach to the 1974 World Cup and although by 1978 he was gone, Coutinho, the PE instructor who had modelled the 1970 team's preparation on that of the astronauts of NASA, had now taken over as manager rather than specialising in his own compartment of the team.

Coutinho, a retired army captain and one-time national volleyball champion, had no pedigree in the game as a manager but he was a good friend of Admiral Helenio Nunes, president of the Brazilian Football Federation, and that made him eminently qualified, in Nunes' eyes, to lead the team into the 1978 World Cup in Argentina. 'If I win the World Cup,' Coutinho said of the expectation in Brazil, 'they will put me in heaven; if I lose I go to hell.' There were occasional gentle hints from Coutinho that the world should not expect a revolt back into style after the aberration of 1974, such as his pragmatic dismissal of the fine Brazilian art of dribbling as 'a waste of time and a proof of our weakness'.

Coutinho stressed powerful, hard tackling as Brazil limbered up for three months inside their zoned-off Teresópolis training camp prior to the 1978 tournament. 'Pressure marking', 'force of play' and 'fighting spirit' were Coutinho's less than lyrical catchphrases as he shaped his team. The new manager, appointed in early 1977, was an enthusiast for European football and wished his players to play with the type of discipline and competitiveness found on that continent. The emphasis on tough tackling was a new element in the game of many of his young Brazilian players, schooled in the Brazilian league, where the emphasis was still placed on skill and they struggled to get it right in the short space of time prior to the World Cup. They could, then, be clumsy and crude in the tackle simply through being the next-best thing to beginners at it rather than through being cynical.

'We have got already the most difficult thing to find – talent,' Coutinho said blithely of his team. 'I cannot provide that – God does that – but I can provide determination, discipline, teamwork.' This was like a Hollywood actress decrying her good looks and acting talent before stating that she was about to train as a hod carrier, as that had been something always missing from her portfolio. The playmaker Zico, at his first World Cup, backed up Coutinho's line for the moment. 'I would prefer to go free,' the man known as 'the white Pelé' said, 'but that is not practical. Europe has forced us to play more systematically because they don't allow space for us to play like in 1970.'

It was not long before Admiral Nunes was offering Coutinho some friendly advice after Brazil had struggled for form in the opening stages of the tournament. 'Admiral Nunes has told Coutinho that he can play any tune so long as it's a waltz,' a Brazilian Football Federation official revealed. 'The admiral has offered his humble opinion of what should be done, which means he has given an order.' Nunes was, in person, even less discreet, describing the Brazil manager as 'a man of scarce technical abilities', something that anyone, possibly even Coutinho, might have been able to suggest on his appointment as manager. Effigies of Coutinho were burned in Brazil and the upshot of it all was that the Brazilian

Football Federation relieved Coutinho of the onerous burden of being solely in charge of team selection after Brazil's second match of the tournament. 'The players and the wise directors,' Nunes said modestly, 'imposed their points of view on Coutinho and made him change that sad panorama to save the honour of Brazilian football.'

Despite their difficulties, Brazil still managed to get within a hair's breadth of the trophy – the sidelining of Coutinho coinciding with a re-emphasis on native skill – and they were pipped for a place in the Final only by Argentina defeating Peru 6–0 and thus bettering Brazil's goal difference in their second-stage group. The Argentina–Peru match, which kicked off hours after Brazil had faced Poland in their final second-stage group game, would gain notoriety with allegations that it might have been fixed for the host nation to get the requisite goals to progress.

'The Peruvians had been having a great World Cup so when that happened it was surprising,' Zico commented. 'What was also surprising was the way Peru played – without any life, without any interest.' It caused Coutinho to claim that Brazil were the 'moral victors' at that World Cup and helped take the heat off him for constricting the team's approach and again placing undue emphasis on muscle. 'Once we played samba and Europe the waltz,' João Saldanha, the former Brazil manager lamented, 'but now we do not even do foxtrot.'

The Brazilians would, though, soon be dancing to a new tune. When Telê Santana was appointed Brazil manager in February 1980, the country appeared set to put behind it the grim memories of the first post-Pelé decade. Santana, aware of the lack of popularity of his immediate predecessors' teams, was determined to find a side that would evoke all that was best in Brazilian football and one that could beat the Europeans through bamboozling them with fluid, easy style, the *jogo bonito*, rather than trying to take them on at an exaggeratedly physical version of their own game. His immediate impact in creating a team of beauty was such that Brazil were heralded as champions elect as they went into the 1982 World Cup in Spain, for which they had warmed up with a 7–0 victory over Ireland.

Santana stated pre-tournament that 'the work was well done, we've done exactly what we should have done and we are ready for the World Cup now,' but he was unwilling to predict how well his team might do. 'In soccer, there is always the unexpected. You never know what might happen in a given game.' The Brazilians had been in a training camp for more than four months, which, as almost always, was the lengthiest time spent together of all the competing nations, and their reliance on inspirational football meant they were routinely compared to their predecessors of 1970. This was no longer the type of defensive, European-style side who had been sent abroad in 1974 and 1978.

Although the Soviet Union took the lead in the first half of the Brazilians' opening match at the 1982 finals, Brazil scored two spectacular goals to win. Scotland too had the nerve to open the scoring, in Brazil's next game, on a balmy Friday night in Seville, but four fine goals in reply ensured the Brazilians' progress into the next round of the tournament. 'They are so good that they are willing to let you take control of the ball and then set out to kid you into passing it where they want it to go,' said Scotland manager Jock Stein. 'To be beaten by what I think'll be the world champions after giving them such a great first half . . . it left a wee bit of joy with us anyway.' Brazil rounded off their group by beating New Zealand 4–0. Bobby Charlton had once suggested, 'It's easy to beat Brazil – you just stop them getting within 20 yards of your goal.' Now, even that logic appeared outmoded, with the Brazilians sending in all sorts of scoring shots from outside the penalty area.

During the match with the Soviet Union, two good calls for penalties against Brazil were turned down by a Spanish linesman, but it might even have done the Brazil team some good to have had their progress slowed by, say, a drawn match at that early stage. Instead, it all looked a bit too easy; as if Brazil could sail through matches with the flaws in a slightly suspect defence immaterial when set against the overpowering strength of their attack.

'To play in the manner of Argentina and Italy is not in our nature. We do not play the game that way. We enjoy our football,' said Zico, with aristocratic snootiness, before meeting both of those nations in the second phase of the 1982 tournament. There was just a hint there that the praise the Brazilians had been receiving for their fine football in the group stage – praise that made the cooing and crowing of an Oscars ceremony look as dishwater-dull as the minutes of congratulation at the annual meeting of a provincial bowling club – had gone to Brazilian heads and might see them trailing clouds of hubris as they took to the field for those contests with their Latin confrères.

It seemed not to matter when Brazil crushed Argentina, their old rivals, 3–1 in the first game of the second group stage. 'If they do not change their style, if they play Brazilian football, they can and should be champions,' César Luis Menotti, a master of wonderfully erroneous predictions, pronounced after Argentina's elimination by the Brazilians. As if to confirm Brazil's floating around on a dangerously over-inflated cushion of self-confidence, Eder, the 1982 team's pin-up playboy, explained before the match with Italy that he knew how the match was going to pan out – with a Brazil win. Not only that but he knew, in advance, the result – a modest 1–0 to Brazil . . . and even, less modestly, the scorer . . . himself. Pelé was less confident. 'Brazil made too many mistakes against Argentina,' he said. 'I have a nasty feeling about the meeting with Italy.'

There would be considerably more goals than Eder expected. Italy twice took the lead but it seemed, when Falcão made the score 2–2, that Brazil, by virtue of superior goal difference in their three-team group, were en route to the semi-finals. Then, with 15 minutes remaining, Paolo Rossi struck the winner that, as he would later describe it, made Brazil cry. While accepting that Brazil were 'superb', Italian full back Antonio Cabrini also suggested that it was to Italy's advantage that Brazil regarded the Italians as 'upstarts and inferior to them' and that the Brazilians were floating on a tide of over-confidence, arrogantly thinking that they could coast their way to the requisite result against Italy.

'We are not invincible,' Brazilian manager Santana said after their elimination by Italy but he remained adamant that if he had to do it all again he would not change a thing. Zico has suggested that the team's exit from that tournament created a sea change in Brazilian football whereby the result became more important than the per-formance – as if the great Brazil sides of the past had played beach-type football, without concern for the result.

Brazil's contest with Italy in 1982 brought a frustration familiar to the national team: when they find the free expression of their talents choked, they struggle to seek an alternative, become depressed and lose their way. As such, Italy are the opponents of their worst nightmares. Against Argentina, Falcão had retreated to his own penalty area with three Argentinians in pursuit, only to wriggle out of that tight spot with a delicate back-heel to a team-mate. The Italians, as Toninho Cerezo had discovered to his cost when his casual pass had allowed Rossi to pounce and make it 2–1, rarely allow such leeway. Brazil had also been unlucky before the start of the tournament when Careca, the striker, was injured and forced to withdraw from the squad. Serginho, his replacement, was something of a blunt instrument up front, so with goals and creation springing largely from midfield, the Italians had been able to concentrate on nullifying that section of the Brazil team while exploiting the wobbly defence.

There was another brilliant intervention from Pelé just before the 1986 tournament in Mexico. The man who, when fit and able, had opted out of the 1974 finals despite the pleadings of his compatriots, was now ready, at the

189

age of 45, to pull on his boots again in aid of the national team, which had been depleted by injury. 'I'm being very serious,' he said. 'I am ready for my fifth World Cup. If you give me two weeks, I'll be able to get into shape to play 45 minutes. Now that teams can make substitutions, it's no problem.'

It was an intervention that could never be mistaken for a vote of confidence in the Brazilian team, again under Santana, but they contributed much to that tournament and were unfortunate in losing in a penalty shootout to France after an effervescent quarter-final. Perhaps there was a lack of a hard winning edge about two teams that were inclined towards the artistic. 'Winning the Cup is important but I won't let football dominate my life when there is so much injustice in the world,' Sócrates, the appropriately named Brazil midfield player, said prior to the meeting with France, while Michel Platini, his French fellow philosopher, offered, 'I don't really enjoy playing in the World Cup. There is so much pressure.' Both men and their teams would soon be allowed plenty of time to think about other things while the Argentinians and West Germans, from whom such wistful comment was near unimaginable, fought out the Final.

For the 1990 tournament the Brazilians reverted to the familiar theme of adopting a hard, dour style for a World Cup that would take place in Europe, in this case Italy. 'This is the Brazil of sweat and sacrifice,' the midfielder Dunga boasted, and now Mario Zagallo, progenitor of the combative Brazil team of 1974, popped up to point the finger at Sebastião Lazaroni, the latest manager entrusted with finding the elusive World Cup-winning formula. 'He has betrayed Brazilian football,' Zagallo said of Lazaroni, who stressed the importance of defending and a sweeper system.

Pelé, of course, had already made his own firm assessment of the team even as it progressed to three victories in the group stage. 'Players are being asked to play as if they are not Brazilian,' he said, alighting on a familiar theme. 'Our national tradition means nothing. Winning is supposed to be everything but can anyone be satisfied with such victories?' He found an unlikely ally in Romário. 'Pelé is right,' Romário said. 'Lazaroni is making mistakes with this line-up and Brazil cannot win the World Cup playing like this.' The dissenting player still found himself named in the side against Scotland but despite victory in that match, the last 16 saw the Brazilians tumble out of the tournament at the hands of Argentina. 'Only the memory of a bad team will survive,' Pelé pronounced, damningly, from on high.

So when Carlos Alberto Parreira's squeaky-tight, safety-conscious version of a Brazil team finally attained the long-awaited victory at the 1994 World Cup, the theory was that it would herald a bright new dawn for the country. After 24 years of perceived failure, in which the spectre of 1970 had hung over a series of sometimes desperate Brazil teams, the Brazilians, now unchained from the shackles of history, would be able to play freely, expressively, expansively in their quest to lift further World Cups. Instead, the triumph of the 1994 team was beginning to look like a shaft of sunlight that had managed to penetrate a gloomy penumbra under which it was Brazil's fate to be forever consigned, replaying over and over the goals of 1970 as colourful consolation for a gloomy present.

So when Brazilians looked at their squad for 2002, they saw only skimpy hopes of success. It was understandable: all they had to console them was the striking talent of Ronaldo, the brilliant invention of Rivaldo, the tricky footwork of Ronaldinho, the penetrating running of Juninho and the slick overlapping of Cafu and Roberto Carlos. Yet Roberto Carlos and Rivaldo would be booed and whistled when turning out for Brazil in the year or so prior to that World Cup – they were perceived by supporters as being rich, remote and, having earned their fortunes in Spain, less than interested in performing for Brazil.

Several of those players had been in the team that had reached the Final in France in 1998 but that had been a team that had stumbled and stuttered to get that far and their tilt at the trophy had been undone by the mysterious fit that took possession of Ronaldo, their great goal-scoring hope, late on the afternoon of the match against France. Edmundo had, at the height of Ronaldo's fit, begun running around shouting that Ronaldo was dying. The racket had woken the other players, who were enjoying a lie-down to conserve energy before the match, and morale had duly plummeted. It seemed impossible that Ronaldo would feature in the match and he was initially omitted from the starting line-up before being dramatically re-instated shortly before kick-off. Speculation would persist that Nike, which had a £25 million contract with the Brazilian national team as well as with several players, including Ronaldo, had insisted that the striker be restored to the team even though he was clearly unfit to play. 'Brazil entered the field under a cloud,' Cláudio Taffarel, the goalkeeper, said of their 3–0 defeat. 'We lost because of ourselves. The problem with Ronaldo was never clear.'

When Brazil turned up for the first World Cup to be held in Asia, the 2002 tournament jointly hosted by South Korea and Japan, the Brazilian press, more than 200 of them, read the runes and decided that this was another impending Brazilian disaster, one that would conclude with them finishing the tournament in a mere third or fourth place, as in 1974 and 1978, or even exiting before the semi-finals, as in 1982, 1986 and 1990. The squad of 2002 had been described during their qualification as a careless, disorganised team and the Brazilian press were unimpressed by Scolari, a gruff, bulky, bear-like individual who would prowl the touchline in polo shirt and tracksuit trousers like a particularly quarrelsome taxi driver. He was a man who would not shirk at offering a rival manager or player a fistfight and one whose tactics at club level had involved instructing his players simply to foul opponents as a means of slowing the game down.

Unimpressed himself by journalists, Scolari was at his grumpy, abrupt best in dismissing their most insolent inquiries of him and his team, not least their incredulousness at his omitting Romário, now 36 but top scorer in domestic football, from his squad, a decision that earned Scolari a denouncement as 'Public Enemy Number One' from one newspaper. 'There are 170 million Brazilians with an opinion on who should be in the team and that's a lot of pressure,' the midfielder Juninho said. 'If you finish second at the World Cup with Brazil, you might as well finish last. To Brazilians, we are always the favourites.'

Or, as Scolari, hands bunched, face downturned, put it succinctly, 'If we don't win, I'm dead meat.' One fan who got close enough to Scolari to berate him for leaving Romário out of his squad received a kick from the manager for his trouble. Stylish football, Scolari stated, was not his priority; winning was. 'Now we have a harmonious group with friendship, without stars, the atmosphere is so much better,' he said of the omission of Romário, who had incurred the new manager's displeasure shortly after his appointment by happily inviting an air hostess into Brazil's training camp.

Johan Cruyff lamented before the tournament kicked off that Brazil looked like a team constricted by their manager, unable to play with the type of freedom that he associated with that nation. 'If we score goals and leave space at the back, the defence gets criticised,' Scolari said. 'If we favour the defence, I'm told we're afraid. I don't know what people want.'

Going into the 2002 tournament, Ronaldo had suffered almost three years of knee injuries and operations that had considerably reduced his prominence in the world game, consequently reducing expectations of him at the finals. He had scored just seven times for Internazionale in Serie A during the season prior to the World Cup – good but not great; and not a record likely to worry excessively his opponents at the finals. Scolari estimated that he was still six months away from full fitness. Rivaldo, on whom Brazil would rely for both creating and scoring, had been handicapped by injury during the 2001/02 season too and had scored just eight goals for Barcelona in La Liga.

To make matter worse, midfielder and captain Emerson, who had held Brazil together tightly as Scolari wrung a place in the finals out of the dying stages of the qualifiers, sustained a serious shoulder injury while playing in goal during training on the day before Brazil's opening match with Turkey. It looked disastrous but proved a blessing, forcing Scolari into fielding a more enterprising Brazil side. He announced a 4–3–2–1 formation that had Juninho at the heart of the midfield three, with Rivaldo and Ronaldinho in advance of him and Ronaldo as the striker.

Being discounted before the tournament would also have a relaxing effect on the players in between the hurly-burly of their matches. 'I think Brazil can do very well in this World Cup precisely because we are not among the favourites,' Ronaldo said. 'Before, especially last time, we would arrive at the World Cup under an awful lot of pressure but now there's a sense that if we lose, we lose.'

It was now the time for Pelé, fielded by Mastercard for the 2002 finals, to act not as a critic but as the inspiration behind a Brazilian renaissance. 'One day I had a visitor at my house – Pelé,' Ronaldo recollected of the three-year period prior to the World Cup when he had frequently been sidelined. 'After injuries like mine, you obviously get very worried but Pelé told me that during the 1966 World Cup he got badly injured and that everyone said he would never play again. Two or three years passed and still nobody believed he would ever play at his best level again

– but he did. He played in the World Cup in 1970 and won it.'

Those critics who had labelled Scolari's team the worst in the history of the Brazil national team were quickly forced into a re-think by the easily palatable performances of that same team. Ronaldo and Rivaldo were both on target in every game as Brazil cruised through their group, scoring 11 goals in the defeats of China, Costa Rica and Turkey. 'All we have to do is concentrate on playing our own game,' Ronaldo said. 'Everything depends on us.'

Argentina and France, the holders, both widely praised beforehand, had been eliminated at the group stage, while neither Germany nor Italy had matched Brazil for style. 'We have come into these World Cup finals and no one has really mentioned us as favourites,' Ronaldo said prior to facing Belgium in the last 16. 'That's strange in a way because Brazil normally are under enormous pressure to succeed. If we don't win the World Cup, the inquests are always endless. Even if we win, there are still people who will find fault. I don't think any side has ever been burdened more greatly than Brazil in the past. But not this time. I think someone up there is helping me this time and when I go out there I know I am going to score. The team is getting better with each game and we can feel our confidence building. We are enjoying ourselves. That's the way of the Brazilians. If you don't enjoy playing football then you can't expect to perform and win. This time we are enjoying it and expecting to win.'

The Belgians were unfortunate in having a 35th-minute headed goal from Marc Wilmots incorrectly disallowed by the referee Peter Prendergast, and Brazil went on to win 2–0. 'The referee apologised after having seen the images on TV but what value does that have?' Wilmots said afterwards. The doubting Thomases were still not convinced, citing weak opposition in the group stage – even though Turkey and Costa Rica had each offered Brazil doughty opposition – while the seat-of-the-pants victory over Belgium had also raised doubts. 'Brazil are utterly devoid of a tactical scheme. What they have is complete disorder,' was the helpful advice offered by Careca, the former Brazil striker. In a curious way, though, such comment would help keep the heat off Scolari's team, in dampening down, to a degree, expectation of them.

Scolari begged to disagree. 'The true characteristics of Brazil and the way I want them to play are coming through,' he insisted before the quarter-final with England, saying that he was glad the old image of him as a footballing Neanderthal was being eradicated by the performances of his team at the finals. 'We have shown we are not just about star players; we have a team that fights for the ball and battles for every minute. I'm very pleased because I'm getting everything I need from them; just like in club football – commitment and dedication.'

Still the critics complained. Brazil, they said, had eased through against Belgium courtesy of a poor refereeing decision. They were suspected of having a leaky defence, as with the team of 1982; and Juninho, the slight midfield player, was said not to be doing enough to justify his place in the team. 'I don't care what people think,' Scolari said of criticism of Juninho's performances. But for all the manager's bluster, he would still drop the player for the remainder of the tournament. The practical Scolari was not one to stick with a player stubbornly as a means of stressing his managerial independence.

'People don't just want us to win,' Juninho said. 'We have to win well. If I pass the ball for 89 minutes and then make a mistake, that's what will be highlighted. In a way, we can't win because whatever happens we get so much criticism. The people have a tradition of not trusting us. In 1982 Brazil had a fantastic team that won four games in a row but didn't end up with the trophy. Now we're playing well, but we have to do more than that because nobody will remember this team if we don't. It's always the same. We had a difficult time qualifying but when we arrived in Korea we felt stronger than before because we've been through so much together.'

England presented another near-immovable obstacle and even went ahead through Michael Owen, but gradually Scolari's side exerted a grip on the game that became more and more powerful and which, once they had it, they did not relinquish. Cafu and Roberto Carlos, the full backs, were such dangerous supplements to Brazil's attacking play that England were forced to deploy David Beckham and Trevor Sinclair, the midfield players, to help out the full backs as their Brazilian counterparts ranged forward. This helped stem one source of danger but left England short as an attacking force and Brazil with an edge in midfield. With so many fine players now hitting form, they were close to unbeatable. Fear of Brazil also convinced Sven-Göran Eriksson, the England manager, to drop five into midfield during the second half, thus reducing England's own threat even further.

'To stay alive and not die was the only thought we had,' Scolari said after Brazil's 2–1 win. 'That was the subject of my team talk.' Even after Ronaldinho, scorer of Brazil's second goal, had been dismissed for a foul on Danny Mills, such was Brazil's control of the match that England failed to get in a shot on goal, disproving the theory that Brazil's defence could be exploited. 'We lost because they were better than us,' Eriksson said. 'When Brazil had to defend, they proved that they could.'

It had not all been seamless style. There had also been evidence of Scolari's gamesmanship – spare balls were thrown on to the field from the bench to delay the game, an old ruse from his days as a club manager in Brazil. Rivaldo also showed that Brazilian super-egotism could still surface. 'What the referee has done could influence not just the fortunes of a nation but the enjoyment of the whole world,' Rivaldo said of Ronaldinho's red card. More often, though, Brazil players at the 2002 World Cup would talk, Zen-like, about staying humble, remaining calm; while Ronaldo and his mother had made a pilgrimage from Rio to the Sanctuary of Our Lady near São Paulo before the tournament to offer thanks for finally getting over his injuries.

For Ronaldo, there was quiet personal motivation after losing years from his career and because of the disappointment at the way the previous World Cup had concluded. 'I cannot explain to you the years of suffering I have had,' he said simply after scoring the goal that beat Turkey in the semi. Less self-effacingly, Ronaldo was by now sporting a haircut that looked as though he had momentarily shoved a night-editor's visor up above his forehead on to his shaven cranium.

'We are finding it a pleasure to be here,' he said before the Final, stressing the unity among the squad. 'It is totally different to 1998 and reminds me more of 1994, although people were more restrained emotionally then. We had players like Dunga and Romário keeping the group together in a tough way. Now we don't have one leader. Cafu is doing his job as captain but we are all on the same level. It is the first time I remember everything being so equal. Cafu is playing his third World Cup Final but even with so much experience he keeps asking questions of us. We are constantly learning together.'

Before each game, Scolari had shown his players video footage of supporters celebrating in the street after wins and of them cast down after defeat. With those thousands, if not millions, of extras helping the cause back home, unknowingly but actively, the Brazilians eased to a 2–0 win over Germany in the Final. It had all been so simple, so straightforward: a productive use by the manager of the talent at his disposal and that talent kept on a tight rein by a fearsome manager, in the right frame of mind to perform at its maximum. Brazil, queried and questioned as they always are, had simply played football better than anyone else is able and when they do that they are just about unstoppable.

The team dispatched to Germany in 2006 was an ageing one, one in which the disco-dancing Ronaldinho suddenly became leaden-footed on the field of play and, with Ronaldo leaden-bellied, they tumbled meekly out of the tournament in the quarter-finals. 'History doesn't talk about the beautiful game,' Carlos Alberto Parreira, back in place as Brazil coach for the finals, had said with a disingenuousness that was almost as mind-boggling as any piece of Brazilian skill, after a stuttering 3–0 victory over Ghana in the last 16. 'It talks about champions. We like the beautiful game but above that we want to be champions.'

Unfortunately for him, Brazil were neither beautiful nor effective. They did set a World Cup record of becoming the first team to win 11 successive games in the World Cup finals and Ronaldo's goal against Ghana made him the record World Cup goalscorer, with 15, but in terms of the bigger picture these were mere baubles. The Brazilians had made the classic holders' mistake of relying on players who had won the previous time but who were no longer hungry enough or capable enough of reaching the levels that had driven them to their previous success. Some of those highly decorated individuals, such as Cafu and Roberto Carlos, appeared to hold too much sway off the pitch, and not very much at all on it. It was Carlos who went missing when Thierry Henry swooped at the back post in the quarter-final with France to deliver the mortal blow to Brazilian hopes of retaining the trophy.

'Differently from the 1982 side, which also had many stars but lost, this World Cup team will not be missed at all,' Tostão, a World Cup winner with Brazil in 1970, said after the 2006 side, favourites to win the tournament, had been ejected from it.

To watch a Brazilian training routine is an eye-opening experience for those who believe they do things off the cuff: the players will sweep round a training ground

201

swinging arms in time, clapping in unison, moving gracefully along all the while, jumping and kicking out their legs in tandem like an especially well-choreographed group of dancers. Witnessing such rhythm, synchronicity and unity it is possible to be hypnotised into thinking that they could never become self-defeating – but they can; and they do. So don't worry about the Brazilians, because they certainly won't be worrying about you.

11

Do Something Strange

THE ARGENTINA TEAM THAT TOOK TO THE FIELD FOR THE 1978 World Cup has to be the most hirsute in the tournament's history. Not only were they hairy but they also appeared to be wearing the shortest shorts ever seen at a finals tournament. These shorts allowed their glistening thighs to gleam under the floodlights and gave them the appearance of a troupe of male dancers assembled for a hen night's delight. At a World Cup that saw several players from a variety of teams wearing the newly fashionable perm, the one sported by Argentina full back Alberto Tarantini had to take the prize as the most outrageous of all. A huge bush, it resembled a guardsman's bearskin that had frizzed out after having been left too long in the drier of a launderette. He was nicely complemented by Argentina's front two, Leopoldo Luque and Mario Kempes, whose long, black hair trailed on to their blue and white shirts like so many spider's legs.

There was a languorous feel to that Argentina team. César Luis Menotti, their suitably long-haired manager, would conduct training sessions bare-chested, looking like a relaxed, holidaying millionaire who had popped off his yacht to visit his favourite restaurant for lunch. The manager was a prize cigarette smoker, as was Kempes – the first thing he would do on awakening of a morning would be to reach for his cigarettes and an ashtray. Despite being allowed those comforts by Menotti, the striker made an indifferent start to the finals that were held in his homeland, failing to score in the opening three matches. This was a situation that needed to be addressed given that Menotti, having resolved to fill his squad only with players from the Argentinian League, had stuck his neck out to make a noticeable exception for Kempes, who was with Valencia in Spain, but whose skills were such that he had been regarded as indispensable.

Despite two wins in those three opening games, Menotti realized that drastic action was required to kick start his star striker's form, so he suggested to Kempes that if he were to shave off his moustache, the goals might start to flow. The player did so and for Argentina's next match, with Poland, Kempes was a man transformed, scooting all over the pitch in search of the ball, and scoring the two excellent goals that demolished the Poles and that put the striker on track to finish as top scorer in the competition. Doing something odd or unexpected can be the trigger for World Cup success.

The seclusion of the Brazil squad at the finals in 1994, in the USA, where they were kept under lock and key in their team hotel by manager Carlos Alberto Parreira, meant that striker Bebeto missed the birth of one of his children. So, in honour of his new son Mateo, he invented the 'cradle-rocking' baby celebration. 'When I scored, I performed a motion as if I was taking him in my arms and rocking him . . .' Not only was it touching, but, amid rumours that Bebeto and his fellow striker Romário did not get on, it helped unite the players. Appropriately Romário had once labelled Bebeto a 'cry baby' but both were side by side swinging their arms in celebration as Brazil remained on course to win the World Cup. That baby celebration was as innovative and creative as almost anything else the Brazilians offered at a World Cup where they prevailed through hard work and tight discipline rather than wild imagination. However, they did show that they knew how to make an entrance, the entire team of Brazil players linking hands every time they walked on to the field of play in an unbroken chain of solidarity that fitted nicely with the emphasis on teamwork in Parreira's side.

Quirky moments help lighten the mood and point the way to success. Jacques Chirac, the French president, seemingly became so carried away by the team's success as they closed in on the World Cup in 1998 that he turned up at the Stade de France with a team shirt emblazoned with the number 23, as if the patrician president was the extra man in the squad. It would not have done in chic Paris for him to actually wear it – *zut alors, non!* But it seemed even more memorable to see him holding it out and shaking it lightly, like a Normandy housewife demurely waving a tea towel to welcome Allied liberators at the end of the Second World War. Prior to the semi-final with Croatia, the midfielder Robert Pires had suggested, 'It would be good to see President Chirac wearing the team colours.' Instead, the president opted to wave them – a sort of halfway house gesture that saw him show his support for the team while maintaining a degree of gravitas. There may have been many agonised hours spent by him mulling over the correct course of political action, but with the French players demanding that their haughty public get behind the team, Chirac's actions helped to demonstrate that it might be OK to lose that frosty cool, although only to a degree.

Then there was Alf Ramsey taking the England team, during the 1966 tournament, to the set of the new James Bond movie and Alf, in his stilted fashion, addressing Sean Connery as 'Seen', to the hilarity of England players such as Bobby Moore. It was an association with a great British success story that resounded with the players. The press had criticised Ramsey in the wake of his team's failure to score in the opening match, with Uruguay, ignoring how the South Americans had frequently placed eight and nine men behind the ball. Their stringent advice to him had been to get straight back down to the training ground and to get back to work with his players. Instead, on the following day, Ramsey took his men to Pinewood Studios to relax, have a drink and mingle with stars such as Connery, Cliff Richard and Yul Brynner. Such style in the face of criticism demonstrated a degree of coolness on Ramsey's part that would be reassuring to his men.

Unpredictable historical events can also have a bearing on a vital World Cup match. The final week of the 1990 World Cup coincided with East and West Germany being reunited 45 years after Germany's defeat in the Second World War had torn them apart. Border controls were removed and the East German Mark joined the Deutschmark. Reunification provided Lothar Matthäus with an extra incentive to win the Final and show off a medal to Joseph, his grandfather, who lived in Magdeburg in East Germany and whom Lothar had not seen for ten years. 'I hope to hug my grandfather soon,' he said. 'I'll do it right after the World Cup. I really look forward to this meeting and all my family will be there. I want to show him my daughters Alisa and Viola and my wife Silvia.'

Perhaps it all gave the Germans a little fillip as they closed in on the trophy, while their quarter-final with Czechoslovakia was coincidentally officiated by one Helmut Kohl, an Austrian, who shared a name with the Chancellor of West Germany. Kohl bizarrely dismissed the Czechoslovakian midfield player Lubo Moravcik for a second booking during the second half after the player had kicked off his loose boot in frustration. Jozef Venglos, the Czechoslovakia manager, suggested that Herr Kohl might not have been entirely neutral. West Germany, in their final match under that name, concluded the week as world champions and the heady atmosphere surrounding the nation appeared to have affected Franz Beckenbauer, the German manager. 'I'm sorry for the other countries,' he said condescendingly after West Germany's 1–0 win over Argentina in the Final, 'but now that we will be able to incorporate all the great players from the East, the German team will be unbeatable for a long time to come.'

That German triumph came as no surprise, but during the 1934 Final, Raimundo Orsi scored Italy's equaliser against Czechoslovakia with a dipping, swerving shot that looked like a strange combination of skill, opportunism and luck. Following the Italians' 2–1 victory, press reporters ribbed him about his 'lucky' goal. An offended Orsi insisted that there had been no luck involved at all and that he had intentionally decided to hit the ball in exactly the way that he had done to score the goal. Not only that but he told the pressmen, he would prove it to them the following day by re-creating his special strike for them. The press duly turned up at the appointed time and hour, as did Orsi. Twenty shots later, he had still failed to reproduce the moment that had lit up the Final for Italy.

'How can they be bored? They have one month to win the World Cup,' Fabio Capello says quizzically of his England team but it helps a gaggle of young men to have something that relieves the mundanity of life inside a training camp at a World Cup. Perhaps the most extraordinary episode of something strange harmlessly distracting a team occurred when Brazil employed a psychologist for the 1958 World Cup, one João Carvalhaes, a friendly, bespectacled, unshaven, professorial type who hovered around the players at their training camp in Sweden. His thinking on the most basic aspects of dealing with players was delightfully complicated and contradictory. He did not believe in addressing players on their own as he felt that that would make any problem they were carrying greater, but he also did not think it a good idea to talk to them collectively. He wanted defenders to rein in their aggression but attackers to tap into it and make more of it. Vicente Feola, the manager, was privately unconvinced. 'What does he know of the feeling among the players?' he pondered of this potential usurper of one of the roles of the manager: that of understanding his players' minds and moods.

After analysing the players, Carvalhaes wrote damningly in his report, 'Pelé is obviously infantile. He lacks the necessary fighting spirit. He is too young to feel aggression and respond with appropriate force. In addition to that, he does not possess the sense of responsibility necessary for a team game.' Garrincha, the winger, was similarly dismissed as having the mentality of a flea with a particularly short attention span, which was absolutely true but which may have helped make him the intrinsically tricky winger that he was. The psychologist's advice and presence was at the behest of Dr Paulo Machado de Carvalho, head of the Brazilian delegation, who said Carvalhaes might be necessary in Sweden in case any nervous player required psychological reassurance before a match.

Carvalhaes was treated as a joke figure by the Brazilian players but another unusual member of the party, Mario Trigo, a dentist, was loved by them not for his skills in looking after their teeth but for his sense of humour and willingness to join in with their practical jokes. Feola, on hearing the psychologist's advice on his players, looked at him levelly, squarely, seriously and responded, 'You may be right. The thing is, you don't know anything about football. If Pelé's knee is ready, he plays.'

Brazil fielded both Pelé and Garrincha, and Pelé, still

only 17 years of age, managed to carry the burden of playing in a World Cup finals so lightly, despite his purported psychological weaknesses, that he scored a hat-trick in the semi-final against France and two in the 5–2 victory over Sweden when Brazil won the Final. As the players performed their lap of honour, Carvalhaes, far from being cowed at seeing the evidence for his advice quashed beyond question, unabashedly helped to carry the flag of Sweden around the pitch. It is difficult to resist the temptation to wonder just what state of mind the psychologist himself was in at that very moment but as with all strange ingredients in a World Cup success, he had had an effect, even if it had been only to strengthen slightly further the players' trust in their manager and themselves in the face of his recommendations.

Plenty of strange goings-on are bound to occur within the confines of a World Cup month. The smallest of them can prove to be a winning factor.

12

Make Yourselves at Home

WHEN THE BALL FELL TO THE BOOT OF ROB RENSENBRINK in the 90th minute of the 1978 World Cup Final he had the potential to change modern history. How he swung at the ball and shaped his shot would not only decide whether the introverted Dutchman could make Holland the only European nation to win the World Cup in Latin America but might also help topple one of the most brutal military dictatorships that that continent had ever seen.

For the Argentina players, watching from around the field, a silence descended like the stealthiest of fogs on the River Plate Stadium. It was, the striker Leopoldo Luque would say, as if the hearts of every Argentinian inside the stadium stopped as Rensenbrink clipped his left-footed shot from the edge of the six-yard box goalwards, past Argentina goalkeeper Ubaldo Fillol. 'The ball was going in,' Osvaldo Ardiles, the Argentina midfield player, says, 'but maybe it was the wishes of all the people that kept it out. It hit the post and from that moment I was certain that we were going to win the World Cup.' Nowhere inside the stadium was relief felt more than in the VIP box, wherein sat General Jorge Videla, the leader of Argentina's bloody junta. Their dictatorship, for the moment, was safe and the prospect of the World Cup going Argentina's way and bolstering their regime was once more alive and well.

Rensenbrink had done well to get his shot away and to go so close to scoring. He would also ponder what might have happened if had managed to score. Frenzied crowds of Argentinians had pounded the Dutch team bus as it drove to the stadium on the day of the match and it had even gone on a detour that had enabled chanting, intimidatory Argentinians to howl in the direction of the Europeans. The Dutch wondered what the reaction would have been had they won the match in that final minute and whether they would even have been allowed to emerge, alive, from the stadium. It may even have been possible that something, subconsciously, was going through Rensenbrink's mind as he lined up his shot and that just when it seemed as if home advantage was about to count for nothing it was instead about to count for everything. If there was a World Cup in which being at home was ever made to count, it was this one.

The comforts of home have become less reassuring to World Cup hosts with each passing competition. Five of the first eleven tournaments were won by the host nation but since Argentina held the tournament in 1978 only one host has triumphed and France, in doing so in 1998, found that being at home only sporadically offered them a distinct advantage, given that they had had to win over an often indifferent domestic public.

In June 2010, South Africa will become the first host nation whose chances of failing to qualify from their group appear stronger than those of reaching the second stage of the competition (although the same was said eight years ago about Japan and South Korea, and both won their group). This is a team that failed to reach the African Nations Cup finals, held in Angola in January 2010. FIFA's world rankings system can be a bit wobbly in places but it does offer a rough guide to a country's standing in world football and, as 2010 began, South Africa were 86th in the world. They were the lowest-ranked nation at the World Cup draw in Cape Town in December 2009. Still, in 1994 the USA, another unheralded host nation, were also widely expected to be the first hosts to fail to qualify from the group stage. Not only did they do so but they achieved that success by eliminating Colombia, Pelé's nominees as likely finalists.

Sammy Nelson, the Northern Ireland full back, summed up the vagaries of confronting a host nation at the World Cup when he and his team-mates faced Spain in 1982. 'It can't come down to 11 men against 11, unfortunately,' he said. 'Nobody makes any tackles in the penalty area. Even if it's a good tackle, the referee gives a penalty. Either that or you are concerned all the time about somebody being sent off for some trivial thing. You can play well for 89 minutes but you can't compete with a referee.'

It is much easier now for a non-host to make themselves feel at home. When Nelson and his Northern Ireland team-mates extended their stay at the Spanish World Cup into the second stage, the accommodation they faced on switching venue was deeply unsatisfactory. England too had trouble with ropey lodgings as recently as the 1980s. Back in the 1960s, Bobby Charlton was disappointed by the reaction of some England players to being eliminated by Brazil in the quarter-finals of the World Cup in Chile, where the England squad had been billeted up a mountain at the remote accommodation of the American Braden Copper Company in Rancagua. 'A lot of players in that team were really quite homesick,' Charlton says. 'There was a lot of laughing and joking afterwards, a couple of them saying they were glad that we'd lost because they'd see their families. I won't mention their names for fear of embarrassing them.'

A hostile or radically different climate, such as the humidity encountered in the Far East in 2002, is another potentially unsettling factor for visiting teams, and a reassuring one for the home side. But for northern European nations, such as England, the conditions in South Africa in June and July are such that the problem of extreme heat, as experienced in recent World Cups closer to home such as those in France, Germany and Italy, may prove to be non-existent. The South African winter, which stretches from May to July, sees temperatures that approximate roughly to summer in Great Britain: somewhere around 20°C during the dry, sunny hours of daylight. At night, the temperature drops drastically to only a few degrees above freezing, equating more to that of an early British spring. Additionally for England, this is the first World Cup for which they have qualified since hosting the tournament themselves in 1966 at which the language of the host country is also their own.

When West Germany defeated Hungary in the 1954 Final it helped that the tournament was being staged in Switzerland, just over the border, allowing 40,000 Germans to roar on their team at each match in the latter stages, while few from communist Hungary could receive dispensation to attend the match. Even more importantly, the rain on the day of the Final fell as though it was never going to stop. For Fritz Walter, the team's playmaker, this was manna, of the sodden kind, from heaven; not only that but the Germans' footwear, boots fitted with newly designed screw-in studs, gave them an advantage over the Hungarians. From that day onwards, heavy rain in West Germany would be known as 'Fritz Walter weather', the silver lining of World Cup memory brightening any cloudy, rainy day.

For a country seeking to settle into their temporary sur-roundings, it can help to attempt a degree of assimilation. Spain and Italy were given near-rapturous support at the 1978 World Cup in Argentina, understandably given that 98 per cent of the population could trace their lineage back to emigrants from those countries who had arrived in Argentina in their grandparents' generation. All the Italians and Spanish had to do was turn up and show their faces on the day.

Others have tried too hard in their attempts at ingrati-ation with the natives. Before Argentina faced Italy in Naples in a World Cup semi-final in 1990, Diego

Maradona sought to enlist the support of the locals, for whom he was a hero in his everyday job at Napoli – just weeks before he had helped them heroically to win the Italian League, the second title in the club's history and the second won through Maradona's influence.

'It upsets me that Italy is now asking for help from the Neapolitans,' he said, pleading with the locals to support Argentina in the semi-final, 'when they are not even considered Italians for the other 364 days of the year. I am sorry that now everybody is asking Naples to think of itself as Italian. Naples has always been forgotten by the rest of Italy – in fact it has always been given slaps in the face.' Pietro Lezzi, mayor of Naples, significant also as the port from which the ancestors of many Argentinians had embarked when emigrating to South America, responded, 'Maradona is a great and famous football champion but this time he has gone too far with opportunist statement. Naples will not be tricked by Maradona's little games.' It worked to a degree – some southerners got behind Italy but others voiced their backing for Maradona, unsettling the Italian players. Argentina won that semi-final on penalty kicks to progress to the Final.

The Argentinians' opponents, West Germany, had enjoyed something akin to home advantage during that 1990 tournament – Andreas Brehme, Jürgen Klinsmann and Lothar Matthäus all played their club football for Internazionale of Milan, in whose Giuseppe Meazza Stadium they played their first five matches. It was a venue, in common with the Stadio Delle Alpi in Turin, where they faced England in their semi-final, that was within easy reach of home, leading once again to hordes of Germans whizzing down the autostradas to provide their team with tumultuous backing. In Rome, for the Final, Rudi Völler and Thomas Berthold were in the stadium where they played their football for AS Roma and found the Italians backing their side in preference to Maradona – perhaps unfairly now voted the ugliest footballer in the tournament by Italian women – who had become an object of scorn after his attempts to turn the Naples crowd against Italy in the semi-final. 'We had the total support of the people,' Völler recalls. 'It was almost a home game for us.'

The softening of international barriers in football, with the modern displacement of so many World Cup-calibre players to leagues outside their own countries, is another factor in home advantage no longer counting for quite so much as in the past. It helped account for the ease with which the Germans had felt at home in that 1990 tournament and, in a world in which a five-star hotel in any major city could be transferred, Monopoly-style, to any other major city, homesickness can be kept at bay that bit more easily. Increased Champions League involvement for the planet's premier stars also means they may be more familiar with high-grade opponents from an opposing country than with those from teams in the nether regions of their own leagues.

It was quite different during the first half-dozen decades of the World Cup, when World Cup squads were mainly drawn from the domestic league of the country that they were representing. Argentina, in 1978, proved a classic example of this, with striker Mario Kempes, then at

Valencia in Spain, the only player in their squad to be employed outside of the Argentinian League.

Daniel Bertoni, another member of that Argentina squad, believes that the Argentinians had been placed among the favourites only because they had home advantage. It was also expected to be an open World Cup, given that this was winter in the southern hemisphere, with the weather being to the advantage of many of the teams, and with evening matches to be played in cold, wintry conditions so the European nations would not be particularly disadvantaged. The Argentinian players, unsure of how they measured up against opponents they rarely encountered, had the fairly modest goal of finishing in the top four. Argentina in 1978 were a moderately talented team, albeit with Osvaldo Ardiles an outstanding midfield player and Kempes a rapier-sharp leader of the line. Italy, France and Holland were all potentially better sides while Brazil and Poland were expected to be able to prove themselves at least their equals. So the military regime had been set the conundrum of how to ensure their team would win the tournament and provide a shot in the arm to a rule that needed a new injection of vitality.

It would surely help, at least a little, that the junta had their own man in Rear-Admiral Carlos Lacoste, a FIFA vice-president no less, as head of the World Cup organising committee. Then there was Artemio Franchi, head of the referees' committee, an Italian who might be expected to do the host nation a turn when necessary, given the historical links between the two countries. The organising committee had gleefully placed Brazil, one of the seeds, and perhaps Argentina's greatest potential rivals, in Mar del Plata, a rainy coastal town, for the opening group stage, an arrangement that left the Brazilians unhappy: the heavy, spongy pitch at the Parque Municipal would prevent the quick changes in acceleration that were key to their game.

Military dictatorships were all the rage in South America in the late 1970s. Brazil had one, as did Peru, Paraguay, Ecuador and Bolivia. General Pinochet, Chile's leader since 1973, began 1978 by lifting a weight from his people's minds, informing them that they need not concern themselves too much with the tedious ins and outs of politics as there would be 'no more elections in the next ten years'. As in Santiago, so in Buenos Aires, where there were between 4,000 and 8,000 political prisoners cramming the jails as the World Cup began, put there after Videla had seized power in a coup in March 1976 and embarked on a 'dirty war' that used torture and executions to eliminate the opposition. 'All the necessary people will die,' Videla had said chillingly on taking power. Those inside the jails were – so far at least – the lucky ones.

Thousands of people had disappeared, snatched off the streets or taken from inside public buildings or homes in broad daylight by secret police, marked out by their habitual dark glasses and the Ford Falcons that they drove to use for their dirty work. The junta were in the process of murdering, in cold blood and without trial, anywhere between 10,000 and 30,000 individuals. The World Cup falling as it did in the midst of this dirty war, it would be hijacked by the junta. There had been several threats from FIFA to withdraw it but football's governors were placated each time by Videla's assurances that the country had the stability to host the tournament.

The junta's coup had, initially, been received with relief by many inside Argentina, given that it was designed to end a campaign of terror by the Montoneros, a left-wing guerrilla group that had itself used kidnappings and executions, but the backlash from Videla's junta had been so brutal that the support for it had withered. One of the regime's favourite methods of murder was to drop victims from aeroplanes into the River Plate, the waterway that gave its name to the 1978 World Cup's premier stadium. Such was the power of the security forces that, soon, it was not only political opponents that were targeted. At a whim, anyone could be picked up off the street, never to be seen again; and informants could have enemies eliminated even if the information given on them was entirely untrue. No one was safe.

In mid-May 1978, three fans queuing for football tickets were injured when police fired during a disturbance caused by some supporters objecting that others were skipping the queue. The official police report claimed that the cause had been a policeman accidentally dropping his gun and it going off. Neither version provided much reassurance to anyone planning on visiting Argentina for the tournament. A bomb exploded at the press centre in Buenos Aires three weeks before the tournament, killing a policeman. Human rights organisations in Holland, Italy, Sweden and West Germany asked the players of those countries to consider withdrawing from the World Cup, but without noticeable success.

The Montoneros insisted that they would not disrupt

the Argentinian people's enjoyment of the World Cup – instead, their plan was to exhort people to buy up tickets for the stadiums and chant 'Argentina campeón; Videla al paredón' (Argentina to be champions; Videla to go hang). The National Union of Journalists handed out to British writers who would attend the World Cup a handy booklet that included Spanish phrases such as 'Please stop torturing me', 'How many journalists have you butchered this year?' and 'Please deliver my body to my family'.

At the World Cup's opening ceremony, Videla dressed up in a fashion he thought would make him respectable in the eyes of the world, but looked instead like a spiv with his slicked back hair and his grey and white Second World War-type thick-pinstriped suit. He used his speech to talk of peace, friendship and freedom. But when Monsignor Juan Carlos Aramburu, the archbishop of Buenos Aires, got to his feet to relay a message from the Pope, who had many priests among the political prisoners in Argentina, the microphones suddenly failed. Videla, expression hawkish, watchful, would be a constant presence at matches in this World Cup and he was due to present the trophy at the Final. To be handing it to anyone other than a blue-and-white-sleeved Argentinian would be disastrous for him and his junta.

The Argentina football team too was attempting to present a new and improved face to the world after years in which it had suffered opprobrium for the low-down and dirty methods employed by its players at World Cup tournaments. After the storm-tossed quarter-final between England and Argentina at Wembley in 1966, Alf

Ramsey had stated that it would not be possible for England to play at their best 'until we meet the right type of opposition; that is, a team that comes out to play football and not act as animals'. His words stung the South Americans so badly that they threatened to withdraw from FIFA entirely.

In 1978, César Luis Menotti's 'left-wing football' was, he said, 'first of all, about scoring more goals than the opposition'. He intended Argentina to win through fluent attacking movements, waves of artistry to mirror the poetry of Borges, the prose of Ernesto Sabato, the music of Chick Corea – artists whom he would name-check frequently. But for all Menotti's espousal of lyrical football, Argentina still relied on a degree of skulduggery that can never entirely be eradicated from their game. They even had a player called Daniel Killer as part of their squad although, perhaps in light of their new image, they had left out his brother.

Their opening match, with Hungary, encapsulated the shades of light and dark intrinsic to the progress of Menotti's team. Argentina's second goal in their 2–1 win, which arrived handily seven minutes from time just as the Argentinian team and crowd had started to become desperate, came after Hungary's goalkeeper Sandor Gujdar had been left sprawled on the ground after an over-enthusiastic charge from striker Leopoldo Luque that allowed Daniel Bertoni to knock the ball into the unguarded net. For all his bulk and forcefulness on the pitch, Luque had been a habitually inconsistent player going into this World Cup. 'I need to feel that people have confidence in me,' he would say. That was no problem to Spanish referee José

Antonio Garrido, whose decision to allow his challenge on Gujdar got Luque's World Cup off to a confident start.

The Hungary manager, Lajos Baroti, had openly stated that he expected the Argentinians to be awarded a couple of penalties to help ease them through the tournament, as and when required. Instead, a couple of red cards came in Argentina's favour, as Garrido finished the match with a flourish, dismissing not one but two angered Hungarian players. First to go was Andras Torocsik, the skilful forward, who had been kicked up and down the field by the Argentinians but who received a second yellow card for hacking down Américo Gallego in frustration after the latest foul on him. Torocsik's first booking had been for throwing the ball away. Tibor Nyilasi was then dismissed in the final minute.

Argentinian physicality was driven by fear that their defence was not quite good enough, but that mattered little when they came up against France in their second match. With tension mounting and Argentina again being held to a draw by a French team that had outwitted and outplayed them for much of the first half, Monsieur Jean Dubach of Switzerland, the referee, took centre stage and awarded an Argentinian penalty right on half-time. Marius Trésor, the France centre back, had been falling over backwards and unable to see the ball when it had hit his arm but Dubach, on the word of his linesman, pointed to the spot. The type of penalty that Baroti had predicted had materialized. Michel Platini equalised early in the second half but the match had turned in Argentina's favour and Luque's bullish shot from outside the penalty area settled the match in Argentina's favour.

The wins over Hungary and France each sparked 48 hours of celebrations, with the streets of Buenos Aires thronged with people of all ages; it was the first time since the generals had taken power that public demonstrations on any scale had been allowed. These helped to give the people a sense of normality and even with young men filling the streets overnight the generals could sleep soundly in the knowledge that with people distracted by Argentinian victories and anticipation of more to come, there would be no element of restlessness in the celebrations.

After the win over Hungary, Argentina became tournament favourites, coming in to 11–4 after Brazil had drawn with Sweden out in Mar del Plata. But the ease with which Argentina had obtained the dubious advantages they required to get the right results was halted, albeit only temporarily, when they faced Italy in their last group game. Even then, an episode that looked unfavourable to the Argentinians in the short term would eventually work well in their favour.

For Argentina against Italy, Abraham Klein of Israel had been appointed referee. 'When I'm on the pitch, only two things are important to me,' he would say: 'being fair to both teams and making my decisions bravely. I think all referees are fair, but not all of them are brave, probably.' At half-time, having lived up to his word, Klein was jeered and scorned frantically and frenetically by the crowd for standing strong in the face of their determination to influence the match in their team's favour and for becoming the first referee to clamp down hard on the Argentinians' persistent and vicious fouling. A second-half goal from

Roberto Bettega settled the match in Italy's favour and although defeat was not quite disastrous for Argentina – their two earlier victories had seen them qualify for the second round – it meant they would have to move out of Buenos Aires, away from their giant River Plate Stadium with the backing of 80,000 city fans, to Rosario and its altogether more modest, scaled-down stadium. Not only that but they would now play in a second-round group with Brazil.

It has to be highly dubious whether this Argentina side would even have qualified from their initial group if the tournament had been staged anywhere other than Argentina. But for that penalty, France would have had a strong chance of going on to beat them because the French, with players such as Dominique Rocheteau, Platini, Trésor and Didier Six, were a quicker, more inventive side, relishing the rebirth of their international team after years in the shadows.

The Argentinians would wear down the will of opponents like a form of drip-drip-drip, drawn-out torture, but their efforts were not all underhand; the team had huge dollops of talent as well. 'He's like a European player,' Mauro Bellugi, the Italy centre back, said of Luque after the European side had defeated the Argentinians. 'He always plays facing the goal.' This, indeed, was key not just to the striker but to the Argentina team in its entirety. They had adjusted, far better than Brazil, to a European style of football: one of pace, direct attacks, facing forward, but still laced with intricate South American skill.

A win over Poland opened Argentina's second-group-stage fixtures and a kicking-fest with Brazil – a 0–0 draw that featured 70 fouls – meant that Argentina's third group game, with Peru, was teed up perfectly to decide whether they progressed into the Final. It would effortlessly surpass for notoriety anything that even the Argentinians had managed in any previous World Cup.

Brazil had found a good passing game to beat Peru 3–0, which was highly respectable against a team that had been enjoying a good tournament. Now, as the Brazilians prepared to face Poland in their final game and Argentina got ready to take on the Peruvians, Brazil asked, quite reasonably, whether the two matches could kick off at the same time. With Rear-Admiral Carlos Lacoste at the helm of the World Cup Organising Committee, this entirely reasonable request must have been considered for all of maybe three seconds before the Brazilians were regretfully told that, no, it was out of the question and that the arrangement whereby Brazil would start their game three hours before Argentina would have to be upheld.

Still, when Brazil beat a good Poland side 3–1, it cast the Argentinian people into gloom for the hour before their match with Peru began. The Brazilians now had a goal difference of six goals for and one against; Argentina had just two goals for and none against. If Argentina were to progress to the Final, they would have to win by at least four goals – a seemingly tough task for a team that had not hit more than two in any of their five matches up to that point.

Prior to the match General Videla visited the Peruvian dressing room to deliver to the opposing team's players a stern, intimidatory lecture on the importance of Latin

American brotherhood and unity. The Argentinians conveniently hit six without reply and that was them in the Final. For the first goal, the Peru centre back was almost like a traffic warden waving through traffic as he stood and watched Kempes motor through to score; the second goal saw Ramón Quiroga, the goalkeeper, so impressive earlier in the tournament, suddenly become almost stationary on the line as Alberto Tarantini's shot went whirling obligingly past him. Peru's defence then opened up regularly for the next four goals. 'We are at our best when we play as if it is all or nothing,' Menotti said, in between long draws on his cigarettes. 'That is the national character.'

Rumours immediately began coursing around Argentina that there had been an attempt to fix the match. The Argentinian version had it that money had been shipped in from Rio by the Brazilians to incentivise Peru to beat the Argentinians; if this was true, it has to have been the least successful bribe in history. The alternative version, the one with more stamina, had it that the Peruvians had laid down to the Argentinians. Argument and counter-argument would rage on the topic for years. Menotti got in a quick defence of his team. 'If Brazil with two forwards could score three against Peru, then it was easy to see that we could score double with five forwards.'

Evidence was put forward of Peruvian attempts to score and of them holding their own for the first 20 minutes until simply, so the story went, collapsing under Argentinian pressure. Juan José Munante had hit the post when the score was goalless and, with Argentina 1–0 ahead, Peru had hit the bar. Still the suspicions remained and tales would emerge of the first batches of millions of pounds worth of grain and food, bound for poverty-stricken Peru, being loaded in Buenos Aires even as the game began. Adding to the suspicion was the fact that Quiroga had been born in Argentina and had become a naturalised Peruvian.

'I never sold myself,' Quiroga says in offering a confusing denial that Argentina 'fixed' the match with Peru. 'Argentina had a brilliant night and we were a disaster. It was just one of those games where everything went wrong. I didn't play badly actually. I conceded six but stopped many other chances. We were unlucky. We hit the post twice. I'm sure the referee was against us; he allowed two goals that were offside.' Allegations would also emerge that the Argentina players had been using amphetamines. No positive tests were recorded, it was suggested, because the urine samples were provided by the team's waterboy who was, naturally, clean of drugs. 'Argentina ran like madmen,' Quiroga says. 'They ran with a speed and a strength that I have never seen. Perhaps it was the excitement of the crowd . . . or maybe it was something else.'

It was a murky matter but, whatever the circumstances, the Argentinians were fixed up for the Final, in which they would meet a Holland team whose skill and toughness they feared enormously. Something would have to be done. The choice of referee for the match was between the impeccable Abraham Klein, the Israeli who had stood up strongly to the Argentinians earlier in the competition, and Sergio Gonella, an Italian. Only Klein had clamped down on the Argentinians' incessant, niggling gamesmanship, the ankle taps, the petty fouls that so disrupted opposing teams. But Gonella, for all his undoubted qualities, could hardly be described as neutral. Such was the affinity inside Argentina for Italy, so rich was it in depth, that cries of 'Italia! Italia!', with an Argentinian accent, resonated around the stadiums where the Italian team played. Artemio Franchi, the Florentine head of the referees' committee, would have the casting vote as to the choice of referee for the Final and he chewed over his options and looked at it from every angle before deciding to opt for his fellow countryman.

Gonella could speak Spanish, the language of Argentina, but not Dutch or English, enabling Menotti's team to make themselves even more at home in the Final. For all that a suitable referee had been found for them, Argentina were in a fairly undesirable situation. The unyielding, furious pressure from their supporters, in tandem with a full-throttle playing style, had put demands on them that looked sure to take their toll eventually, particularly against a cool Dutch team unlikely to be fazed by fouling or fans. But what the Argentinians did have going for them was that they used a unique style of football, designed for a team playing at home in front of 80,000 bellicose fanatics: a hit or miss, high-tempo format, created to unsettle defenders by playing short, staccato passes in and around them, passes that were angled from one moving man as he twisted and turned to another one doing the same, aiming always, ultimately, for Luque or Kempes. It was exciting, cavalier, risky, it looked almost miraculous that it ever came off at all; and for all that the aficionados might rail against the way the Argentinians had been favoured, it was a form of exciting football that won admiration from television viewers around the world.

Not that the Argentinians would concentrate solely on football and cast off their essential character just because they were in the Final. First, they allowed the Dutch to take the field before them and then kept their opponents waiting on the pitch – the din from the partisan crowd ringing in their ears – for eight minutes before joining them. Once the national anthems had been played and the players had shaken hands, Osvaldo Ardiles suggested to Daniel Passarella, the Argentina captain, that the plaster cast that René van der Kerkhof was wearing on his arm would be dangerous for any player given a whack by it mid-match. So Passarella enlisted the help of Gonella, who duly took Van der Kerkhof by the arm like an errant schoolboy and led him off the pitch, amidst Dutch protests that they would all leave the field. 'If that's how you want it you can play the World Cup Final on your own,' Johan Neeskens said threateningly to Passarella.

The Dutch were of the belief that this was another piece of gamesmanship from the Argentinians, designed to unsettle their European opponents: Van der Kerkhof, after all, had been wearing the cast since sustaining an arm injury against Iran in Holland's opening match and they felt that the Argentinians could have registered any objections long before kick-off. Ardiles insists that it was a spur-of-the-moment matter and that if he had known the trouble it would cause, he would have kept his mouth shut.

It still meant that bad feeling between the teams had

been created even before a ball had been kicked and, with Van der Kerkhof restored to the action with extra padding applied to his arm in case of injury to any stray Argentinian boot that might find its way in his direction, the game finally began, way behind schedule. Menotti was reputed to smoke four packs of cigarettes in the course of each match and soon there was smoke billowing from his dugout, as the Dutch showed no signs of being worn down by the attempts of Argentina at waging psychological warfare. All this despite Rudi Krol and his team feeling that the referee was so biased that, as Krol put it, they wondered whether he might feel as though he was playing for Argentina, so many fouls and clear handballs from the Argentinians did he allow to pass. The pick of the many Argentinian infringements was Daniel Bertoni's elbowing of Neeskens and three blatant handballs by centre back Luis Galván to break up Dutch attacks. An unconcerned Gonella allowed play to continue freely on each of those occasions.

A first-half goal from Kempes – a player who was 50 per cent of the Argentina team, according to Johan Neeskens – was equalised by Dick Nanninga late in the game, then Rensenbrink missed his chance to win it in the final minute of the 90. Extra time saw the tackling grow more desperate, the Argentinians' excesses still going unchecked by Gonella, and Kempes and then Bertoni swivelled and swayed through the Dutch defence to score the typically hectic goals that won the Argentinians their first World Cup. The second goal encapsulated the mixture of skill, luck and opportunism that characterised the Argentina team. Kempes slalomed stylishly past two

Dutch defenders, having his shot blocked by Jan Jongbloed, only for it to hit the striker's trailing heel and, with two Dutch defenders and Kempes, all angular action and flowing hair, flailing for the ball in the six-yard box, the striker managed to get the sole of his boot to it and nudge it over the line.

Menotti insisted afterwards that he would stick with his plan to retire after the World Cup, one that he had announced when he had been under severe criticism pre-tournament; six months before the finals there had been speculation that he might be about to be replaced by Juan Carlos Lorenzo. 'I want to be able to open a cupboard without a football player falling out,' he said after the match. Videla presented the World Cup, a tarnished trophy, to Daniel Passarella, and the military regime could reflect on money well spent in hosting a tournament that had presented a clean image abroad. The vanquished Dutch, meanwhile, were unable to attend the post-match banquet at the Plaza Hotel in downtown Buenos Aires because they could not be given assurances as to their safety. The Argentinian hosts would be left to please themselves – just as they had been allowed to do through-out the competition.

13

Get Into Shape

WHEN RUN-OF-THE-MILL LEAGUE FOOTBALLERS SIT DOWN to watch the faraway World Cup action on their television screens, they must do so with a sigh of apprehension. Tactics at a World Cup are so fluid and difficult to pinpoint that they can be problematical for even the greatest exponents of the game. 'It wasn't such a tactical game as you see today but that's how football was then,' Franz Beckenbauer says glowingly on reminiscing about the 1966 World Cup Final. 'We didn't think much about tactics. Today there is too much emphasis on tactics and not enough on talent and technique. When we got the ball all we thought about was to go forward. Perhaps it was a little naive. The game now is much more athletic but not so good to watch. It's all about security. First of all, you mustn't lose. In 1966, our priority was always that we wanted to win.'

That all sounds fine and warm and sentimental for a

long-gone age and you can almost feel the reassuring heat as you bask in the cosy fireside glow of Franz's nostalgia. Except that Franz seems to have overlooked one tiny, minor detail, which is that, for all his abundance of talent and desire to attack with devil-may-care abandon, he spent the entire 120 minutes against England at Wembley on 30 July 1966 sticking to Bobby Charlton like a particularly large piece of chewing gum, sacrificing his own instinctive creativity to prevent the England midfielder performing. The duo were so well matched that they just about cancelled each other out. It is not that Franz has forgotten about this: it is a facet of that game that the German remembers well despite his rose-tinged memories of international football in the 1960s. He also recalls concluding the game completely worn out after chasing the tireless Charlton around Wembley's green swathes. 'At the time he was the best player in the world,' Beckenbauer says of Charlton, 'and he also had lungs like a horse. I never remember being as exhausted as I was playing that afternoon.'

It seems impossible for Franz to be right on both accounts and yet, somehow, he is. The most sophisticated tactical formations are often put into play at World Cups but their code can almost always be cracked by the world's best players. Tactics add an element of science to the game but players give it heart. Beckenbauer smothered Charlton that day in 1966 but the West Germans could not snuff out the eager attacking instincts of other England players such as Alan Ball and Geoff Hurst, both of whose play on the day epitomised the desire to push forward with which Franz recalls his era. That is why

Franz is not wrong in holding a seemingly contrary opinion on that match. England's victory at Wembley in 1966 was framed by Alf Ramsey's tactics, but it was individual initiative that gave them the edge over the West Germans.

Halfway through the 1966 tournament, Ramsey appeared to discard instantaneously more than a century of British tradition by fielding a formation that contained no wingers. A shudder must have travelled through all of the watching wide boys, although perhaps not George Best. Decades later, when asked where he had been on the day of the Final, Best could not remember, even though he had been drinking in the action inside Wembley Stadium. He had no need to look on and worry about his skills being sidelined, but less exalted contemporaries did. Following the 1966 World Cup, Football League managers in England rushed to adopt Ramsey's 4–4–2, making wingers an unprotected species in the consequent cull. During the next decade, 2,000 fewer goals were scored in English football.

England's 2–0 victory over Spain on a freezing December night in Madrid six months before the 1966 finals had been the first time Ramsey's 4–4–2 system had been shown to work effectively and so pleased was he after that match that, in a rare show of ebullience, he spoke of 'this precious gem', shaping his hands into a football. The message was that he had found a pleasing means of retaining the ball, which he would sometimes describe to his players as 'a lump of gold' – something you don't want to lose. Yet classifying that England team as a 4–4–2 presents the problem of how Bobby Charlton fitted into it: at the 1966 finals he wore a number 9 on his back, but was supposedly one of the four midfield players in Ramsey's 4–4–2. 'I tried nine centre forwards in three years,' Ramsey said, 'but I knew months, even years, before the World Cup that Bobby Charlton would have a number 9 on his back.' This is further evidence that tactical formations can often be regarded only as a fairly rough guide as to exactly what is happening on the field of play.

Nobby Stiles demolishes the notion of rigidity suggested by this fixed formation, even, confusingly, describing Ramsey's system not as 4–4–2 but as one more like a 4–2–2–2. 'The talk was that we played the 4–3–3 system but that was a load of rubbish,' Stiles says. 'The fluid movement of the team was unbelievable. There was a back four. I played in front of the back four. I had Alan Ball on the right of me, Martin Peters and Bobby Charlton in front of me and then the two front men. Alan Ball used to make runs across the field to Martin and get the full backs overlapping.'

When Argentina won the World Cup in 1986 with a radical 3–5–2 formation that had at its base three large but mobile central defenders, it was the turn of squat full backs around the world to suddenly begin wondering about their shelf life. The decision of Carlos Bilardo to go with three instead of four at the back was a radical move – the first time since the 1950s that a change in tactical formation had reduced rather than increased the number of players who formed the ultimate barrier in front of the goalkeeper. The manager was criticised on the basis that he had to be mistaken – but the addition of a central defender made his teams more constrictive inside the penalty area, while the replacement of full backs with wing backs gave him five, six or even seven players defending when his team was under pressure, and extra attacking options when they were on the front foot. The demands on the joints of the new wing backs also provided plenty of extra work for orthopaedic surgeons everywhere. The two markers and the libero provided the team with a solid platform for Jorge Burruchaga, Diego Maradona and Jorge Valdano to spring forward. No one had any solidly fixed positions in the team other than the back three; the other players had the opportunity to make runs and move as they saw fit, given that the extra man in midfield afforded plenty of cover.

Perhaps the most surprising tactical pioneers have been the Brazilians, not least because they are rarely associated with rigidity and fixed form. It seems de rigueur for television voice-overs previewing Brazil at World Cup time to focus, patronisingly, on how they hone their talents on sunbathed beaches and in the rutted backstreets that run through their *favelas* – images of children doing just this are usually accompanied by a gentle *bossa nova* soundtrack, complete with persistent flute, that makes it all seem so liltingly easy and natural. Yet for all that Brazil are rightly revered for their great fluidity of movement and instinctive brilliance, they too have been responsible for tactical changes that have transformed football the world over. Tactical discipline has been key to every one of their World Cup triumphs.

Prior to the World Cup of 1958 the favoured team formation worldwide had been 2–3–5 – two full backs, behind a midfield consisting of a centre half, a right half and a left half, with five forwards. The Hungarians, in 1954, had tinkered with this formation, allowing centre forward Nandor Hidegkuti to drop off the forward line, but he remained, for all that, a forward nonetheless. For the tournament in Sweden, Brazil formalised the revolution away from the old orthodoxy that saw teams fielding five forwards and that saw defence as the poor relation of attack. The Brazilians withdrew the centre half and the left half into defence – doubling its strength from two to four – and brought one of the forwards, the inside right, into midfield, thus creating the 4–2–4 formation. It provided them with an expanded back line while losing little in attack, given that the left and right backs could range forward into midfield when necessary, to join up with their wingers. It helped, naturally, that Brazil could field players of the calibre of Nilton Santos, a quick, skilled, athletic full back, and ultra-inventive attackers such as Didi, Garrincha, Vavá and Pelé.

Further tinkering for 1962 saw the Brazilians modify their system to create 4–3–3. The manager, Aymoré Moreira, in working with a team of seasoned players, several of whom were over 30, believed he needed to bulk out the midfield, so Mario Zagallo was transformed from being a left winger into a player who worked his way up and down on the left side of midfield, a move that helped to earn him the nickname 'the Ant'. In 1966, Ramsey took this a step further by pulling another man into midfield to create his hardworking 4–4–2.

Yet the most radical Brazilian tactic – taking those three previous modifications almost to the extreme – was ignored, seemingly entirely, by the world, when it was adopted in 1970. That blissful ignorance of the team's shape demonstrated how a tactical format is simply the chassis of a team. As with a high-performance car, effectiveness is entirely dependent on what lies under the bonnet. The tactical framework that housed the Brazil team of 1970 went unnoticed; it is as if it is irrelevant or even irreverent to discuss something as mundane as that team's structure, as if they simply played off the cuff from start to finish in the sweltering heat of Mexico. A squad that adopted the utmost professionalism, sequestered together for months in a training camp, who were put through the same conditioning programme as NASA's astronauts to prepare them for the altitude of Mexico, supposedly followed all of that intricate preparation by just strolling out on to the field of play and leaving everything to chance once they had crossed the white line, as if they were ambling on to their local park for a Sunday afternoon bounce game.

Instead, the Brazil of 1970 offered perhaps the finest example of how a tactical framework, regardless of how sophisticated, only becomes particularly prominent when those that it houses lack the charisma and style to provide it with a gilded disguise. That was most definitely not the case with the team of Pelé, Jairzinho and Roberto Rivelino, who, back then, were working their magic within a tactical system that only became widely prevalent from the 1990s onwards and that is often seen as a signifier of how the modern game is becoming increasingly cautious. The Brazilians, in that glorious summer of supposed abandon for football, were using 4–5–1.

It had nagged at Zagallo before the 1970 World Cup that Pelé and Tostão might prove to be too similar to work successfully as a pairing up front. Through pulling Pelé back into an advanced midfield role, Zagallo resolved the problem. Crucially, Tostão remained up front as a spearhead, the sole forward, stretching the play and often leaving Pelé unmarked and free, as the opposition's two central defenders would be unsure whether to stay put or to be pulled out of position in pursuit of him.

'I knew there would be a lot of changes,' Zagallo said of taking over the Brazil team, 'because I didn't accept 4–2–4. There's no way we could have won the World Cup using that system. I'm happy to see the team in terms of 4–5–1. We brought our team back behind the line of the ball. We didn't want to give space for Europeans to hit us with quick counter-attacks so we played as a block, compact, leaving only Tostão up field. Jairzinho, Pelé and Rivelino all tracked back to join Gérson and Clodoaldo in the midfield. So we saved our energy, dropped back and then, when we won possession, the technical quality of the team stood out.' His tinkering with the team did not see him spared criticism. 'In 1970 I was an idiot, *loco*, a donkey,' he says, 'because I put Rivelino on the left wing. I was accused of trying to turn the clock back to 1958.'

Watch the Brazilians in 1970, and look again at some of those famous goals that were knocked in from all angles as the sunburst-yellow shirts spread their warmth around the world and provided classic cameos of action to be cherished for ever. Watch Pelé or Jairzinho in the Brazilians' opening match, with Czechoslovakia, as time and again Czech attacks are broken up and they pick up the ball to go racing through towards goal from deep within their own half. Frequently, the only player in the Czech half is Tostão, the lone forward. That this is counter-attacking football is easily overlooked because of the mesmeric spell cast by the Brazilians' graceful action and close control, while the uncertainty and anticipation as to what they will do next means that thinking about their tactical shape seems almost superfluous. The directness that is usually associated with counter-attacking – the intention of catching the opposing defence on the hop simply by running hard at them and exploiting undefended space – seems to be absent. It is there, but it is bundled up with a variety of other aspects of the game, such as the type of step-overs, quick flicks, close-quarters deception and changes of pace that made the Brazil players unique.

Watch the instance when Pelé collects the ball and attempts to catch out Ivo Viktor, the Czech goalkeeper, by lobbing him from within his own half. It begins with a Czech attack being intercepted and broken down and the only player in the Czech half as Pelé's shot from inside the centre circle goes past Viktor's left-hand post is Tostão, the lone striker. Even then he too is only just inside Czech territory. Watch the Brazilians' fourth goal in this match. When Pelé, well inside his own half, feeds Jairzinho, the latter is the only Brazilian in the Czech half but the whirl of action as he bends and sways away from four defenders before shooting low past Viktor covers up the fact that the bulk of the Brazilians are behind the ball and in their own part of the field. You will see that this is yet another counter-attack, regardless of how sophisticated and attractive the manner in which it is dressed. Look at Jairzinho's goal in the semi-final with Uruguay: as he takes a pass from Tostão on the halfway line, Jairzinho is the only Brazil player further advanced than the centre circle, and again it is his weaving trickery and cheetah-like pace that gets the goal rather than weight of numbers in attack.

Zagallo's belief was not that attack was the best form of defence but that attacking players were. 'We were seen as an attacking team, because of the goals we scored,' Pelé says, 'but in actual fact when the ball went into our own half we all went back. Only Tostão stayed up front.' When Brazil's opponents sat back and attempted to absorb pressure, as with the Italians in the Final, it made life easier for the Brazilians, who could then feel free in attacking, knowing that eventually their guile and style would prevail. Skill and speed of thought then came to the fore and the Brazilians' 4–1 victory over the best-drilled defenders in the tournament was their most emphatic triumph of all. Pelé suggests that the Brazil team that won the 1958 World Cup was more talented, but that the 1970 winners were better organised – not the epithet usually applied to that team and its works.

At Zagallo's first training session in early 1970, Pelé told the new manager that he understood that it was Zagallo's right to drop him if necessary but stressed that the one thing to which he would object strenuously would be to be messed about. Prior to that tournament there had even been some doubts raised about Pelé's ability to make an imprint on the fourth World Cup in which he was to participate. Jozef Marko, the Czechoslovakia manager, had described the Brazilian as 'a spent force'. Zagallo had not only made him key to his plans but had refreshed his role in the team and allowed him to shine.

The most seemingly democratic of all tactical styles followed, with the arrival of 'total football' in the early 1970s. It chimed with the times. People were restlessly asserting their rights more and more at the beginning of the new decade, and the Holland team that espoused 'total football' presented themselves in a fresh, freedom-loving fashion. Long haired and with love beads around their necks, they looked entirely in tune with youthful popular culture and their tactical outlook was an appealingly egalitarian one. There was to be no discrimination inside a team, seemingly no hierarchy, in that every player was equally valued and was supposedly expected to be able to do the job of any other. In theory, at any time, a defender could appear in a forward's position and vice versa. This was a team casting off oppressive labels.

'People talk of "total football" as if it is a system,' Dutch midfielder Arie Haan said, 'something to replace 4–2–4 or 4–3–3. It is not a system. As it is at any moment, so you play. That is how we understand. Not one or two players make a situation but five or six. The best is that with every situation all 11 players are involved but this is difficult. In many teams maybe only two or three play and the rest are looking. In the Holland team when you are 60 metres from the ball you are playing.'

The idea of interchanging positions worked to an extent: Holland's key second goal against Brazil that put them in the 1974 World Cup Final saw Rudi Krol, a defender, burst through into space to take a pass from

Rob Rensenbrink and then cross from the edge of the penalty area with the alacrity of an inside forward for Johan Cruyff to clip the ball into the Brazilian net. But the idea that the Dutch were constantly in flux with players bobbing about all over the field without being in fixed positions simply never happened . . . could not happen. Holland would use Cruyff as their principal forward, with Johan Neeskens in central midfield, and one or both of them would often drift wide, at will, and play someone else through the middle; but those two players were still key to all of Holland's attacking movements. Cruyff was incredibly quick, with supreme close control, incisive imagination and decisive finishing, the complete player in any era and in any system. Neeskens was the perfect midfield player, tough in the tackle, precise and clever in his distribution, good in the air and with a powerful shot.

There was still something of smoke and mirrors about the whole 'total football' idea, as Rinus Michels, the Holland manager, all but admitted in the midst of the 1974 World Cup. 'Without Cruyff I have no team,' he said, giving the game away somewhat. Cruyff, a player with a strong claim to being the best ever, made the Dutch team tick – he genuinely did have a free, floating role, one reminiscent of that adopted by Argentinian Alfredo Di Stéfano, who transformed attacking play in the 1950s. As with Di Stéfano, Cruyff had the all-round awareness and ability to pop up all over the field to start attacks or to drag markers out of position and create space for teammates. 'Cruyff is 70 per cent of our team,' said the normally reticent Dutch midfielder Wim Jansen in the midst of the tournament. 'He is a great man, our leader off the field and on the field. He has the affection and respect of all of us.' Not so much total football, then, as total Johan.

It sometimes went unnoticed that West Germany too were utilising total football, minus the colour and flair and flamboyant style of the Dutch and without anyone as brilliantly versatile as Cruyff. But they played total football nonetheless, with players exchanging positions when the progress of the game or a particular move demanded it. Theirs was a more disciplined version, of course, with Franz Beckenbauer, a defender, as their great totem. He had the demeanour of a bank clerk, in contrast to the excitable, unpredictable Cruyff, who looked and often behaved like the leader of the latest student sit-in. Yet Beckenbauer had been as revolutionary as any Dutchman in the manner in which he brought the ball out from the back to spark attacks, join in with them and even score himself from time to time. If the Dutch seemed to be gaudy, eye-catching impressionists, the Germans were more of the hard-edged but equally revolutionary Bauhaus school. It was a distracting illusion, given that the Holland international players of the 1970s were as tough and deliberately physical as anyone, and more so than most.

England were not renowned for tactical versatility but suddenly embraced 3–5–2 early in the 1990 tournament and it helped propel them to the semi-finals. After a dull 1–1 draw with the Republic of Ireland, Bobby Robson sprang on the world an England team with three at the back for the second group game, against Holland, Mark Wright, Terry Butcher and Des Walker being the three central defenders. With Holland going 4–5–1, it meant that the danger of having an underemployed four-man defence and an overworked midfield was averted. It also allowed more cover for Paul Gascoigne, indisciplined tactically, to work his magic without his absences from key areas having a costly effect on the team. The three men at the back added more strength to the centre of the defence, the better to combat Marco van Basten, the Dutch striker, even if it meant Butcher, a left-sided player, being used on the right. A 0–0 draw, which England edged in terms of creditworthiness, gave Robson's team a morale-boosting confidence that helped sustain them for the rest of the tournament.

A fresh footballing form can, like any fashion, soon look hackneyed. When 3–5–2 was unwrapped by Argentina at the 1986 finals it was quickly taken up by West Germany, although when the two sides met in the Final that year it was still the human factor that would see the game sway back and forth. Lothar Matthäus marked Diego Maradona for the opening hour of the match, and although Argentina went 2–0 ahead, Maradona was more subdued than in the preceding games at that World Cup. 'I marked him well,' Matthäus said, 'because in those 60 minutes he was never decisive. Then Beckenbauer put Förster on him and I began to play my normal game. We got back on terms but it wasn't enough. Maradona's flair allowed Burruchaga to win the game.'

With Matthäus elsewhere, one poked pass forward from Maradona had opened up the West Germany half for Burruchaga to run through and score. During the early days of 3–5–2, its inbuilt flaws could be overlooked in the dazzling shock of the new but by the 1994 World Cup, only the Germans held fast to this style, which, with the space it left unguarded on the flanks, made it highly vulnerable to quick-thinking wingers.

By USA '94 almost everyone had retreated to a version of 4–4–2, sometimes with split strikers making it a 4–4–1–1. Brazil, the winners, played a regular 4–4–2, with playmaker Raí at the point of the midfield diamond and the more obdurate Mauro Silva at the rear. With the doughy talents of Dunga and Mazinho filling the centre of a stuffy central midfield, the full backs were expected to get up and service the two strikers.

The back four is now a hardy perennial for World Cup teams, with managers tending to tinker with midfield as the means of getting the most from their teams. France went 4–3–2–1 at the 1998 finals in a formation that had by then been around for a few years and was known as the 'Christmas Tree' because of the way it had a strong, broad base and tapered off into a point. Supporters of Newcastle United and Rangers would agree that Stéphane Guivarc'h, who would feature for those British clubs after that World Cup, fitted well into the role of the fairy on top. Guivarc'h had been scoring prolifically in the French League – and had been top scorer in France in the two seasons prior to the World Cup – but quite stunningly managed to cruise through the tournament without troubling the net once.

Aimé Jacquet's formation matched the talent at his disposal. He was blessed with fine defenders such as Laurent Blanc and Marcel Desailly, centre backs who were so accomplished that Lilian Thuram was moved to right back, and even finer midfield players. But the strikers in his squad were too young, injured or off form. Jacquet had been searching furiously for a striker in the years preceding the World Cup but with little success so, lacking goalscorers, he fielded a team in a formation that fitted his players' strengths. Nicolas Anelka, David Trézéguet and Thierry Henry were all on the fringes of the team but all were in their late teens and early twenties, and although Trézéguet and Henry figured now and then in the World Cup, it all came just a little bit too early for them to be encumbered with serious responsibility.

For the Final, Didier Deschamps sat centrally in front of France's back four as a bolster behind Emmanuel Petit, Christian Karembeu and Zinédine Zidane, with Youri Djorkaeff behind Guivarc'h. Anyone wishing to be finicky about all this might describe it as a 4–1–3–1–1 system, the field having been compartmentalised into finely differentiated areas of influence, with each player having a refined role as if he was one of the Sun King's courtiers. In contrast, Brazil were almost unsophisticated and peasant-like with their 4–2–2–2 formation.

Just Fontaine, the France striker who scored a record 13 goals at the 1958 finals, had warned shortly before the 1998 tournament that a team with a lone striker could not win the World Cup because they could not have all the chances falling to the same player. For all that France had to make do with limited firepower up front, they were still a powerful attacking force, as no fewer than nine Frenchmen and even a South African, putting through his own goal, would score for them in the tournament – everyone except their principal striker Guivarc'h.

It seemed symbolic of France, the great creators, that among their players Djorkaeff had the best goalscoring record going into the finals. Although he sometimes partnered Guivarc'h up front, he saw himself as principally a midfield player. Djorkaeff would score just once in the finals and that with a penalty in the match with Denmark, the third group game for France, in which Jacquet rested a number of first-choice players, given that the French had already qualified for the knockout stage.

The confusion for spectators in this new world of players wearing numbers that are disconnected to their role on the field, and in which flexibility and fluidity reign, was encapsulated by Telê Santana, the Brazil manager, as he spoke of attacking play in 1982. 'Wingers are players like any other and the fact that they have 7 or 11 on their backs in no way obliges them to stay glued to the line. Today, attackers are called on to move about endlessly. Men must burst through on the flanks but that doesn't mean it's the exclusive task of a special player.'

Even with saturation satellite coverage of football in the twenty-first century and managers who are familiar with tactical variation, it is still possible for the astute manager to enjoy a tactical triumph now and again, while the opponent isn't looking, as it were. Marcello Lippi used several different tactical formations during the 2006 World Cup. He put five in midfield to match and stifle the Czechs in the Italians' third group game, which they won 2–0. In the memorable semi-final with Germany he went to four forwards in extra time when the midfield was increasingly being bypassed. It was end-to-end football by that point and 'our defence was much better than

Germany's,' Lippi suggested in explanation of his move. In the Final, as Italy tired, he took off Francesco Totti, the forward, replacing him with the defensive midfielder Daniele De Rossi, but maintained Italy's attacking potential by moving Andrea Pirlo forward. The consequence was to make Italy more solid, without handing France the initiative.

All this was possible because, Lippi said, 'Italian players are the best tactically in the world. That's an honest opinion. I'm not saying that it's the best-looking football but it's the hardest because, whatever team you play, you are always going to have great difficulty when playing them.' Lippi's favoured style had been 4–3–1–2 but he could transform that into 4–4–2 when wishing to hold a lead; or a 4–2–4 as against Germany in the semi-final when he wished to seize the day; and a 4–5–1, as seen against the Czechs.

'It's unfair to say that we play a defensive game,' Lippi had said before the finals. 'We've changed, although we have, of course, remained true to our traditions. All pre-tournament favourites inevitably begin by focusing on their traditions and later innovate.' The Italian defence had performed extraordinarily well at that World Cup, Gianluigi Buffon reinforcing his reputation as the world's finest goalkeeper, while the back four of Fabio Cannavaro, Marco Materazzi, Fabio Grosso and Gianluca Zambrotta grew ever more impressive as the tournament approached its conclusion. For all the strength in Italy's defence, they still required Andrea Pirlo and Rino Gattuso to work hard as the first line of defence at the back of midfield. Pirlo, from a wealthy background, can take on the appearance of an over-indulged child slowly developing into an adult dilettante, but his assiduousness in closing down opponents was especially notable in a player recognised principally for his delicate touch and creative powers.

Italy in 2006 were no longer the cautious side that would habitually retreat into defence but that defensive heritage, in which drilled discipline and adherence to fixed positioning is essential, had done them no harm in allowing those in more pliable positions to help the team metamorphose into something quite different. Once again World Cup winners had demonstrated the seeming contradiction that, when it comes to tactical shape, flexibility and not rigidity is the essential ingredient.

14

You've Won It Once . . .

I SOMETIMES SEEMS FACILE TO LINK ENGLAND'S 1966 World Cup victory to the nation being at the epicentre of the swinging sixties but there is a logical link. Alf Ramsey, who possessed the demeanour of a dogged civil servant, may not have appeared to have had much in common with the radical changes that were taking place in British art, cinema, television, fashion and popular music during that decade, but he had broken down barriers as much as the leading denizens of those other disciplines, albeit more discreetly and quietly, as befitted his unassuming nature.

On his appointment as manager in 1962, Ramsey had insisted that he be solely responsible for selecting the players for the England team. This meant that he wrested control of that matter away from the patrician Football Association committee who had previously picked the side. This revolutionary, evolutionary step paved the way for England's future success and allowed the new manager enough confidence to state, quite audaciously, that 'England will win the World Cup in 1966.'

England had already made four unsuccessful bids to host the tournament. Had they been successful then, with a selection committee carrying out the most important job of all, their chances of victory might have been significantly reduced. As it was, the 1966 tournament fitted the spirit of the times in Britain, as an England team that blended skill and discipline with colourful improvisation, not to mention some controversial selections from Ramsey, proved unstoppable en route to one of the most exciting Finals of all, with West Germany.

That victory in the 1966 World Cup had a bit of nearly everything needed to land the world championship – without specialising too much in anything. The team enjoyed a bit of luck in the Final when Geoff Hurst's shot bounced down from the bar and was ruled by the match officials to have crossed the line. They pioneered a tactical innovation in using a 4–4–2 system but only adopted it halfway through the tournament; made the very most of home advantage by playing all six games at Wembley stadium; struck gold in a year when there was no need to worry about the Brazilians; survived a mini-crisis when the FA and the press put pressure on Ramsey to eject Nobby Stiles from his squad; had at the helm an eccentric manager; and enjoyed a slowish start. All of these factors came into play, but no single one of them would quite predominate in the way that some other winning nations have needed something extreme to happen to drive them to World Cup victory.

Perhaps the most remarkable thing about England's

victory was how straightforward it all seemed – not easy but straightforward, attained calmly and strategically. Bobby Charlton maintains that winning the European Cup with Manchester United in 1968 was a more difficult undertaking. 'I never thought the World Cup was that difficult,' Charlton says. 'We were the favourites, the best team, we were at home, we only had six matches to play.' England's win in 1966 was a typically moderate British victory – not too much of anything but enough of everything.

It was a tournament that began with all the fizz of a cup of lukewarm, milky tea. 'Thousands of people who bought tickets for this match in block form in order to obtain a ticket for the Final presumably did not trouble to use their ticket for tonight's match,' an FA spokesman said with wonderful understatement, after Wembley had been more than 10,000 short of capacity for England's opening match, with Uruguay. Ramsey used the flat performance of his team in a stolid 0–0 draw to work the trick of both playing down expectation of easy progress and maintaining that the ultimate victory was possible. 'With regard to the mass-hypnotism after the draw,' he said after the Uruguay game, 'when everybody thought England was in an easy group, I said at the time that there were 15 others and that nothing was going to be easy but I still believe that we are able to win the World Cup.'

Unlike some host nations who flopped in front of their own supporters, England efficiently extracted every ounce of advantage from that special situation but tempered it with moderation in the well-modulated 2–0 victories over Mexico and France that saw them emerge from the opening stage as group winners. The sense of steadiness and togetherness vital inside any World Cup-winning squad was helped by such matters as an agreement reached that, in the event of England winning the World Cup, the £22,000 on offer would be divided equally among all 22 members of the squad.

Ramsey was continually tinkering with his team, fine-tuning it like a perennially dissatisfied car mechanic in the approach to the tournament. Martin Peters would later be described as being 'ten years ahead of his time' by the manager but he only just made the 1966 team with days to spare, being given his debut in the final pre-tournament friendly, against Yugoslavia. Alan Ball, the midfield player, was dropped after the opening match with Uruguay and replaced with Peters for the second game, with Mexico, before being restored alongside Peters for the knockout phase.

It says much about those times that Wembley remained not filled to capacity for all of England's group matches. But after a torpid start to the World Cup, England started to look lively the moment when Bobby Charlton picked up the ball 49 yards from goal against Mexico and went streaking forward with it before hitting a 25-yard shot into the top corner of the net. The yellow ball flying from Charlton's foot and through the air was almost like a flare to signal the moment for mass enthusiasm for the World Cup finally to be properly released.

English enthusiasm was curtailed slightly by the loss through injury of Jimmy Greaves, the svelte striker who had had three stitches inserted in his leg after the game with France. As England prepared to face up to

Argentina, Geoff Hurst, a bulkier, more robust player, replaced Greaves and Ball returned to the team in place of Ian Callaghan, leaving England without a winger. Ramsey expected the match against Argentina to be a severe test for England but the Argentinians were lacking the type of discipline necessary to push Ramsey's team as hard as he had expected. Argentina had been in a state of flux before travelling to Europe and had even been reportedly on the point of withdrawing from the tournament, during the spring, after their entire coaching staff resigned, but Juan Carlos Lorenzo had been recruited as manager in April and he had brought with him a brutally rational approach to the game.

Ramsey had been well aware of the type of thing that was in store for his team from the South Americans and had briefed them on the need to retain their self-discipline throughout the match, regardless of the provocation. Lorenzo and his players had already been warned about their poor conduct, following wild behaviour from them in their match with West Germany, but the effect had been a bit like leaving a parking ticket on a bank robber's get-away car. 'Whenever I beat an Argentinian I could expect to be tripped, body-checked, spat at or dragged to the ground,' Bobby Charlton recalls.

Matters came to a head after 35 minutes of the first half when Antonio Rattín, the Argentina captain, was dismissed for 'violence of the tongue', as Rudolf Kreitlein, the West German referee, would describe it. Rattín had been harrying Kreitlein like a nagging harridan and so Kreitlein stopped the game to send off Rattín and buy himself some peace; or so he thought. Instead, he found himself engulfed in vigorous protest from the Argentina players and their representatives on the bench during an eight-minute period during which Rattín's dismissal was debated furiously. Late in the match, Hurst, latching on to a clever, diagonal cross dispatched by Peters from the midfield area, headed the only goal of the game, with alacrity, past Antonio Roma. It was significant that such a cross should come from behind Hurst, the centre forward, in Ramsey's winger-free team.

Rattín would insist that he had only been asking Kreitlein for an interpreter to be called so that the referee could explain why he was persistently pulling up Argentinians – several players had already been booked by the time of Rattín's dismissal. 'I do not approve of the conduct of our players and officials,' Dr Menendez Betly, of the Argentinian Football Association, said the following day, 'but they were provoked by the referee. He was absolutely biased in favour of England. The referee and those who selected him were, in my opinion, responsible for the trouble. He was against Argentina from the start. I apologise to the huge crowd for our not being able to show them that we can play skilful football.'

There was no need for the good doctor to issue such an apology – indeed it would have been more appropriate for the huge crowd to have issued Dr Betly, Juan Carlos Lorenzo, Rattín and everyone in the Argentina team with a vote of deep and sincere thanks and for the FA to have made them fixtures on their Christmas card list. Had Lorenzo's men poured all of their efforts into deploying their undoubted talents with a football, the South Americans would have been formidable opponents; as it was, even amidst all their gamesmanship, the game had been a close thing, with Argentina opening up the England defence and going close to scoring on more than one occasion.

The Argentinians' indiscipline instead provided England with a rallying point and the impetus to defeat Portugal in the semi-final and then, a week later, West Germany in the Final. 'When I started playing I didn't even know about the World Cup but to actually get to win it – wow!' Charlton would reflect. 'I knew things would never be the same again.' He was right: that was so not only for those players but for England too, who are the World Cup winners who have endured the longest wait for that elusive second trophy. Four decades on, winning the World Cup has become a national obsession.

Hurst, scorer of the hat-trick in the Final, mowed the lawn and washed the car on the day after victory, making up for his neglect of familial duties during his absence at the tournament. It is difficult to imagine England's modern, outrageously well-rewarded players indulging in such activities at any time: their lawns are too vast and the cars in their collections too numerous. During the 1966 World Cup, daily life carried on as normal even if there were people dancing in the fountains in Trafalgar Square on the night of the Final. Now, at a World Cup, the month or so during which it takes place finds national flags attached to domestic vehicles as if they were diplomatic carriages of state and normal working practices are suspended on the days of England matches.

Amid the excessive expectations of the modern era, it has been hard for previous England managers and players to maintain a sense of perspective. 'We are not as good as we think we are,' Steven Gerrard, the England midfield player, said after a team described as 'abysmal, embarrassing and dreadful' by George Cohen, the 1966 winner, had been eliminated in 2006. 'We talked ourselves up too much. In future tournaments we must learn to be humble. Be calm. We went around Germany blowing our own trumpet and returned home mute with embarrassment. Me and the other players constantly claimed we could win the World Cup – it was stupid,' Gerrard admitted.

Wayne Rooney, the focus of England's hopes in 2010, and one who should have learned from the Sven-Göran Eriksson experience, concurred. 'Saying we were going to win it doesn't help, and we were guilty of that. The expectation is always far too high and that is a problem. We built ourselves up and the press whipped the country up into a frenzy and then slaughtered us for not playing well.' In advance of the 2010 tournament Fabio Capello has tended to play things low-key; his repeated stating, pre-tournament, that he would settle for an England–Italy Final seems to be something of an aberration.

One of the most important characteristics that the England team possesses going into the 2010 tournament is having a manager who seems utterly resistant to the type of furore and frenzied fanaticism that surrounds modern English assaults on the World Cup. Flowing on almost naturally from the conservative outlook of Fabio Capello has been the development of a settled team that is well-balanced and hard to beat and whose solid structure provides the type of platform for a player of world-class ability, in the person of Wayne Rooney, to thrive at a

World Cup finals, in much the same way as Romário thrived on being allowed the freedom to bounce around looking for goals in front of the solid body of men behind him during the 1994 tournament.

'I know of no man who can match him when it comes to understanding of the world game. He used to leave us almost breathless with the way he could go through every player in the opposing team, picking out his strengths and weaknesses as if he saw him play every day of the week. Rarely, if ever, was he proved wrong with his diagnosis.' Bobby Moore was speaking of Alf Ramsey; it is not hard to imagine a modern England player saying the same of Capello. As with the Italians in 2006, England go into the World Cup with two successive disappointing tournaments behind them and with several players who underwent those experiences and who now share the burden of proving that they can seize the day, and that this group of players, of whom so much has been expected for so long, can come good at last.

15

Facts and Figures

A 'league table' of World Cup winners to illustrate where they stand in terms of overall victories and goal difference:

	P	W	D	L	F	A	Pts	Success rate
Brazil 2002	7	7	0	0	18	4	21	100%
Brazil 1970	6	6	0	0	19	7	18	100%
Uruguay 1930	4	4	0	0	15	3	12	100%
France 1998	7	7	0	0	12	4	21	100%
Italy 1938	4	4	0	0	11	5	12	100%
Brazil 1958	6	5	1	0	16	4	16	93%
West Germany 1990	7	6	1	0	15	5	19	93%
Italy 2006	7	6	1	0	12	2	19	93%
Argentina 1986	7	6	1	0	14	5	19	93%
Brazil 1962	6	5	1	0	14	5	16	93%
Brazil 1994	7	6	1	0	11	3	19	93%
England 1966	6	5	1	0	11	3	16	93%
Italy 1934	5	4	1	0	12	3	13	90%

Uruguay 1950	4	3	1	0	15	5	10	87.5%
West Germany 1974	7	6	0	1	13	4	18	86%
West Germany 1954	6	5	0	1	25	14	15	83%
Argentina 1978	7	5	1	1	15	4	16	79%
Italy 1982	7	4	3	0	12	6	15	79%

* Matches that resulted in a draw but were settled by a penalty shootout are classified as a win or loss dependent on result of the shootout
** Three points given for a win; one for a draw
*** Standings rated firstly on percentage success rate and then on goal difference
**** Adjusted to allow for tournaments in which fewer games were played than in modern times

A 'league table' of host nations to show how they did at their own World Cup:

	P	W	D	L	F	A	Stage reached
Uruguay 1930	4	4	0	0	15	3	Winners
Argentina 1978	7	5	1	1	15	4	Winners
West Germany 1974	7	6	0	1	13	4	Winners
Italy 1934	5	4	1	0	12	3	Winners
France 1998	7	7	0	0	12	4	Winners
England 1966	6	5	1	0	11	3	Winners
Brazil 1950	6	4	1	1	22	6	Second
Sweden 1958	6	4	1	1	12	7	Second
Germany 2006	7	6	0	1	14	6	Third
Italy 1990	7	6	0	1	10	2	Third
Chile 1962	6	4	0	2	10	8	Third
South Korea 2002	5	4	1	2	8	6	Fourth
Mexico 1986	4	3	1	1	6	2	Quarter-finalists
Mexico 1970	4	2	1	1	5	4	Quarter-finalists

Switzerland 1954	4	2	0	2	11	11	Quarter-finalists
France 1938	2	1	0	1	4	4	Quarter-finalists
Japan 2002	4	2	1	1	5	3	Second round
Spain 1982	3	1	2	2	4	5	Second round stage
USA 1994	4	1	1	2	3	4	Second round

* Matches that resulted in a draw but were settled by a penalty shootout are classified as a win or loss dependent on result of the shootout

** Standings rated firstly on percentage success rate, then on goal difference and then on goals scored

A table of goalscorers restricted solely to the leading scorer from each of the World Cup winners:

	Games played	Goals scored
Ronaldo (Brazil, 2002)*	7	8
Jairzinho (Brazil, 1970)	6	7
Pelé (Brazil, 1958)	4	6
Max Morlock (West Germany, 1954)	5	6
Mario Kempes (Argentina, 1978)*	7	6
Paolo Rossi (Italy, 1982)*	7	6
Pedro Cea (Uruguay 1930)	4	5
Silvio Piola (Italy, 1938)	4	5
Juan Schiaffino (Uruguay, 1950)	4	5
Diego Maradona (Argentina, 1986)	7	5
Romário (Brazil, 1994)	7	5
Geoff Hurst (England, 1966)	3	4

Angelo Schiavio (Italy, 1934)	4	4
Garrincha (Brazil, 1962)*	6	4
Luca Toni (Italy, 2006)	6	4
Vavá (Brazil, 1962)*	6	4
Gerd Müller (West Germany, 1974)	7	4
Lothar Matthäus (West Germany, 1990)	7	4
Thierry Henry (France, 1998)**	6	3

* Also leading goalscorer in the tournament overall
** Thierry Henry is the only leading goalscorer for his country who did not play in the World Cup Final

Age of each World Cup-winning manager:

Uruguay 1930	Alberto Suppici	31 years old
Italy 1934	Vittorio Pozzo	48 years old
Italy 1938	Vittorio Pozzo	52 years old
Uruguay 1950	Juan López	42 years old
West Germany 1954	Sepp Herberger	57 years old
Brazil 1958	Vicente Feola	48 years old
Brazil 1962	Aymoré Moreira	50 years old
England 1966	Alf Ramsey	46 years old
Brazil 1970	Mario Zagallo	38 years old
West Germany 1974	Helmut Schön	58 years old
Argentina 1978	César Luis Menotti	39 years old
Italy 1982	Enzo Bearzot	54 years old
Argentina 1986	Carlos Bilardo	47 years old
West Germany 1990	Franz Beckenbauer	44 years old
Brazil 1994	Carlos Alberto Parreira	51 years old
France 1998	Aimé Jacquet	56 years old
Brazil 2002	Luiz Felipe Scolari	53 years old
Italy 2006	Marcello Lippi	58 years old

A 'league table' showing penalty shootout records:

	Shootouts	Scored	Missed/saved
Germany*	4	18	1
France	4	16	5
Argentina	4	13	5
Italy	4	13	7
Brazil	3	10	3
Spain	3	10	4
England	3	7	7
Romania	2	8	3
Ireland	2	7	3
Mexico	2	2	5
Belgium	1	5	0
South Korea	1	5	0
Sweden	1	5	1
Bulgaria	1	3	1
Ukraine	1	3	1
Portugal	1	3	2
Holland	1	2	2
Yugoslavia	1	2	3
Switzerland	1	0	3

* Includes West Germany

A 'league table' comprising all Brazil teams in the finals:

	P	W	D	L	F	A	Pts	Success rate
Brazil 2002	7	7	0	0	18	4	21	100%
Brazil 1970	6	6	0	0	19	7	18	100%
Brazil 1958	6	5	1	0	16	4	16	93%
Brazil 1962	6	5	1	0	14	5	16	93%
Brazil 1994	7	6	1	0	11	3	19	93%
Brazil 1950	6	4	1	1	22	6	13	83%

Brazil 1982	5	4	0	1	15	6	12	80%
Brazil 1986	5	4	0	1	10	1	12	80%
Brazil 2006	5	4	0	1	10	2	12	80%
Brazil 1978	7	4	3	0	10	4	12	79%
Brazil 1990	3	3	0	1	4	2	9	75%
Brazil 1998	7	5	0	2	14	9	15	71%
Brazil 1938	3	2	0	1	9	8	6	67%
Brazil 1974	7	3	2	2	6	4	11	57%
Brazil 1954	2	1	1	1	8	5	4	50%
Brazil 1930	2	1	0	1	5	2	3	50%
Brazil 1966	3	1	0	2	4	6	3	33%
Brazil 1934	1	0	0	1	1	3	0	0%

* Matches that resulted in a draw but were settled by a penalty shootout are classified as a win or loss dependent on result of the shootout

Number of goals scored and number of different goalscorers in the winning team:

	Played	Goals scored	Number of different goalscorers
Uruguay 1930	4	15	6
Italy 1934	5	12	5
Italy 1938	4	11	4
Uruguay 1950	4	15	6
West Germany 1954	6	25	8
Brazil 1958	6	16	6
Brazil 1962	6	14	6
England 1966	6	11	4
Brazil 1970	6	19	7
West Germany 1974	7	13	7
Argentina 1978	7	15	6
Italy 1982	7	12	6

Argentina 1986	7	14	6
West Germany 1990	7	15	6
Brazil 1994	7	11	5
France 1998	7	12	10
Brazil 2002	7	18	6
Italy 2006	7	12	10

Full line-ups of teams in every World Cup Final, with information about key participants:

World Cup Final 1930
Centenario Stadium, Montevideo, Uruguay

Argentina 2
Peucelle 20, Stabile 37

Uruguay 4
Dorado 12, Cea 57, Iriarte 68, Castro 89

Uruguay: Ballestrero, Nasazzi, Mascheroni, Andrade, Fernandez, Gestido, Dorado, Scarone, Castro, Cea, Iriarte

Argentina: Botasso, Della Torre, Paternoster, Juan Evaristo, Monti, Suarez, Peucelle, Varallo, Stabile, Ferreira, Mario Evaristo

'If we don't win today, we're dead,' José Nasazzi, the Uruguay captain, told his team-mates prior to the match against Argentina at the Centenario Stadium, a stadium built to mark both 100 years of Uruguayan independence and the staging of the World Cup. Uruguay's 4–2 victory provoked riots that saw the Uruguayan Embassy in Buenos Aires besieged by a mob. The World Cup had started as it meant to continue.

World Cup Final 1934
PNF Stadium, Rome, Italy

Czechoslovakia 1
Puc 76

Italy 2
Orsi 81, Schiavio 95
(after extra time)

Czechoslovakia: Planicka, Zenisek, Ctyroky, Kostalek, Cambal, Krcil, Junek, Svoboda, Sobotka, Nejedly, Puc

Italy: Combi, Monzeglio, Allemandi, Ferraris, Monti, Bertolini, Guaita, Meazza, Schiavio, Ferrari, Orsi

'It was the strength of desperation,' Angelo Schiavio, the Italy forward, said on how he had summoned up the reserves of energy to score the goal that made the result 2–1 and won the World Cup during extra time in the Final against Czechoslovakia. Vittorio Pozzo, the Italy manager, had controversially obtained victory while using several oriundi, *players born outside Italy, most often in South America, but with Italian ancestry.*

World Cup Final 1938
Stade de Colombes, Paris, France

Hungary 2
Titkos 8, Sarosi 70

Italy 4
Colaussi 6, 35, Piola 16, 82

Hungary: Szabo, Polgar, Biro, Szalay, Szucs, Lazar, Sas, Vincze, Sarosi, Zsengeller, Titkos

Italy: Olivieri, Foni, Rava, Serantoni, Andreolo, Locatelli, Biavati, Meazza, Piola, Ferrari, Colaussi

'To have him in your team meant to start 1–0 up,' Vittorio Pozzo, the Italy manager, said of Giuseppe Meazza, his ruggedly creative team captain, the brightest star in Italian football and a key inside forward in a sprightly Italian team that was adept at exploiting the counter-attack. Pozzo, described as the 'father of Italian football' is the only manager to have helmed successive World Cup triumphs.

World Cup Final 1950
Maracanã Stadium, Rio de Janeiro, Brazil

Brazil 1
Friaça 47

Uruguay 2
Schiaffino 66, Ghiggia 79

Brazil: Barbosa, Augusto, Juvenal, Bauer, Danilo, Bigode, Friaça, Zizinho, Ademir, Jair, Chico

Uruguay: Maspoli, Gonzalez, Tejera, Gambetta, Varela, Andrade, Ghiggia, Perez, Miguez, Schiaffino, Moran

'Drastic action necessary to prevent World Cup competition flopping,' W. Capel-Kirby, the distinguished British journalist, had telegrammed home on arrival in Rio de Janeiro for the finals after the late withdrawals of France, Portugal and Scotland had left the tournament lopsided, with 13 competing nations. The melodramatic conclusion, with 200,000 Brazilians in the Maracanã seeing their team upstaged by Uruguay, instead made the first post-war World Cup legendarily dramatic.

World Cup Final 1954
Wankdorf Stadium, Berne, Switzerland

Hungary 2
Puskas 6, Czibor 8

West Germany 3
Morlock 10, Rahn 18, 84

Hungary: Grosics, Buzansky, Lantos, Bozsik, Lorant, Zakarias, Czibor, Kocsis, Hidegkuti, Puskas, Toth

West Germany: Turek, Posipal, Kohlmeyer, Eckel, Liebrich, Mai, Rahn, Morlock, Ottmar Walter, Fritz Walter, Schafer

'If we had been beaten by a better team I wouldn't have minded second place,' Gusztav Sebes, the Hungary manager, said after one of the great World Cup upsets. Yet his own words contained the secret of his side's defeat: the West Germans were the better team, even if Sebes quite probably had the better collection of players. On going 2–0 down inside the opening ten minutes, the reaction of the Germans had been not to give in but to show what they were made of – and they did. The 1954 finals saw the highest average number of goals per game – 5.38.

World Cup Final 1958
Rasunda Stadium, Stockholm, Sweden

Brazil 5
Vavá 9, 32, Pelé 55, 90, Zagallo 68

Sweden 2
Liedholm 4, Simonsson 80

Brazil: Gilmar, Djalma Santos, Bellini, Orlando, Nilton Santos, Didi, Zito, Garrincha, Vavá, Pelé, Zagallo

Sweden: Svensson, Bergmark, Axbom, Borjesson, Gustavsson, Parling, Hamrin, Gren, Simonsson, Liedholm, Skoglund

'I think this kid has got a good future,' Jack Kelsey, the Wales goalkeeper, had said on encountering Pelé in the quarter-finals. Within a week the 17-year-old Brazilian had attained near immortal status, scoring half of Brazil's goals in the semi-final with France and their hugely entertaining tussle with Sweden in the Final. The goal-happy latter stages were entirely in keeping with the high-scoring tournament.

World Cup Final 1962
Estadio Nacional, Santiago, Chile

Brazil 3
Amarildo 17, Zito 69, Vavá 78

Czechoslovakia 1
Masopust 15

Brazil: Gilmar, Djalma Santos, Mauro, Zozimo, Nilton Santos, Zito, Didi, Zagallo, Garrincha, Vavá, Amarildo

Czechoslovakia: Schroiff, Tichy, Pluskal, Popluhar, Novak, Kvasnak, Masopust, Pospichal, Scherer, Kadraba, Jelinek

A smiling Garrincha and a confident Nilton Santos performed ball-juggling tricks on demand for the cameras prior to the 1962 Final and their confidence was not misplaced as Brazil cruised to victory. 'Was this the new Pelé?' was the thought that Amarildo's exemplary performance in the match brought into the mind of Pelé himself. Amarildo's impact on that game was such that it left Pelé, on the sidelines for the Final because of injury, insecure about his future in the Brazil team.

World Cup Final 1966
Wembley Stadium, London, England

England 4
Hurst 18, 101, 120, Peters 78

West Germany 2
Haller 12, Weber 90
(after extra time)

England: Banks, Cohen, Jack Charlton, Moore, Wilson, Ball, Stiles, Bobby Charlton, Peters, Hunt, Hurst

West Germany: Tilkowski, Hottges, Schulz, Weber, Schnellinger, Haller, Beckenbauer, Overath, Seeler, Held, Emmerich

This was a terrific match that raged from end to end with the verve, vigour and honest effort of a British cup-tie. England and West Germany produced a World Cup Final like no other and one that was fitting for a tournament held in Britain, where the first international match had been played and the rules of the game instituted. 'It takes two teams to make a match of the nature we saw today and Germany were a very, very good side and it is most unfortunate that there had to be a losing team,' Alf Ramsey, the England manager, said honourably after England had proved to be the better of the two teams in extra time.

World Cup Final 1970
Azteca Stadium, Mexico City, Mexico

Brazil 4
Pelé 18, Gérson 66, Jairzinho 71, Carlos Alberto 86

Italy 1
Boninsegna 37

272

Brazil: Felix, Carlos Alberto, Brito, Piazza, Everaldo, Jairzinho, Clodoaldo, Pelé, Gérson, Rivelino, Tostão

Italy: Albertosi, Burgnich, Cera, Rosato, Facchetti, Bertini (Juliano 75), Mazzola, De Sisti, Domenghini, Boninsegna (Rivera 84), Riva

Italy, leg-weary after a draining extra time semi-final played three days earlier, sat back and attempted to soak up Brazilian pressure but their opponents created too much of it for even an Italian defence to resist. All of the goals were wonderful but Brazil's fourth, scored on the overlap by right back Carlos Alberto, after a move that had begun on the other side of the defence, was the consummate team goal. 'I get reminded about my goal in the 1970 World Cup Final every single day of my life,' Carlos Alberto says. 'It never gets on my nerves – it would be more annoying if no one asked anything at all.'

World Cup Final 1974
Olympiastadion, Munich, West Germany

Holland 1
Neeskens 2 (pen)

West Germany 2
Breitner 25 (pen), Müller 43

Holland: Jongbloed, Suurbier, Rijsbergen (De Jong 69), Haan, Krol, Jansen, Neeskens, Van Hanegem, Rep, Cruyff, Rensenbrink (René Van der Kerkhof 46)

West Germany: Maier, Vogts, Schwarzenbeck, Beckenbauer, Breitner, Bonhof, Hoeness, Overath, Grabowski, Müller, Hölzenbein

The first Final to feature a penalty-kick got not one but two, but it was a fine piece of instinctive striking from Gerd Müller that won the match for West Germany. It was Müller's 14th

World Cup finals goal, and he would remain the World Cup's record scorer for more than three decades. Holland, galvanised by Johan Cruyff, had been captivating throughout the tournament, but produced their most disjointed display in the Final. 'It's a pity that Johan Cruyff didn't play,' Helmut Schön, the West Germany manager, said, tongue in cheek, on what he saw as Cruyff's subdued performance in the match.

World Cup Final 1978
Estadio Monumental, Buenos Aires, Argentina

Argentina 3
Kempes 38, 105, Bertoni 116

Holland 1
Nanninga 82
(after extra time)

Argentina: Fillol, Olguin, Galván, Passarella, Tarantini, Ardiles (Larossa 67), Gallego, Ortiz (Houseman 75), Bertoni, Luque, Kempes

Holland: Jongbloed, Poortvliet, Krol, Brandts, Jansen (Suurbier 73), Neeskens, Haan, René van der Kerkhof, Willy van der Kerkhof, Rep (Nanninga 59), Rensenbrink

'I will come as a substitute and score in the last ten minutes,' said Dick Nanninga in advance of the match, making one of the greatest of World Cup predictions – the Dutchman's header eight minutes from time equalising Mario Kempes' first-half opener. Urged on by a frantic 80,000 crowd and helped by a compliant referee, Argentina sealed victory in extra time but it was a victory that left a bitter aftertaste. 'Whether we like it or not,' Osvaldo Ardiles, the Argentina midfield player, says, 'we helped a genocidal junta stay in power by winning the competition.'

World Cup Final 1982
Bernabéu Stadium, Madrid, Spain

Italy 3
Rossi 57, Tardelli 69, Altobelli 81

West Germany 1
Breitner 83

Italy: Zoff, Collovati, Scirea, Gentile, Cabrini, Oriali, Bergomi, Tardelli, Conti, Rossi, Graziani (Altobelli 8) (Causio 88)

West Germany: Schumacher, Kaltz, Stielike, Karl-Heinz Förster, Bernd Förster, Breitner, Briegel, Dremmler, Rummenigge, Littbarski, Fischer

Antonio Cabrini became the first player to miss a penalty-kick in a World Cup Final, scuffing his effort wide during a goalless, niggly first-half. Dino Zoff, at 40 the oldest player to receive a World Cup winner's medal, captained the Italian team, emulating Gianpiero Combi, the goalkeeper who had captained Italy to victory in 1934. 'I was never over-excited in my career but those moments were completely different,' Zoff said. 'I was so confused that I came close to hugging and kissing the Queen of Spain, Sofia, before receiving the trophy. Fortunately, I realised in time that it was not the right thing to do.'

World Cup Final 1986
Azteca Stadium, Mexico City, Mexico

Argentina 3
Brown 23, Valdano 55, Burruchaga 83

West Germany 2
Rummenigge 74, Völler 80

Argentina: Pumpido, Ruggeri, Brown, Cuciuffo, Giusti, Batista, Burruchaga (Trobbiani 89), Enrique, Olarticoechea, Valdano, Maradona

West Germany: Schumacher, Brehme, Jakobs, Förster, Berthold, Matthäus, Magath (Hoeness 62), Eder, Briegel, Rummenigge, Allofs (Völler 46)

Rarely has a World Cup-winning team relied so enormously on one man as Argentina did on Diego Maradona in 1986. His emotional demeanour and expressive talents spurred his team-mates on to victory. 'When Germany scored to make it 2–2 in the Final, I said to myself, "The Cup is leaving me, no, please, no,"' Maradona says with his usual dramatic flourish. 'Then, when I set up Burruchaga for the winner, I said, "You returned it to me, thank you."' The suggestion of divine intervention is appropriate for a man who relied on the 'Hand of God' to get past England in the quarter-finals and who produced a series of heavenly performances in Mexico.

World Cup Final 1990
Stadio Olimpico, Rome, Italy

Argentina 0

West Germany 1
Brehme 85 (pen)

Argentina: Goycochea, Ruggeri (Monzón 46), Simon, Serrezuela, Sensini, Basualdo, Burruchaga (Calderón 54), Troglio, Lorenzo, Maradona, Dezotti

West Germany: Illgner, Buchwald, Kohler, Augenthaler, Berthold (Reuter 74), Hässler, Matthäus, Littbarski, Brehme, Völler, Klinsmann

A negative tournament that broke records for the fewest goals per match ended in an appropriately unfortunate fashion. Argentina not only became the first World Cup finalists to fail to score but provided the first player to be sent off in a World Cup final, Pedro Monzón, only for him to be followed off the

276

field by Gustavo Dezotti. 'The 1990 Final was not a beautiful match,' Rudi Völler, the West Germany striker, says of a game settled by Andreas Brehme's penalty, 'but you don't get praised only for the performance in the Final but for the performance during the whole tournament. And we played a great tournament.'

World Cup Final 1994

Pasadena Rose Bowl, Los Angeles, USA

Brazil 0

Italy 0

Brazil won 3–2 on penalties

Brazil: Taffarel, Jorginho (Cafu 22), Aldair, Márcio Santos, Branco, Mazinho, Mauro Silva, Dunga, Zinho (Viola 106), Bebeto, Romário

Italy: Pagliuca, Mussi (Apolloni 34), Baresi, Maldini, Benarrivo, Berti, Dino Baggio (Evani 94), Labertini, Donadoni, Roberto Baggio, Massaro

'It's a death sentence,' Carlos Alberto Parreira, the Brazil manager, said of the task of leading Brazil to World Cup success. 'You can't have fun in this job. It will only be a pleasure if we win the World Cup.' The first goalless Final, a tight, tactical battle, reflected the pressure on both Parreira and Arrigo Sacchi, the Italy manager, and was an unfortunate denouement to a colourful tournament. Romário, the Brazil striker, admitted that the spectacle had not been acceptable even if winning still tasted sweet.

World Cup Final 1998
Stade de France, Paris, France

Brazil 0

France 3
Zidane 27, 45, Petit 90

Brazil: Taffarel, Cafu, Junior Baiano, Aldair, Roberto Carlos, Dunga, Leonardo (Denilson 46), César Sampaio (Edmundo 74), Rivaldo, Bebeto, Ronaldo

France: Barthez, Thuram, Leboeuf, Desailly, Lizarazu, Deschamps, Karembeu (Boghossian 56), Zidane, Petit, Djorkaeff (Vieira 75), Guivarc'h (Dugarry 66)

'We were just like one big family,' Christophe Dugarry, the France striker, says of the team that finally won the World Cup for the nation whose Jules Rimet had devised the competition and who had kept the original trophy, named in his honour, under his bed during the dark days of the Second World War. The scenes that accompanied victory had not been seen in France since the Liberation. A vigorous French side had swept aside a Brazilian one that was in bits after Ronaldo's fit on the afternoon of the match.

World Cup final 2002
International Stadium, Yokohama, Japan

Brazil 2
Ronaldo 66, 78

Germany 0

Brazil: Marcos, Cafu, Lucio, Edmilson, Roberto Carlos, Kleberson, Gilberto, Roque Junior, Ronaldinho (Juninho 85), Rivaldo, Ronaldo (Denilson 90)

Germany: Kahn, Frings, Linke, Metzelder, Bode (Ziege 84),

278

Schneider, Ramelow, Jeremies (Asamoah 77), Hamann, Neuville, Klose (Bierhoff 74)

'We had a great team, the best I ever played in,' Ronaldo says of the Brazil that defeated Germany in straightforward fashion in the 2002 Final. 'We had Rivaldo, Ronaldinho, Roberto Carlos, Cafu, me . . . It was a team where we could find a goal in every minute in every way and win every game.' Ronaldo's decisive second goal came when Oliver Kahn, Germany's imposing goalkeeper, made a rare mistake and spilled the ball into the Brazil striker's path. A strange aspect of this match was that these two long-proven heavyweights of World Cup tournaments were meeting for the first time in a match in the finals.

World Cup Final 2006
Olympiastadion, Berlin, Germany

France 1
Zidane 7 (pen)

Italy 1
Materazzi 19

Italy won 5–3 on penalties

France: Barthez, Sagnol, Thuram, Gallas, Abidal, Makélélé, Ribery (Trézéguet 100), Zidane, Vieira (Diarra 56), Malouda, Henry (Wiltord 107)

Italy: Buffon, Zambrotta, Cannavaro, Materazzi, Grosso, Gattuso, Pirlo, Camoranesi (Del Piero 86), Totti (De Rossi 61), Perrotta (Iaquinta 61), Toni

A tight, taut match revolved around Zinédine Zidane, as so much else had in a distinguished career that had been blighted by disciplinary indiscretions, and this, his last game as a player, was in character. He gave France the lead with a risky chipped

penalty that only just fell behind the line. Marco Materazzi headed an equaliser for Italy but when the Italians' goalscorer later taunted Zidane he reacted with a headbutt that saw him dismissed in extra time. 'It happened and I can't pretend it wasn't me,' Zidane says. France, who had had the edge in extra time, prior to Zidane's dismissal, went on to lose the penalty shootout, the first the Italians had won at a World Cup finals in four attempts.

How They Won the World Cup 2010

Group A

South Africa	v	Mexico
Uruguay	v	France
South Africa	v	Uruguay
France	v	Mexico
Mexico	v	Uruguay
France	v	South Africa

Group B

South Korea	v	Greece
Argentina	v	Nigeria
Argentina	v	South Korea
Greece	v	Nigeria
Nigeria	v	South Korea
Greece	v	Argentina

Group C

England	v	USA
Algeria	v	Slovenia
Slovenia	v	USA
England	v	Algeria
Slovenia	v	England
USA	v	Algeria

Group D

Serbia	□ v □	Ghana
Germany	□ v □	Australia
Germany	□ v □	Serbia
Ghana	□ v □	Australia
Ghana	□ v □	Germany
Australia	□ v □	Serbia

Group E

Netherlands	□ v □	Denmark
Japan	□ v □	Cameroon
Netherlands	□ v □	Japan
Cameroon	□ v □	Denmark
Denmark	□ v □	Japan
Cameroon	□ v □	Netherlands

Group F

Italy	□ v □	Paraguay
New Zealand	□ v □	Slovakia
Slovakia	□ v □	Paraguay
Italy	□ v □	New Zealand
Slovakia	□ v □	Italy
Paraguay	□ v □	New Zealand

Group G

Ivory Coast	v	Portugal
Brazil	v	North Korea
Brazil	v	Ivory Coast
Portugal	v	North Korea
Portugal	v	Brazil
North Korea	v	Ivory Coast

Group H

Honduras	v	Chile
Spain	v	Switzerland
Chile	v	Switzerland
Spain	v	Honduras
Chile	v	Spain
Switzerland	v	Honduras

Second Round (last 16)

Match

1	A1	v		B2
2	C1	v		D2
3	D1	v		C2
4	B1	v		A2
5	E1	v		F2
6	G1	v		H2
7	F1	v		E2
8	H1	v		G2

Quarter-finals

Match

Q1	5	▢ v ▢		6
Q2	1	▢ v ▢		2
Q3	3	▢ v ▢		4
Q4	7	▢ v ▢		8

Semi-finals

Match

Q1	▢ v ▢		Q2
Q3	▢ v ▢		Q4

World Cup Final 2010

Soccer City Stadium, Johannesburg, South Africa

▢ v ▢

284

Bibliography

Newspapers and Journals

The following publications provided most useful background information in my research for this book:

FourFourTwo
The Independent
Independent on Sunday
Observer
The Sunday Telegraph
The Sunday Times
The Times
When Saturday Comes
World Soccer

Books

Castro, Ruy, *Garrincha* (Yellow Jersey Press, 2005)
Glanville, Brian, *The Story of the World Cup* (Faber & Faber, 1993)
Hunt, Chris, *World Cup Stories* (Interact Publishing Ltd, 2006)
Jamrich, Klara and Taylor, Rogan (editor and translator), *Puskas On Puskas* (Robson Books, 1997)
Lichtenberger, Uli-Hesse, *Tor!* (WSC Books, 2003)
Maradona, Diego, *El Diego* (Yellow Jersey Press, 2005)
Ruhn, Christov, *Le Foot* (Abacus Books, 2000)

My thanks also to Roy Rajber in the press office of the German Football Association.

Picture Acknowledgements

FIRST SECTION

Page 1
World Cup Final ball: © National Football Museum; 'Win or die!': Italian team, 1934: both © Press Association Images; Hungarian team, 1954: © Getty Section

Pages 2 and 3
Argentina, 1978 (top left): © Action Images; Argentina, 1978 (top right and centre): Menotti: Kempes: all © Press Association Images; Maradona and Bilardo, 1986: Maradona and Bilardo, 2010: both © Getty Section

Pages 4 and 5
Feola, 1958: © Getty Section; Pelé: © Press Association Images; Garrincha, 1962: © Getty Section; Brazil, 1970: © Press Association Images; Carlos Parreira: © Getty Section; Romário, 1994: © Action Images; Scolari, 2002: © Press Association Images

Pages 6 and 7
Bearzot, 1982: © Getty Section; Bearzot etc on flight home: © Press Association Images; Rossi, 1982: Cannavaro, 2006: both © Getty Section; Der Spiegel: © 31/1977 DER SPIEGEL; Pozzo: © Getty Section

Page 8
Lippi, 2006: Gattuso: both © Press Association Images

Index

Adidas 140
Alfonsín, President Raúl 38, 42–3
Allofs, Klaus 23
Amaral, Paulo 72
Amarildo 271
Anelka, Nicolas 248
Antognoni, Giancarlo 110, 122, 127
Ardiles, Osvaldo 211–12, 218, 230, 274
Argentina
  appointment of Maradona as manager
    (2008) 44–5, 80
  reputation for dirty methods
    employed by players 221–2
  Videla's junta coup 219–20
  World Cup (1930) 70–1, 267
  World Cup (1966) 221–2, 256–8
  World Cup (1978) 31–2, 185, 203–4,
    217–32
    allegations of amphetamine use 228
    Final against Holland 211–12,
      228–32, 274
    game against France 223
    game against Italy 224–6
    game against Peru and allegations
      of match fixing 185, 226–8
    opening games 222–3
    style of football 229–30
    vicious fouling 225
  World Cup (1982) 36, 39, 121–2, 188
  World Cup (1986) 35–43, 67
    Bilardo as manager 24–7
    development of strength and
      togetherness of side 39–40
    Final against Germany 23–5, 35,
      42, 246–7, 275–6
    offering of captaincy to Maradona
      by Bilardo 35–6, 37–8, 40
    pre-tournament run-up 33–4
    press criticism 116
    qualifying campaign 38
    quarter final match against England
      and 'hand of God' goal by
      Maradona 18, 19–20, 41–2,

      77–8, 79–80, 83
    tactics 236–7
    welcome home for team after
      victory 43
  World Cup (1990) 100, 215–16
    defeat by Cameroon 26
    Final against Germany 43–4, 86–7,
      102–3, 276–7
  World Cup (2006) 130
  World Cup (2010) qualification 44
Aston, Ken 116
Auld, Andy 70
Austria 7

Babo, Lamartine 175–6
Bafokeng Sports Campus 17–18
Baggio, Roberto 87, 172
Bahkramov, Tofik 80–1
Ball, Alan 234, 236, 255, 256
Ballack, Michael 164
Barbosa, Moacyr 178
Barnes, John 41, 113
Baroti, Lajos 223
Batista, João 36
Battiston, Patrick 91, 93
Bearzot, Enzo 32, 108, 110, 116–18,
  126, 127, 128
Bebeto 170, 205
Beckenbauer, Franz 24, 97–8, 245
  World Cup (1966) 81–2, 233–4
  World Cup (1970) 147
  World Cup (1974) 83, 84, 130,
    142–3, 151–2, 153
  World Cup (1986) 32
  World Cup (1990) 32, 94, 96, 101–2,
    207
Beckham, David 198
Belgium
  World Cup (2002) 196–7
Bellone, Bruno 93
Bellugi, Mauro 225
Bennaceur, Ali 77, 78
Bergeroo, Philippe 58

288

INDEX

289